EFGHIJ
PQRS
XYZ

ghijkl
rstuv

Helvetica Medium is the standard typeface for all graphics for the New York City Transit Authority. It is to be used for all permanent and temporary signage for stations, rolling stock, garages, yards and other facilities.

The alphabet shown is for reference only; it should not be reproduced. Typography for sign production may be obtained from a variety of commercial sources.* Alphabets must match the weight of the characters illustrated on this page. Helvetica Condensed or Italic or other typefaces are not to be used.

*A listing of different sources of typography will be found on page —.

Letters are not to be altered by shortening mechanical

Next train →

Helvetica and the
New York City Subway System:
The True (Maybe) Story

Paul Shaw

The MIT Press | Cambridge, Massachusetts and London, England

Paul,
Did I tell you that your report is terrific?
That is the final statement on the subject.
Hugs, Massimo

Dedicated to the memory of Bob Noorda (1927–2010)

Revised Edition
Copyright © 2011 Massachusetts Institute of Technology
Text copyright © 2009, 2011 Paul Shaw

An earlier, limited edition of this book was published in 2009 by Blue Pencil Editions.
An earlier version of the essay appeared online at AIGA Voice, November 2008.

Library of Congress Cataloging-in-Publication Data
Shaw, Paul.
Helvetica and the New York City subway system : the true (maybe) story / Paul Shaw. —
Rev. ed.
    p.   cm.
Includes bibliographical references.
ISBN 978-0-262-01548-6 (hardcover : alk. paper)
1. Helvetica type—New York (State)—New York. 2. Subways—New York (State)—
New York. 3. Signs and signboards—New York (State)—New York—Lettering. I.
Title.
Z250.5.H45S53   2011
686.2'24—dc22

2010039985

Design: Paul Shaw and Abby Goldstein
Typefaces: AG Old Face, Berthold Akzidenz Grotesk BQ,
 Monotype Grotesque, and Trade Gothic Next
Produced by Scott-Martin Kosofsky, The Philidor Company,
 Rhinebeck, NY. www.philidor.com

Printed and bound in China by Everbest
10 9 8 7 6 5

CONTENTS

FOREWORD

The history of the New York subway system has been a continual struggle between centripetal and centrifugal forces. Opened in 1904, the city's first subway, a line of the Interborough Rapid Transit Company (IRT) that went from City Hall in lower Manhattan to the Bronx, was acclaimed for its high speeds. IRT express cars surpassed forty miles per hour, faster than any other urban railway in the world. Speed shrunk distance and unified the city. Built at a time when most New Yorkers lived below 14th Street in southern Manhattan and when outlying areas were thinly settled, the IRT stimulated the residential development of northern Manhattan and the Bronx. That helped make an economic and social unit of Greater New York, which had been formed six years earlier by the consolidation of the five separate boroughs of Manhattan, the Bronx, Queens, Brooklyn, and Staten Island into a single municipality.

Conflicts between the Interborough and the City of New York exerted centrifugal pressures, however. When the IRT refused to construct more lines that might have diluted its profits, the municipal government countered its monopoly power by trying to induce another transit company to build a separate subway, an approach that led to the authorization of a second stage of sub-

way construction, in 1913. This dual contract system, as it was known, called for new lines to be built by the Interborough Rapid Transit Company and by a second company, the Brooklyn Rapid Transit Company (BRT), later renamed the Brooklyn-Manhattan Transit Corporation (BMT). The IRT already operated its original subway and both it and the BRT ran older elevated lines that they had added through mergers. The dual system, though, more than doubled the city's rapid transit mileage, reaching beyond the built-up territory to serve outlying portions of the Bronx, Queens, and Brooklyn. Thanks to the dual contracts, by the 1920s New York's subway system had become the longest and most heavily patronized in the world. But the dual contracts also fragmented the subways. Because the IRT and BMT competed with each other, passengers had to pay full fares to transfer from one company to the other. Even more bizarrely, each company's maps usually omitted its rival's routes.

A third subway network, the Independent Subway System (IND), opened between 1932 and 1940. While the earlier IRT and BMT lines were publicly owned and privately operated, protests about their monopolistic behavior and poor passenger service led the municipal government to own and operate the IND itself. Private

(half title) "Typography alphabet." (detail) From Metropolitan Transportation Authority. *Graphics Standards: Signage.* New York: Michael Hertz Associates, 1988, n.p. (See **206** for full image.)

1 (frontipiece) Illuminated sign. Lefferts Boulevard (A). The letters are a handcut version of Standard Medium. (2008)

2 (copyright page) Illuminated sign. Fourth Avenue–9th Street (F/G/R), 1933. (2009)

3 (opposite page) Entrance kiosk, City Hall (4/5/6), c.1904. Designed by Heins & LaFarge. Closed December 21, 1945.

subway ownership came to a complete end in 1940, when the IRT and BMT, in poor financial condition, were acquired by the City of New York and combined with the IND into a single network run by a single operator. To a surprising extent, however, the three divisions continued to function separately. IND and BMT cars are larger than IRT cars and do not fit IRT tunnels. More fundamentally, for decades the subway has been so short of funds that it has been slow to authorize construction projects intended to link the divisions into a coherent whole by, for example, linking together stations and corridors.

Today, this problem of fragmentation has been further compounded by suburban growth. Although the subways and the commuter railroads are now part of the Metropolitan Transportation Authority (MTA), the subways are confined within the city's boundaries and do not have very good connections with the commuter railroads. Because employment, residence, and leisure in metropolitan New York is becoming increasingly interconnected, the MTA can be expected to put added emphasis on projects like East Side Access, which will provide a new terminal for the Long Island Rail Road under Grand Central Terminal that

will drastically shorten commuting times for residents of eastern Queens and Long Island who travel to the east side of Manhattan.

Paul Shaw makes clear that these counter-pressures between unification and fragmentation extend even to subway signage. In untangling the complicated story of the subway's typeface, Shaw makes a valuable contribution to our understanding of the subway and to printing history. His essay is the most original piece about the subway's history that I have read in a long time.

Clifton Hood

Professor of History, Hobart & William Smith Colleges; author of *722 Miles: The Building of the Subways and How They Transformed New York* and the forthcoming *Striving for Distinction: Economic Elites and the Making of New York City, since 1754*.

4   Mosaic tile directional sign. 14th Street (F/V), 1940. (2005)

5   Porcelain enamel station entrance sign. From an unidentified station on the IRT no. 4 line north of 167th Street, c.1918.

4

INTERBOROUGH
RAPID TRANSIT CO.
UPTOWN TO WOODLAWN.
DOWNTOWN VIA LEX. AND 4TH AV.
TO GRAND CENTRAL,
CITY HALL, SOUTH FERRY AND BROOKLYN.
CHANGE AT 149TH ST. FOR TIMES SQ., PENN. STATION,
SOUTH FERRY, WALL STREET AND BROOKLYN
VIA BROADWAY AND 7TH AVENUE.
TO SO. FERRY VIA 6TH AND 9TH AVE. ELEVATED.

5

INTRODUCTION

There is a common belief that Helvetica is the signage typeface of the New York City subway system. This belief has been reinforced by *Helvetica*, Gary Hustwit's popular documentary about the typeface. But it is not true—or rather, it is only somewhat true. Helvetica *is* the official typeface of the MTA today, but it was *not* the typeface specified by Unimark International when they created a new signage system at the end of the 1960s. Why was Helvetica not chosen originally? What was chosen in its place? Why is Helvetica now used? When did the changeover occur? To answer those questions this essay looks at the history of the New York City subway system, the history of transportation signage systems in the 1960s, the history of Unimark International, and the history of Helvetica. These four strands are woven together to tell a story that ultimately transcends the simple issue of Helvetica's presence in the New York City subway system. [1]

Paul Shaw

Department of Communication Design, Parsons School of Design
Department of Art History, School of Visual Arts

6/7 **(opposite page) Porcelain enamel girder signs. Forest Hills–71st Avenue (E/F/G/R/V).** The girder column on the left is set in Standard Medium; the one on the right is set in Neue Helvetica Medium. (2008)

8 **Porcelain enamel station sign. Beach 98 Street–Playland (A/S).** The porcelain enamel sign in the rear, with Playland obscured, is set in Standard Medium while the newer metal one in front is in Helvetica Medium. (2009)

Note in the footnotes and captions references to images in the book are indicated by the relevant number in bold type within parentheses and without the prefix "fig."

1. Gary Hustwit, *Helvetica: A Documentary Film.* (Brooklyn: Swiss Dots Productions, 2007.) Hustwit's film includes images of signage and other graphics from the subway system in its montage of Helvetica in use in New York City.

8

THE LABYRINTH

As any New Yorker—or visitor to the city—knows, the subway system is a labyrinth. This is because it is an amalgamation of three separate systems, two of which incorporated earlier urban railway lines. The current New York subway system was formed in 1940 when the IRT (Interborough Rapid Transit), the BMT (Brooklyn-Manhattan Transit) and the IND (Independent) lines were merged. The IRT lines date to 1904, the BMT lines to 1908 (when it was the BRT or Brooklyn Rapid Transit), and the IND to 1932. Portions of the IRT and BMT lines began life as elevated train lines, some of which are as old as 1878. [2]

9 (opposite page) Terracotta initial.
Atlantic Avenue (2/3), 1908. (2006)

10 Terracotta initial. Spring Street (6),
1905. (2008)

2. For detailed information on the evolution of the New York City subway system see Philip Ashforth Coppola, *Silver Connections*. (Maplewood, New Jersey: n.p., 1984–1999), 4 vols.; and nycsubway.org.

Note the New York City subway system continues to evolve. Following the initial publication of this book budgetary cutbacks forced the MTA to reduce service. On June 27, 2010 the V and W were discontinued; the M (re-colored orange) re-routed to replace the V in Manhattan and Queens; the G terminated at Long Island City / Court Square; and the Q extended to Astoria Boulevard. *These route changes are not reflected in the text, notes or captions of this new edition.*

10

11–17 Selected IRT and BMT mosaic station names. Note the variations in serif and sans serif lettering styles.

11 Brook Avenue (6), 1919. (2008)

12 28th Street (1), 1918. (2008)

13 Times Square (7), 1917. (2009)

14 Prince Street (R/W), 1917. (2005)

15 South Ferry (1), 1904. (2008)
This station is no longer in operation. A new South Ferry station, linked to the Whitehall Street station (R/W), opened in March 2009.

16 Rector Street (1), 1918. (2008)

17 Wilson Avenue (L), 1928. (2008)

11–17

18–23 Selected IND mosaic station names. Note the subtle variations in the sans serif lettering and the renaming of some stations.

18 Liberty Avenue (A), 1948. (2008)

19 163rd Street–Amsterdam Avenue (C), 1932. (2007)

20 Bergen Street (C/G), 1933. (2008)

21 Fordham Road (D), 1933. (2007)

22 Briarwood–Van Wyck (E/F), 1937. Originally Van Wyck Boulevard, the station was renamed upon community request in 1997. This avoided confusion with the Jamaica–Van Wyck Boulevard station (E) that opened in late 1988. (2008)

23 23rd Street–Ely Avenue (E/V), 1933. (2009)

The first "signs" in the New York City subway system were created by Heins & LaFarge, the architects of the IRT. In 1904 they established the now-familiar tradition of mosaic station names on platform walls. The name tablets were composed of small tiles in both serif and sans serif roman capitals (figs. 11–17). The BRT/BMT followed suit under Squire J. Vickers who took over the architectural duties of Heins & LaFarge in 1908. Neither line had a uniform lettering style even though the designs were prepared in the architects' studio and then shipped in sections to the stations. Thus, there is a surprising amount of variety within the mosaic station names. Smaller directional signs—with arrows indicating exits from each station—were also made in mosaic tile in both serif and sans serif roman capitals (figs. 26–30). Vickers simplified the decorative borders surrounding the name tablets but did not alter the lettering styles of either the IRT or the BMT. However, when the IND was established in 1925, he created a new style of sans serif capitals to accompany the stripped-down decoration of the stations (figs. 18–23). These letters, inspired by Art Deco, were heavier and more geometric than the earlier sans serifs which were rooted in 19th c. grotesques. They used larger, more uniform tiles than the IRT and BMT mosaics. However, the IND's directional mosaic signs employed lighter sans serif capitals and were made of smaller tiles. [3]

24 Mosaic tile directional sign. 14th Street (F/V), 1940. H & M Tunnels refers to the Hudson & Manhattan Railroad (now PATH). (2005)

25 Porcelain enamel directional sign, probably Union Square (4/5/6/N/Q/R/W), late 1920's or 1930s. The "14th Street Subway" was the Canarsie Line (L) that opened in 1924.

26–29 Selected IRT, BMT and IND mosaic tile directional signs. Note the use of serif and sans serif lettering.

26 Rector Street (1), 1918. (2008)

27 Lorimer Street (L), 1924. (2009)

28 21st Street–Van Alst Avenue (G), 1933. (2007)

29 28th Street (R/W), 1918. (2008)

30 Court Street (M/R), 1920. This is one of two mosaics in the system with text set in blackletter. (2008)

3. "...[T]he mosaic was of the cut variety, that is, the body is burned in strips, glazed, and then broken into irregular shapes. The designs are set by hand and shipped in sections with paper pasted on the front. These sections are set against the wall flush with the tile. In certain stations the color bands and name tablets are a combination of mosaic and hand-made tile." Lee Stookey, *Subway Ceramics: A History and Iconography of Mosaic and Bas Relief Signs and Plaques in the New York City Subway System.* (New York: Lee Stookey, 1994), p. 61. "Like the Victorians in general, who responded to a nineteenth-century explosion of new fonts by mixing and matching, Heins & LaFarge used both serif fonts (letters with fine lines finishing off the main strokes) and sans serif (no such fine lines), all uppercase. In general, they preferred serif lettering for sculptural faience or terra-cotta plaques like the flowery 'BH' monogram at Brooklyn Borough Hall and sans serif for flat surfaces, whether ceramic or glass tile mosaics." New York Transit Museum [Carissa Amash], *Subway Style: 100 Years of Architecture & Design in the New York City Subway.* (New York: Stewart, Tabori & Chang, 2004), p. 138. "He [Vickers] also changed his typography in response to European developments. Modernist European typography preferred the bold look of the sans-serif [sic], and embraced new fonts with names like 'Futura'." *Subway Style*, p. 141.

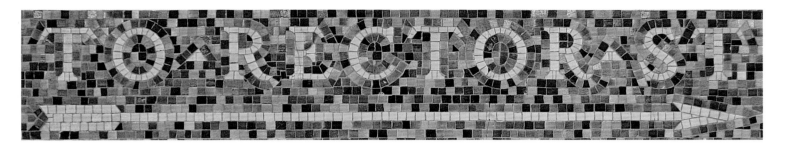

TO RECTOR ST

TO LORIMER ST. SOUTH SIDE

L.I. CITY AND JAMAICA

TO 28TH STREET

Church of the Holy Trinity

26–30

31

31 Mosaic tile column sign. Bushwick–Aberdeen (L), **1928.** (2008)

32–38 Selection of porcelain enamel or glazed tile directional signs. Note the variety of lettering styles, tile configurations and colors.

32 Liberty Avenue (A/C), **1948.** Two-letter tiles. (2008)

33 50th Street (C/E), **1932.** Single letter tiles. Note the arrow in parts. (2008)

34 Euclid Avenue (A/C), **1948.** Two letter tiles. (2008)

35 Forest Hills–71st Avenue (E/F/G/R/V), **1936.** Note the single tile for ordinal **ST.** (2008)

36 Bleecker Street (6), **1918.** (2007)

37 Wall Street (2/3), **1918.** Two-letter tiles. (2008)

38 Beverly Road (2/5), **1920.** Name in three sections. (2008)

32–38

Heins & LaFarge also "hung large, illuminated porcelain-enamel signs over the express platforms, using black type [actually handlettering] on a white background and painted station names on the round cast-iron columns." The latter were replaced in 1918 when Vickers commissioned enamel signs from both Nelke Signs (later Nelke Veribrite Signs) and the Baltimore Enamel Company. The two companies continued to make enamel signs throughout the 1930s, placing them on girder columns as well as cast-iron ones. Vickers' goal was to make it easier for riders to quickly recognize their stop upon entering a station. The abbreviated station names on the porcelain enamel signs were rendered in condensed sans serif capitals derived from common signpainting models (fig. 36). For the IND Vickers also added a second set of modular tiles—white letters and arrows on a black background—for the smaller directional signs (fig. 33). These were integrated into the station walls rather than being attached to the platform columns. The lettering of these signs is in a spur serif style—common in 19th c. signpainting manuals—that is reminiscent of social invitation typefaces such as Copperplate Gothic. [4]

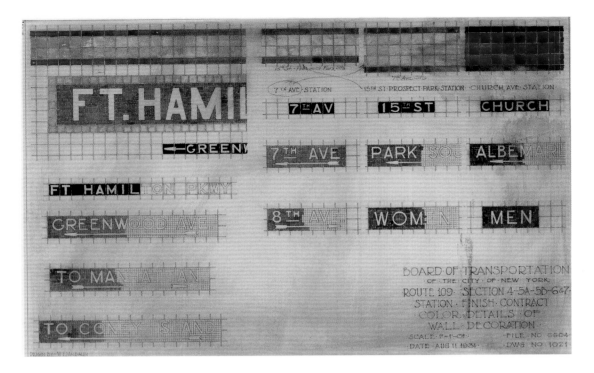

4. *Subway Style*, p. 138. Two examples of these porcelain enamel column signs are shown on p. 153. For an early 20th c. version of this lettering style see Spurred Commercial Gothic (with spacing guides) in Thomas E. French and Robert Meiklejohn, *The Essentials of Lettering: A Manual for Students and Designers.* (New York: McGraw-Hill Book Company, Inc., 1909), figs. 18 and 19, pp. 20–21. The spacing guides suggest French and Meiklejohn's book may have been used by the porcelain enamel companies.

39 IND ceramic ornamentation and glazed tile designs. Fort Hamilton Parkway (F) and 15th Street–Prospect Park (F). Rendering. August 11, 1931.

40 Mosaic tile restroom sign. Bergen Street (2/3), 1920. (2009)

41 Cut stone restroom sign. Fulton Street (4/5), 1905. (2008)

39–41

Beginning in the early 1950s, stations began to be systematically lengthened to accommodate newer and longer cars. The station walls were covered with simple glazed tiles in dull green, brown, blue and other solid colors. Station names were baked on in white spur-serif capitals. These were superseded by ochre tiles with standardized black spur-serif letters and, later, geometrically-constructed condensed sans serif letters. (The Grand Street station, which will play an important role in this story, has Delft blue letters rather than black or white ones.) [5]

As if this plethora of signs was not enough the subway system also had a bewildering variety of other porcelain enamel signs and handpainted signs. The porcelain enamel signs, either hung from the ceiling or posted on the walls, were directional as well as informational (fig. 49). The directional signs included those on the outside of the station entrances as well as those intended for the corridors and platforms underground. Many of the informational signs warned against behavior that was criminal, dangerous or unhealthy: no peddling wares, no leaning over the tracks, no crossing the tracks, no smoking, no spitting, etc (figs. 42, 43, 249, 250, 285). The directional and informational signs were made by Nelke Veribrite Signs and the Baltimore Enamel Company while the behavioral ones were the product of the Manhattan Dial Company. Most were lettered in some form of sans serif capitals—regular, condensed, square-countered, chamfered, outlined—though some were in bracketed or slab serif roman

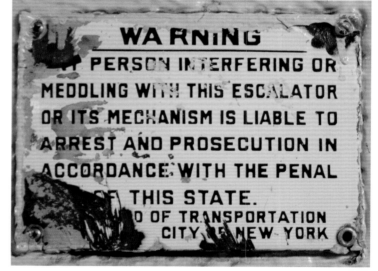

42–43

5. There is little information on these signs. See nycsubway.org for a rough dating of their appearance in various stations. A prime example of these often overlooked station identification signs are those in the Grand Street station. These can be precisely dated to 1967.

6. Examples of the large directional signs and smaller behavioral ones can be found in *Subway Style*, pp. 141 and 150–151 as well as at The Transit Museum in downtown Brooklyn. The chaotic welter of signs in stations c.1965 is evident in photographs in William Lansing Plumb, "Telling People Where to Go: Subway Graphics." *Print* XIX:V (September/October 1965): 13–23 and in *Subway Style*, p. 140.

The sans serif capitals are similar to alphabets the signpainters called Egyptian, Block or Plain letters. For instance, see Frank H. Atkinson, *Atkinson Sign Painting: A Complete Manual Self-Educational.* (Chicago: Frederick J. Drake & Company, 1909), pp. 169 and 191. Also see New York Gothic in James Eisenberg, *Commercial Art of Show Card Lettering* (New York: Van Nostrand, 1945), plates 4 and 5.

7. Several of these handpainted signs are reproduced in Plumb (1965), pp. 13–23. The most amusing of them reads, "Hiya Folks. Do you know that your subway system is the fastest, safest & cheapest mode of transportation in the world today." (77)

42 Porcelain enamel prohibitory sign, pre-1938.

43 Porcelain enamel warning sign. Grand Central Station (7), pre-1953. (2008)

capitals. They were usually white letters on a colored background, often dark green for the IND and dark blue for the IRT and BMT; though some were black on a white background. There was no house style. [6]

Handpainted signs were added to the subway system as far back as the mid-1930s—maybe earlier—and were still being used three decades later (figs. 44, 46). (In fact, some can still be seen today at stations such as Forest Hills–Continental Avenue in Queens.) Some were temporary in nature—lettered on easel boards—and others were more permanent. The latter, usually informational in nature—such as the location of toilets—were painted on corridor walls in red and black grotesque capitals. There is evidence that when they faded or became scuffed, they were simply repainted (fig. 46). [7]

44–46

47 Porcelain enamel directional sign.
    Saratoga Avenue (3), 1920. This
    station has the only two such signs
    still surviving in the system. (2010)

48 Porcelain enamel directional sign.
    34th Street–Herald Square
    (N/R/Q/W), probably 1920s. (1970s)

49 Porcelain enamel station platform sign.
    Kings Highway (B/Q), c.1926. (1980s)

50 Painted destination sign. Coney
    Island–Stillwell Avenue. (1995)

47–50

51 **Painted lettering over two-letter porcelain enamel tiles. Liberty Avenue (A/C), c.1956?** The IND Fulton line was originally planned to extend to Richmond Hill but in 1956 it hooked up instead with a section of the Liberty Avenue Elevated (BMT). (2008)

52 **Painted station entrance sign (detail). Unidentified BMT station.** Note the porcelain enamel lettering underneath.

51–52

.4. Division codes and service categories
also to be named on interior station signs,
with directions to other platforms if needed:

BRINGING ORDER OUT OF CHAOS

That this overlapping array of sign systems was an untenable mess was recognized as early as 1957 when George Salomon, (1920–1981), typographic designer at Appleton, Parsons & Co., made an unsolicited proposal to the New York City Transit Authority (NYCTA) entitled "Out of the Labyrinth: A plea and a plan for improved passenger information in the New York subways" (figs. 53–57). The unpublished typescript anticipated many of the suggestions for overhauling the signage of the subway system that Unimark would make a decade later. Salomon suggested that the distinctions among the IRT, BMT and IND be abolished and replaced by five major trunk lines and eleven subsidiary routes. The trunk lines would be color-coded and identified by a letter and the branch lines by a derivative letter/number combination. Thus, Salomon's system consisted of the Lexington Avenue line (B, blue), the Broadway BMT line (C, purple), the Sixth Avenue line (D, orange), Seventh Avenue line

(E, red), and Eighth Avenue line (F, green). The Seventh Avenue line branched off into single lines, desig-nated E1 through E5. Similar markings were used for the other subsidiary lines. Salomon proposed that the color-coding be used for the trains, signage and maps to ensure consistency and uniformity throughout the subway system. He also wanted the signage to be standardized. His preference was for signs to be set in Futura Demibold—which he claimed was the most legible face available—set in white on a black background and supported by large directional arrows. Salomon concluded his proposal by stating, "It's a big job. But for the sake of the subway itself and for the sake of the city it serves and for the people of that city it must be done soon." [8]

53 (opposite page) George Salomon. "Out of the Labyrinth: A Plea and a Plan for Improved Passenger Information in the New York Subways." (c.1957), p. 23, fig. 4.

54 George Salomon. "Out of the Labyrinth: A Plea and a Plan for Improved Passenger Information in the New York Subways." (c.1957), p. 17, fig. 3.

8. Salomon, George, "Out of the Labyrinth: A plea and a plan for improved passenger information in the New York subways." [1957], last page. See also *Subway Style*, p. 141. Salomon's proposal exists as an unnumbered typescript with pasted-on photostats in the Archives of The Transit Museum, Brooklyn. Salomon's choice of Futura is not surprising since it was one of the most popular sans serif faces in American graphic design in the 1950s. Univers, Helvetica and Folio were not yet available in the United States and Akzidenz Grotesk (Standard) was just beginning to be discovered. Little is known about George Salomon. He worked as a graphic designer from 1947 to 1960, including freelance assignments for the New York City Transit Authority from 1957 to 1959, before becoming a journalist and comunity relations worker. At the time he penned his proposal he was working for Appleton, Parsons & Co., a design and printing firm in Manhattan, and living in Yonkers. See "Business Notes," *New York Times*, February 17, 1947 and "Advertising News and Notes," *New York Times*, April 12, 1950. For Salomon's family history see The Leo Baeck Institute at the Center for Jewish History http://findingaids.cjh.org/?pID=480697. Salomon's interest in transportation systems must have been longstanding since he wrote a letter to the New York Times a decade earlier complaining about the failure of the ferries to properly join up with the subway system; and in May 1955 he sent the TA a proposal entitled "Orientation". Salomon, George, "Letters to Editor." *New York Times*, 1946. The latter was kindly brought to my attention by Peter B. Lloyd. See his website http://www.metronexco.com/research.htm.

54

55 George Salomon. "Out of the Labyrinth: A Plea and a Plan for Improved Passenger Information in the New York Subways." (c.1957), p. 16, fig. 1.

56 George Salomon. "Out of the Labyrinth: A Plea and a Plan for Improved Passenger Information in the New York Subways." (c.1957), p. 23, fig. 3.

57 George Salomon. "Out of the Labyrinth: A Plea and a Plan for Improved Passenger Information in the New York Subways." (c.1957), p. 16, fig. 2.

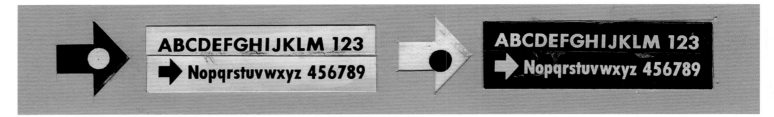

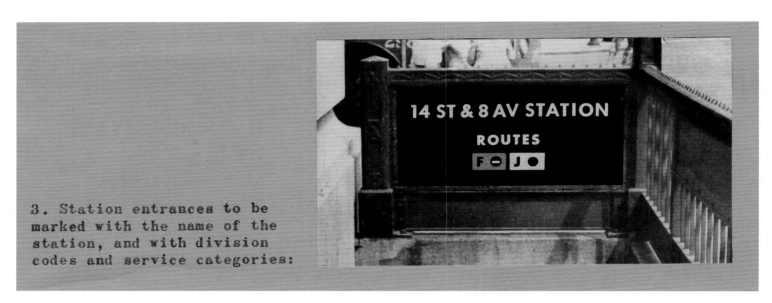

3. Station entrances to be marked with the name of the station, and with division codes and service categories:

2. Consistent use of the standard lettering, and of the mark or parts of it:

55–57

14

The only one of Salomon's ideas that was taken up by the TA was his suggestion for a color-coded route map. His design of a map for the subway system, heavily influenced by Henry Beck's famous map for the London Underground, was published in 1958. It was the first official map issued by the TA (the shortened name of the NYCTA) since its inception in 1953—and the first to show the entire system. (Maps issued by its predecessor, the Board of Transportation, were produced by private companies such as Hagstrom Maps.) Salomon's map was not as ambitious as his "Out of the Labyrinth" ideas (fig. 58). The IRT lines were colored black, the BMT lines green and the IND lines red. The map was set in a mix of News Gothic, News Gothic Bold, Standard and Times Roman—but no Futura. [9]

Apparently, the TA did make some kind of an attempt in 1958 to improve the signage within the subway system. It engaged Ladislav Sutnar, the pioneer of information design, to design exit signs for the stations but they were not "properly implemented" by the TA's sign shop—a portent of what Unimark was to face a decade later (fig. 59). No further details about the assignment are known. [10]

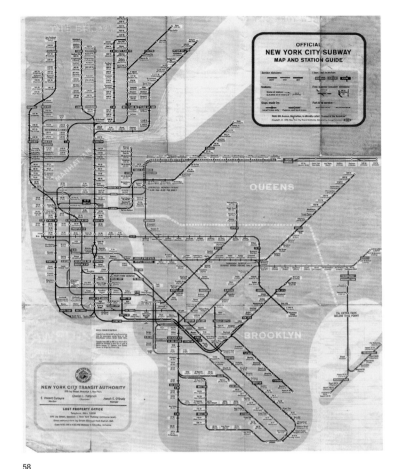

58

58 **Official New York City Subway Map and Station Guide, 1958.** Designed by George Salomon.

59 **Proposed Exit sign by Ladislav Sutnar, 1958.** From "Making New York Understandable," *Print* XVI:IV (July/August 1972), p. 64.

9. *Subway Style*, pp. 163 and 172–173. The 1958 map can also be seen at ursasoft.com/maps/NewYork/newyork-notes.html and subway.com.ru/maps.htm. A detail is reproduced in Mark Ovenden, *Transit Maps of the World*, 2nd rev. ed. (London: Penguin Books, Ltd., 2007), p. 033. The map was a winner in the information design category of the AIGA's Design and Printng for Commerce competition in 1959. Although the map is signed by Salomon alone the AIGA credits also cite Peter De Nare, Jr. The typefaces used are identified in the AIGA catalogue entry. See designarchives.aiga.org/entry.cfm/eid_16014. Ovenden's claim that Salomon "introduced the Akzidenz-Grotesk font to the system" (p. 032) overstates the importance of its

appearance on the 1958 map. Salomon's 1958 map was the basis for subsequent NYCTA maps until 1967 when it was superseded by the Goldstein/D'Adamo map.

10. Sutnar's carefully designed lettering was replaced by "ordinary shop type"—Futura in the accompanying photograph. "Making New York Understandable," *Print* XVI:IV (July/August 1972), p. 64. This is the only known mention of Sutnar's work for the NYCTA. It does not appear in Iva Janáková et al, *ladislav sutnar: prague—new york—design in action*, (Prague: Museum of Decorative Arts in Prague and Argo Publishers, 2003) nor in any of Sutnar's own writings. The July/August 1972 issue of *Print* served as the catalogue for the exhibition "Making New York Understandable", an exhibition organized by advertising designer William McCaffrey and sponsored by the Art Directors Club. It took place at the New York Cultural Center in the former Huntington Hartford Building at Columbus Circle.

59

TRANSPORTATION SIGNAGE SYSTEMS IN THE 1960s

The 1960s saw an interest among urban planners, architects and graphic designers, both here and in Europe, in the systematic design of signage for cities, highways, railways, subways, and airports. At the beginning of the decade greater attention to the issues involved in urban signage was sparked by the near simultaneous publication of *Lettering on Buildings* by Nicolete Gray (1960) and *Sign Language for Buildings and Landscape* by Mildred Constantine and Egbert Jacobson (1961). Unfortunately, Gray did not examine transportation system signage and Constantine and Jacobson devoted only a few sentences and images to the topic, primarily focusing on above-ground signs for the Paris Métro and London Underground. Their lone image of signage within an underground railway system was, surprisingly, from the Philadelphia subway. [11]

One reason for this lacunae is that, at the time, coordinated subway sign systems were rare. New York was not the only major city to have a visual mess underground. Even the famed Paris Métro was plagued by a welter of different styles of signs that was not brought under control until 1971 when Métro, designed by Adrian Frutiger and based on his Univers typeface, was introduced. The lone exception to this state of affairs was London where Johnston Railway Sans—designed by calligrapher Edward Johnston at the behest of Frank Pick, Publicity Manager at London Transport—had been in use since 1916 for signage as well as on posters and advertising. [12]

60 (opposite page) Signage. The Oceanic Building, Heathrow Airport, 1961. Designed by Colin Forbes using Airport alphabet.

11. This survey of 1960s-era transit systems does not take into account those in Chicago, Philadelphia, Rome, San Francisco (Bay Area Rapid Transit or BART) or Montreal since none of them have any direct bearing on the issues discussed in this book.

12. For detailed information on Edward Johnston's Railway Sans see Justin Howes, *Johnston's Underground Type.* (London: Capital Transport, 2000) and for the mosaic name tablets in the London Underground see Douglas Rose, *Tiles of the Unexpected Underground: A Study of Six Miles of Geometric Tile Patterns on the London Underground.* (London: Douglas Rose, 2007). Details on the genesis of Adrian Frutiger's Métro typeface are in Heidrun Osterer and Philipp Stamm, eds., *Adrian Frutiger Typefaces: The Complete Works.* (Basel, Boston & Berlin: Birkhäuser Verlag AG, 2008), pp. 244–247.

The first coherent transportation sign system of the 1960s was created by Colin Forbes (b.1928) in 1961 for The Oceanic Building at Heathrow Airport (fig. 60). Now called Terminal 3, The Oceanic Building was the second terminal to be built at the airport. Forbes' sign system for it employed modular panels with sans serif lettering in black on white (though white on black was allowed for some levels of information) combined with arrows. Guidelines for spacing and sizing the letters were an essential aspect of the system. For the lettering, Forbes, who had a solo practice at the time, hired a young Matthew Carter (b.1937) to design a custom grotesque. The design, eventually called Airport, was based on Standard (as Akzidenz Grotesk was called at that time in England) which Forbes praised for its "simple, bold, easily identifiable letterforms with an individual but unaggressive personality" (fig. 61). Carter drew a special weight, increased the x-height and amended several individual letters (principally replacing the angled terminals of **c**, **e** and **s** with horizontal ones). [**13**]

The result looked a lot like Helvetica Medium. Forbes acknowledged this years later in *A Sign Systems Manual* (1970) when he wrote, "Since this amended design was produced a new typeface, Helvetica, has been issued. Helvetica incorporates many of the adaptations made to Standard and it is now often used for signs by reproducing directly from printers' and filmsetters' type." In 1960, when the signage for The Oceanic Building was being planned, Forbes and Carter were unaware of the existence of Helvetica. "If we'd known about it," Carter said in 2007 to Alice Rawsthorn of the International Herald Tribune, "I'm sure we would have used it, since it's a much better typeface than the one I drew." [**14**]

All of the elements of The Oceanic Building sign system resurfaced in other transportation sign systems of the 1960s. In November 1964, work on the M1 (Red) line, the first of the

13. Crosby, Fletcher, Forbes, *A Sign Systems Manual.* (New York and Washington: Praeger Publishers Inc., 1970), pp. 16–55. The book slides over the exact dating of the Oceanic Building project. Information confirming the genesis and dating of Airport was provided by Matthew Carter. Matthew Carter to author, 5 July 2008. For a full chronology of the various terminals at Heathrow Airport see http://www.milesfaster.co.uk/information/heathrow-airport/heathrow-history.htm. Fletcher/Forbes/Gill was formed in 1962; Crosby/Fletcher/Forbes in 1965. Since 1972 the firm has been known as Pentagram.

14. *A Sign Systems Manual*, p. 16. Despite Forbes' admission that Airport was inferior to Helvetica—and that Helvetica was available in England after 1965—the typeface was released for general use by Berthold AG c.1968. Rawsthorne, Alice, "Helvetica: The little typeface that leaves a big mark," *International Herald Tribune*, April 1, 2007.

61 Airport alphabet by Matthew Carter, 1960.

62–65 *Pagina 4* **(Gennaio 1964).** Bob Noorda, "Studies for signs and indicator board in the Milan underground–Studi per la segnaletica della metropolitana Milanese / Etudes pour la signalisation du metropolitain Milanais.".

62 Character legibility tests by Bob Noorda. *Pagina 4* **(Gennaio 1964), p. 8.** The "broader character" is Noorda's modified version of Akzidenz Grotesk.

61

three-line Metropolitana Milanese, was completed. The station designs were by Franco Albini and Franca Helg while the signage was by Bob Noorda who was also responsible for suggesting the color coding of the system's three lines. At the time, Noorda (1927–2010)—a Dutch designer who had moved to Italy in 1952 and gained a reputation for his work as art director of Pirelli— had his own design firm in Milano. His sign system for the Milano Metro involved modular enamel strip signs placed along the station walls at consistent intervals. Along with the platform signage Noorda designed route diagrams, neighborhood maps, clockfaces and posters for each station. The entire Milano Metro won Noorda and the architects the Premio Compasso d'Oro in 1964. [**15**].

The lettering for the Milano Metro signs was a modified version of Helvetica drawn by Noorda himself (fig. 63). Finding the available weights of Helvetica to be either too bold or too light, Noorda created an intermediate weight. He also reduced the height of the capitals and ascenders and the depth of the descenders to make a more compact design. Several characters were drawn following those of Akzidenz Grotesk: **Q**, **R** and **2** for instance. The letters were designed to be white reversed out of a red matte background. Station names and exit signs were set in all caps while informational signs were set in upper- and lowercase characters. Noorda established a spacing system for his custom typeface. [**16**]

15. For detailed information on Noorda's work for the Milano Metro see Bob Noorda, "Studies for Signs and Indicator Board in the Milan Underground–Studi per la segnaletica della Metropolitana Milanese– Etudes pour la signalisation du Metropolitain Milanais," *Pagina* no. 4 (Gennaio 1964), pp. 4–13; Bob Noorda in "Transportation Graphics," *Dot Zero* 5 (Fall 1968), pp. 38–41. The *Dot Zero* article is an edited version of Noorda's talk at the symposium "Transportation Graphics: Where Am I Going? How Do I Get There?" organized by Mildred Constantine and held at the Museum of Modern Art on October 23, 1967. Limited accounts of the project are contained in Toon Lauwen, *Bob Noorda*. Eindhoven: [Z]OO Producties, n.d. [1994?] and Nico Ventura, ed., *Bob Noorda Design*. (Ferrara: MusArc, 2005), pp. 42–45. The account in Giorgio Fiorvanti, Leonardo

Passarelli and Silvia Sfligiotti, *La Grafica in Italia*. (Milano: Leonardo Arte, 1997), p. 137 is marred by inconsistent dating. The Red Line was the first line of the Metropolitana Milanese to be completed, followed by the Green Line in 1969 and the Yellow Line in 1990.

16. Noorda's signage was used for the Green and Yellow Lines but in the late 1990s it was altered by Inarea, a Milanese design agency. It became glossy instead of matte and a modified version of Arial replaced Noorda's custom typeface. (Several older signs have survived.) (**66**) Recently there has been an attempt to revive Noorda's typeface (newly digitized by Michele Patané). See the unpublished report *Relazione sulle proposte Inarea per la segnaletica della Metropolitana di Milano* by James Clough (May 2009).

Tests for legibility of characters

Prove per la leggibilità
dei caratteri

Expérience de légibilité
des caractères

8-9. *Two basic types of already-existing characters (one narrow, the other broad) were tried out for their legibility as seen from various angles. Better results were obtained with the broader character.*
Per garantire la leggibilità delle scritte in prospettiva sono stati studiati i risultati in due tipi base di caratteri già esistenti, uno più stretto, l'altro più largo: la leggibilità prospettica è maggiore nel carattere più largo.

8
9

Pour s'assurer de la légiblité des inscriptions en perspective, on a soumis à l'étude les résultats de deux types de caractères de base déjà existants: un type de caractère étroit et un autre plus large. La légibilité en perspective s'est avérée meilleur avec le caractère plus large.

82

ABCDEFGHIJ KLMNOPQR STUVWXYZ 1234567890 abcdefghij klmnopqrst uvwxyz

12. *Alphabet, complete with numbers, capitals and small letters, in the character adopted for the Milan underground.*
Alfabeto, completo di maiuscole, minuscole e numeri, con il carattere adottato per la Metropolitana Milanese.
Alphabet complet de majuscules, minuscules et de nombres; caractère adopté par le métropolitain milanais.

After fixing the type of character, details of the character itself were worked out

Stabilito il tipo di carattere, studio del carattere stesso

Aprés établissement du type de caractère, étude du caractère lui-même

10. *The character adopted for the Milan underground is derived from the kind known as «grotesque». Boldface and clear versions of «grotesque» turned out to be too light or dark when enlarged as required. Bob Noorda worked out a modification which only affected the «eye» of the character, the height of the «grotesque» remaining unchanged.*
Il carattere adottato dalla metropolitana

è una derivazione del carattere tipografico «grottesco». I «grotteschi» chiari e neretti, ingranditi secondo le esigenze, risultavano troppo chiari o troppo scuri. Bob Noorda ha studiato una modifica che riguarda soltanto l'occhio del carattere; l'altezza è rimasta quella del «grottesco».
Le caractère adopté par le métropolitain est un dérivé du caractère typographique «grotesque». Les «grotesques» clairs et gris-noirs, agrandis selon les besoins, apparaissaient trop clairs ou trop obscurs; Bob Noorda a étudié des modifications concernant seulement les bouches des caractères, la hauteur restant celle du «grotesque».

10

11

11. *A system of variable spacing between letters was planned: one space-unit between two «round» letters, or between an upright and an oblique one, no space-unit between an oblique and «rounds» letter, two between «round» and upright ones, three between two upright ones.*
E' stato studiato un sistema di spaziatura che, attraverso unità di misura, stabilisce esattamente la quantità di spazio da lasciare tra qualsiasi tipo di lettere. Una unità tra due lettere rotonde o tra una diritta e una obliqua, zero unità tra una lettera obliqua e una rotonda, due unità tra una lettera rotonda e una diritta, tre unità tra due lettere diritte.
On a étudié également un système d'éspacement qui, moyennant une unité de mesure, établit l'espace que l'on doit laisser entre les divers types de lettres. Une unité, entre deux lettres rondes, ou entre une lettre droite et une oblique; zéro unité entre une lettre oblique et une ronde, deux unités entre une ronde et une droite, trois unités entre deux lettres droites.

9

13-15. *The indicator strip is twice as high on platforms; its upper half becomes white, and carries information additional to the station names on the other half.*
La banda della segnaletica si raddoppia in banchina e prende una parte superiore bianca, necessaria per la segnaletica minore della stazione.
La bande de signalisation se double sur le quai et la partie supérieure est blanche, précaution indispensable en raison de la signalisation mineure de la station.

16. *The arrows are in circles, resulting in a geometrical form which allows the central part to be moved round without affecting its legibility. This system has a precedent in the signs at London Airport.*
Le frecce sono inscritte in cerchi, forma geometrica che permette di far ruotare la figura interna garantendone sempre la leggibilità. Questa soluzione ha una precedente esemplificazione nella segnaletica dell'aeroporto di Londra.
Les flèches sont inscrites en cercle, forme géométrique qui permet de faire tourner la figure interne, en en garantissant la légibilité. Cette solution a un précédent dans la signalisation de l'aéroport de Londres.

13
14
15
16 17

USCITA
GORLA   GORLA

← SESTO S. GIOVANNI

Corso Buenos Aires →

← USCITA

17. *Signs for the telephones.*
La segnaletica degli apparecchi telefonici.
Signalisation des appareils téléphoniques.

11

Bisceglie / Rho -

65–66

63 Milano alphabet by Bob Noorda, 1964. *Pagina 4* (Gennaio 1964), p. 10. In his notes for the 1967 "Transportation Graphics" symposium at the Museum of Modern Art, Noorda wrote, "Having decided on Helvetica typeface, I found that the medium was too heavy and the light too light, when used in negative on a red background. I therefore designed a modified version. The importance being to get a more open body with shortened ascenders and descenders." But close examination of the Milano alphabet suggests that Noorda actually modified Akzidenz Grotesk instead. Note the retention of the key characters **J**, **Q**, **R**, **2** and **5**.

64 Comparison of Akzidenz Grotesk to Milano alphabet by Bob Noorda. *Pagina 4* (Gennaio 1964), p. 9.

65 Elements of the Metropolitana Milano signage system by Bob Noorda. *Pagina 4* (Gennaio 1964), p. 11.

66 Illuminated directional sign. Duomo station (M3, Yellow line), Metropolitana Milano, 1990. (2008)

Dark on light letterform

67–68

Noorda was not the only designer in the early 1960s dissatisfied with Helvetica as a face for transportation signage. In 1964 Jock Kinneir (1917–1993) and Margaret Calvert (b.1936) of Kinneir Calvert Associates designed Rail Alphabet as part of a comprehensive sign system for British Railway done in parallel with a full corporate identity program by Design Research Unit (DRU) (fig. 67). Their typeface was a modified version of Helvetica Bold, available in both positive and negative versions. The capitals, ascenders and descenders were all reduced while the **J**, **Q**, and **2** were modeled after Standard. The individual letters—as well as arrows and the new British Rail logo—were made as individual artwork tiles for easy assembly and spacing. The British Rail identity, including Rail Alphabet, was unveiled in 1965. [17]

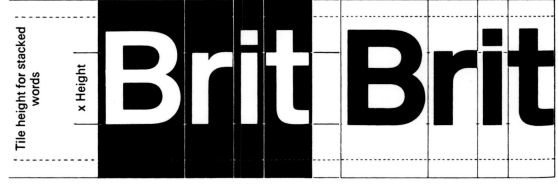

69

17. "Our first viewing of Akzidenz Grotesk was in the book *Lettera*, Volume I. Neue Haas Grotesk appeared much later, in a mailer... (Soon to be renamed Helvetica, as you know). The interesting point is that there were 3 designers, all working independently, round about the same time, on a Helvetica influenced signing face. These were Mathew Carter for [Fletcher, Forbes, Gill], Gerald Barney DRU, and me, starting with our work for the Ministry of Health, around about 1963." Margaret Calvert email to author, 24 June 2009. The story behind the Rail Alphabet can be found in several places: Jock Kinneir in "Transportation Graphics." *Dot Zero* 5 (Fall 1968), pp. 5–11; Robert Spark, "Face-life for BR," *Design 1965 Journal*, pp. 46–51; nationmaster.com/encyclopedia/Rail-Alphabet; designmuseum.org/design/ jock-kinneir-margaret-calvert; and vads. ahds.ac.uk/diad/article.php?year= 1965&title=193&article=d.193.32. It is also included in *A Sign Systems Manual*, pp. 58–59; and Walter Diethelm, *Signet, Signal Symbol*. (Zurich: ABC Verlag, 1984), pp. 88–89. It should be noted that Kinneir used Standard in his signage for the 1957 Gatwick Airport renovation. The Rail Alphabet was subsequently adopted for the Danish State Railways (DSB). It was redesigned and released by A2/HK/SW (Henrik Kubel and Scott Williams) as a digital font called New Rail Alphabet in 2009.

67 Rail Alphabet by Jock Kinneir and Margaret Calvert, 1964. Rail Alphabet, an "amended" version of Helvetica Bold, was subsequently used for British Airports Authority signage (1968) and Danish State Railways (DSB) signage (1971).

68 Signage. King's Cross railway station, British Rail, 1960s. Designed by Kinneir Calvert Associates.

69 Explanation of "artwork tile" method of spacing Rail alphabet in both positive and negative versions. From Crosby, Fletcher, Forbes, *A Sign Systems Manual*. (1970), p. 58.

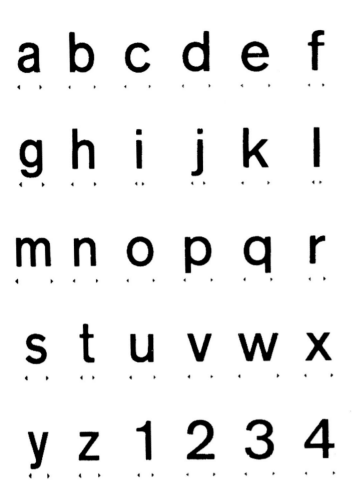

70

Work on Amsterdam's Schiphol Airport, designed by M. Duintjerand Kho Liang Le, was begun in 1962. The design of its sign system was carried out by Benno Wissing (1923–2008) of Total Design who used an altered Standard—ascenders and descenders chopped down—as the typeface (fig. 70). With the exception of the gate designations, the signs were set in all lowercase letters. The colors were a combination of black and white on either yellow or green backgrounds. The system was publicized in 1965 but the airport did not open until two years later. [18]

The same year that the Red Line of the Metropolitana Milanese opened, plans for modernizing the Boston subway system were announced. The newly-created Massachusetts Bay Transportation Authority (MBTA) awarded the contract for station renovation in January 1965 to Cambridge Seven Associates, a multi-disciplinary architectural and design firm led by architect Peter Chermayeff.

71

18. The dating of the Schiphol signage is not wholly clear. *A Sign Systems Manual*, pp. 60–61 dates the signage to 1965; Broos, Kees, *design: Total Design*. (Utrecht: uitgeverij Reflex, 1983), pp. 53–55 says 1967; Smit, Gees-Ineke, "*Schiphol: The development of an airport,*" in *Holland in Vorm: Dutch Design 1945-1987* edited by Gert Staal and Hester Wolters ('s-Gravenhage: Stichting Holland in Vorm, 1987), pp. 33–37 shows the altered Standard typeface but provides no date; and Paul Hefting, Koosje Sierman and Dingenus van de Vrie, *Benno Wissing: Grafische & ruimtelijke ontwerpen*. (Rotterdam: Museum Boijmans Van Beuningen and NAi Uitgevers, 1999), pp. 62–63 says that Wissing began work on Schiphol signage in 1962 but provides no end date. If this date is correct, then the assignment would have predated the formation of Total Design in 1963, thus providing an explanation for why it was Wissing and not the more celebrated Wim Crouwel who carried out the assignment.

70 Schiphol alphabet by Benno Wissing, 1965. From Crosby, Fletcher, Forbes, *A Sign Systems Manual*. (1970), p. 61. The Schiphol alphabet designed by Benno Wissing is a modified version of Standard Medium.

71 Signage. Schiphol Airport, 1965–1967. Designed by Benno Wissing of Total Design.

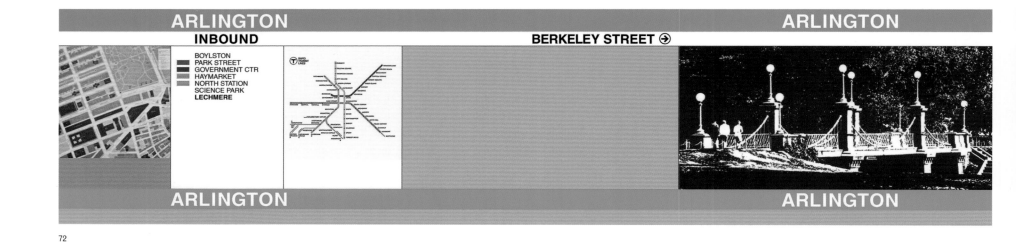

The design partners in the firm, Ivan Chermayeff (b.1932) and Tom Geismar (b.1931), were responsible for the station graphics. They created a new symbol for the Boston system (a black sans serif T in a circle), color-coded its four lines (and renamed them red, blue, orange and green), designed a Beck-inspired diagrammatic map, and established a uniform typographic style for all signage in the subway and bus system. [19]

The enamel signs were split in half horizontally with white lettering on a colored background at the top for the name of each station and black letters on a white background below for additional information about each stop. The typeface, used on maps as well as the signs, was Helvetica Medium (figs. 72–75). "As to the choice of Helvetica, it's a bit fuzzy," Geismar has recently said, "but I recall that we were generally excited to have a machine-set version, and felt that it's directness was appropriate to our whole effort to simplify and clarify the MBTA transit system. Also, as part of the program, I had designed the T in the circle to identify and re-name the system, and that featured a very simple, Helvetica-like T." The MBTA signage was publicly introduced in August 1965 but the first renovated station—Arlington Street—did not open until October 1967. It was the first transportation signage system to use Helvetica without modifications. [20]

72 Prototype of station wall panel with neighborhood map, system map and photomural of neighborhood landmark. Arlington Street, Boston (MBTA), 1965. Designed by Chermayeff & Geismar.

73 Entrance sign with T logo. Arlington Street, Boston (MBTA), 1965. T logo and signage designed by Chermayeff & Geismar. (1968)

19. Cambridge Seven Associates was founded in 1962 by Peter Chermayeff, Louis J. Bakanowsky, Paul Dietrich, Terry Rankine, Alden Christie, Ivan Chermayeff, and Thomas Geismar. The firm integrated work in architecture, urban design, planning, exhibitions, graphic, and interior design. songdo.com. The Boston T renovation project is detailed in Joan M. Lukach, "Transportation: Design in Transit: Boston's Revitalized Subway System," in *Print* XXII:II (March/April 1968), pp. 62–67; Chermayeff, Peter in "Transportation Graphics," *Dot Zero* 5 (Fall 1968), pp. 32–37; Patricia Conway George, "Mass Transit: Problem and Promise." *Design Quarterly* 71 (1968), p. 21; and Peter Blake, "Boston's MBTA," in *Subways*. (New York: Cooper-Hewitt Museum, 1977). The project used Arlington Street as a pilot station. Contemporary reactions to its opening in 1967 include Scott Kelly, "Boston transit: team design and fractious fans," *Industrial Design* 14/5 (June 1967), pp. 64–70; "Subways Can Be Beautiful," *Time*, October 20, 1967 and John H. Fenton, "Imported Ideas Improve Boston Subways," *New York Times*, November 27, 1967. The Institute of Contemporary Art in Boston held an exhibition dedicated to the program in 1967.

20. Chermayeff and Geismar's graphics for the Boston T are shown in Ivan Chermayeff, Tom Geismar and Steff Geissbuhler. *designing*. (New York: Graphis Inc., 2003), pp. 274–275. The dating of their work comes from Tom Geismar. Tom Geismar to author, 30 April 2008. The T logo was inspired by the symbol used by the Stockholm Tunnelbana. "Mass Transportation," *Industrial Design* (November 1966), p. 34 described the signage as being set in an "easily-read modified Helvetica typeface" but it provided no details. In contemporary photographs of the signage, the typeface does not appear to have been altered but it is difficult to tell since there are no lowercase letters. Geismar says that Standard was used for the MBTA's stationery.

74

75

WARNING
...AR OVER EDGE OF PLATFORM
8

TO EAST SIDE OF LEXINGTON AVE.
AND IRT UPTOWN TRAINS
USE STAIRWAY AT FAR END OF PLATFORM
...OWN TRAINS

ET & UPTOWN
ON AVE LINE

ESCALATOR · STRE
↑ IRT DOWNTOWN

YELLOW LINE

59
LEX.
AVE.

NO
Standing

P4A

THE NYCTA AND UNIMARK INTERNATIONAL

76 (opposite page) Signage at 59th Street–Lexington Avenue subway station, April 18, 1968.

At the same time that Milano was opening the first line of its new metro system and Boston was overhauling its "T", the New York City subway was still bumbling along. But the 1964/1965 World's Fair in Flushing pressured the TA to improve its image and information graphics. They commissioned a new logo from Sundberg-Ferar, an industrial design firm responsible for designing a new subway car, and they created special strip maps (set in Futura) for use on the no. 7 Flushing Line (fig. 79). The TA also decided to hold a competition for a new map. [21]

The 1964 NYCTA map competition was apparently the idea of Len Ingalls, Director of Public Information and Community Relations at the agency, who was eager to see if the London Underground map's color coding could be applied to the New York City subway map. The contest—which was judged by Harmon H. Goldstone (1911–2001), head of the New York City Planning Commission, and Jerry Donovan, cartographer for *Time* magazine—drew only nine entries. Four were awarded $3000 prizes but none were chosen

as a winner. The best of them, Raleigh D'Adamo's submission, emulated London's seven-color coding system but was deemed "too complex for general use". Goldstone later said that there was no winner "because a good map is not possible for a system which lacks intellectual order and precision". In the wake of this disaster, Prof. Stanley A. Goldstein (b.1923), a professor of engineering at Hofstra University, was hired as a consultant in January 1965 to devise a map that would successfully solve the color-coding problem posed by New York City's tangled subway system. Six months later he submitted a 39-page report entitled "Methods of Improving Subway information" that went beyond ideas for a new map to include suggestions on "train designations, car information and station information". Goldstein's recommendations did not bear immediate fruit, but they set in motion the events that eventually led the NYCTA to hire Unimark International. [22]

---

21. The opening of Shea Stadium in 1965 was a second reason for the creation of the no. 7 strip maps. Their design was cribbed from the London Underground. Examples can be seen in *Subway Style*, p. 175. Sundberg-Ferar was established in Walled Lake, Michigan in 1934 by Carl W. Sundberg (1911–1982) and Montgomery Ferar (1910–1982). They designed several subway cars for the Budd Company. new.idsa.org. The logo they designed consisted of an intertwined lowercase blue **t** and red **a** sloped to the right (**79**).

22. Details of the 1964 map competition are from Neil Sheehan, "Subways a Maze to Uninitiated," *New York Times*, September 18, 1964; "3 Win Transit Authority Prizes for Designs of Subway Maps," *New York Times*, October 17, 1964; and Peter Blake, "Get Off at N, 1, 2, 3, 7, SS, QB, RR, NX, EE—The Crossroads of the World," *New York Magazine*, April 8, 1968, p. 108. They have been confirmed by Prof. Stanley A. Goldstein. Stanley A. Goldstein to author, 6 August 2008. See also Harmon Goldstone in "Transportation Graphics." *Dot Zero* 5 (Fall 1968), p. 44. Information on Len Ingalls' role comes from John Tauranac. John Tauranac to author, 11 August 2008. Leonard Ingalls was a former reporter for the *New York Times* who was appointed Director of Public Information and Community Relations at the TA in July 1964, a position he held through the end

of the 1970s. Peter B. Lloyd kindly shared with me R. Raleigh D'Adamo's copy of the competition guidelines issued by the New York City Transit Authority, July 30, 1964.

Prof. Stanley A. Goldstein, who had an interest in mathematical puzzles, was recommended to the TA by a mutual friend at the New York City Planning Commission. His report made the following recommendations for a new map to replace the Salomon-derived existing one: 1. letters and numbers should be used to designate all routes—the IRT already had numbered lines and the IND lettered ones, but the BMT had neither; 2. each of the 36 lines should be rendered in one of six colors; 3. the underlying geographic shapes should better represent the contours of New York City—with some distortion allowed out of a need to maintain maximum clarity;

4. some slight alterations to the strict angles of lines should be allowed to fix erroneous relationships among lines and stations; 5. stations should be indicated by colored geometric shapes that distinguish between express and local stops; and 6. lettering should be in black and in a typeface that is the most legible. Goldstein's six colors were taken from the Munsell Color System which was the industrial standard at the time. For further information on the Munsell Color System see Joy Turner Luke, *The Munsell Color System A Language for Color* (New York: Fairchild Publications, 1996). (The Pantone Matching System was not as widely established then as it is today.) The recommended "type font" was "Navy Aeronautical Medical Equipment Laboratory Letters and Numerals, (MIL-C-18012)" or something equivalent that had a line width-to-height

ratio of 1:6 and a letter width-to-height ratio of .65:1. Stanley A. Goldstein, "Methods of Improving Subway Information," New York City Transit Authority, 1965, pp. 9, 15, 21–22, 27 and 29.

The new Milano Metro finally came to the notice of the American design community in 1965. Industrial designer William Lansing Plumb, in the September/October 1965 issue of *Print*, compared the London, Milano and New York—but not Boston—subway systems. He angrily described the latter as "grimy, dingy and slumlike", complaining that the original beauty of the mosaic decorations of Heins & LaFarge and Vickers had been covered over in the intervening decades by dirt and grime, by advertising and by newer signs (fig. 76). Plumb also criticized the new TA logo by Sundberg-Ferar as dated (fig. 79). In contrast he praised Noorda's graphics—including his use of a "modified grotesque" typeface—for the Metropolitana Milanese, suggesting that they could be applied to New York City. Plumb's suggestion proved prescient [23]

In late 1965 Massimo Vignelli (b.1931), a Milanese graphic designer, moved to New York City. He had come to the United States to head up the New York office of Unimark International, an international design consultancy established earlier that year. The firm was the brainchild of Vignelli and Ralph Eckerstrom (1921–1996), former design director of Container Corporation of America (CCA). The two men, who had first met in Chicago in 1958 while Vignelli was teaching at the Institute of Design at the Illinois Institute of Technology on a Moholy-Nagy Fellowship, shared a similar philosophy of design. In establishing Unimark

Hiya Folks
DO YOU KNOW -
THAT YOUR SUBWAY SYSTEM IS
THE FASTEST, SAFEST & CHEAPEST
MODE OF TRANSPORTATION
IN THE WORLD TODAY
PLEASE CO-OPERATE
BUY YOUR TOKENS FOR THE WEEK

77

23. Plumb (1965), p. 13. Plumb's article was a follow-up to an appearance he made on WNBC-TV's "New York Illustrated" in 1965 to discuss "New York subways as a design environment". Plumb was not alone in his views about the New York City subway. In February 1967 Mayor John V. Lindsay's Task Force on Urban Design, led by David A. Crane, released its report. "The Threatened City: A Report on the Design of the City of New York by the Mayor's Task Force" called the subway, "the most squalid public environment of the United States: dank, dingily lit, fetid, raucous with screeching clatter; one of the world's meanest transit facilities." Quoted in Steven V. Roberts, "Mayor Hires Consultants to Study Street Design," *New York Times*, November 14, 1967.

24. This summary of Unimark's genesis comes from a conversation with Jan Conradi to author, 26 July 2008. Conradi has since written the definitive history of Unimark International, a design firm that has not gotten its full due in general histories of graphic design. *Unimark International: The Design of Business and the Business of Design* (Baden, Switzerland: Lars Müller Publishers, 2010) expands upon her graduate thesis: Helms, J.C., "A Historical Survey of Unimark International and Its Effect on Graphic Design in the United States." (MA thesis, Iowa State University, 1988). The website www.unimark-international.com, created in 2004 by Kevin Rau with input from Conradi, have been superseded by the new book. Also see Bob Noorda and Francesco Dondina, *Bob Noorda: Una vita nel segno della grafica.* (Milano: Editrice San Raffaele, 2009), pp. 90–91.

Ralph Eckerstrom (1922–1996) was president of Unimark International. Prior to the formation of the firm he was director of design at Container Corporation of America from 1956 to 1964. Eckerstrom served on the board of directors for the International Design Conference in Aspen, Colorado and was elected Chairman of the 1962 International Design Conference on the Environment. After Unimark, he became president of Mobium Corporation, a design subsidiary of R.R. Donnelley and Sons.

James K. Fogleman (1919–2003) was part of the design team that developed the Lockheed P-38 Fighter. In World War II he served as a USAF bomber pilot. From 1950 until 1964 he was director of design for the American offices of CIBA Corporation, the Swiss pharmaceutical company.

Jay Doblin (b.1920) began his career as a designer for Raymond Loewy Associates in the 1940s. From 1955 to 1969 he was the director of the Institute of Design at the Illinois Institute of Technology. He introduced "systems design" and "methodology" to design education. Ann Lee Morgan, ed., *Contemporary Designers.* (London: MacMillan Publishers, 1984), p. 158.

Larry Klein (1928–1997) began his career in industrial design, working for a variety of firms in the Chicago area—including Klein/Wasserman and Sieber & McIntyre—before joining Unimark. Although he was a Unimark founder, his tenure with the company was brief. He left it to re-establish his own firm, and later was chairman of the exhibition department of the Field Museum. He wrote *Exhibits: Planning and Design* in 1986.

Information on the careers of Noorda and Vignelli prior to the creation of Unimark International can be found in *Contemporary Designers*, pp. 455–456 (Noorda) and p. 610 (Vignelli). The New York office of Unimark was originally overseen by Walter Kacik before Vignelli's arrival in New York. Information to the contrary by Jan von Holstein at trex.id.iit.edu/events/strategyconference/2006/perspectives_jsvh.php has not been substantiated.

they sought to wed American marketing to European modernist design. Along with Vignelli and Eckerstrom, the other founding partners of the firm were Bob Noorda, Jay Doblin, James K. Fogleman, and Larry Klein. Herbert Bayer, the former Bauhausler, served as a consultant, giving Unimark immediate legitimacy. [24]

Within months of Vignelli's arrival in New York, Unimark gained a plum assignment. New maps meant new signs. In May 1966 the NYCTA, on the recommendation of the Museum of Modern Art, hired the firm to advise it on signage and to assess Prof. Goldstein's report. The recommendation came from Mildred Constantine (1913–2008), Associate Curator in the Department of Architecture and Design at MoMA. It is likely that the Transit Authority turned to Constantine because of her longstanding interest in signs and her intimate knowledge of graphic design. She curated the exhibition Signs in the Street at MoMA in 1954 and later co-authored *Sign Language for Buildings and Landscape*. She was on the Board of Directors of the AIGA and was very familiar with graphic design firms, especially the nascent Unimark. Constantine had met both Vignelli and Eckerstrom in 1959 when all three served as jurors on the Art Directors Club of Chicago competition. And, most important of all, she was aware of Noorda's graphics for the Metropolitana Milanese from having served in 1964 on the United States selection committee for the 13th Triennale di Milano. Unimark had the connections and it had the experience. [25]

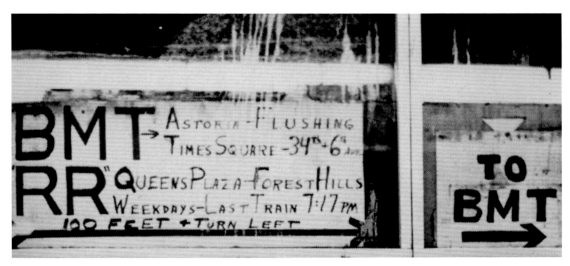

78

79

25. The NYCTA's decision to finally act on Prof. Goldstein's report may have been spurred by fears of reduced ridership in the wake of the debilitating subway strike that occurred in January 1966. The rudimentary nature of Goldstein's suggestions for improving train designations, car information and platform information—he was more interested in "the name and destination of incoming trains"—paved the way for the NYCTA to bring in signage specialists. "Methods of Improving Subway Information," p. 35. Information on Mildred Constantine's role in the NYCTA's hiring of Unimark comes from several sources: Mildred Constantine to author, 15 May 2008; Massimo Vignelli to author, 29 April 2008; and Blake (1967), p. 108. Blake writes, "His [O'Grady's] agents approached one

Mildred Constantine, of the Museum of Modern Art (ahah!) and asked Connie to 'suggest, not recommend' some names of professional graphics types who might be able to revamp the subway map and the existing subway signs…. Connie suggests, but does not recommend, three outfits, including the team of Massimo Vignelli and Robert Noorda, who had done the handsome graphics in Milan's two-dozen-stop mini-subway system." This hilarious account has the ring of truth to it. At the time, Peter Blake (1920–2006), an architect and architectural critic, was editor in chief of *Architectural Forum*. Earlier in his career he had been a curator at the Museum of Modern Art alongside Constantine. Blake does not identify the other two firms that Constantine recommended to the NYCTA,

but the most likely ones would have been Cambridge Seven Associates and Kinneir Associates. Other possibilities could have been Lester Beall and Rudolph de Harak. The dating of the Unimark contract is based on "Subway Studying Color-Centric Guide," *New York Times*, May 20, 1966.

77 Handpainted sign at unidentified IRT subway station, c.1965. From William Lansing Plumb. "Telling People Where to Go: Subway Graphics." *Print* XIX:V (September/October 1965), p. 13.

78 Token booth with handlettered directional signs. 42nd Street–Times Square (1/2/3/S), 1965. From William Lansing Plumb. "Telling People Where to Go: Subway Graphics." *Print* XIX:V (September/October 1965), p. 15.

79 New York Transit Authority (TA) logo, 1964. Designed by Sundberg-Ferar.

CINTURATO PIRELLI

With the hiring of Unimark it seemed that the NYCTA had finally realized the need to rectify the Piranesian situation underground. But the assignment was brief—Unimark was expected to submit their report by September 1966—and ultimately very unsatisfying. In the summer Noorda flew to New York to carry out a detailed survey of the traffic flow at five key subway stations: Times Square, Grand Central Station, Broadway/Nassau, Jay Street and Queensborough Plaza (figs. 83–85). Previously the NYCTA had sent him architectural drawings of each station, but they were not at the same scale and he had difficulty coordinating them. Noorda spent three weeks as a "mole" tracking the paths of commuters in these stations to find the essential message points—entering/exiting, transferring, etc.—for each sign. He plotted decision points on a tree diagram (fig. 86). And, as in Milano, he viewed signs in perspective to test their legibility. He and Vignelli then created a modular sign system with different components for the arrows, route designations—using the color-coding proposed earlier by Goldstein—and train inform-ation (figs. 88–89). The text was black on a white background; the typeface was Standard Medium. Three sizes of type were estab-lished to distinguish different levels of information. A modular support system for the signs—in which they fit into black metal channels suspended from the ceiling by black struts—was created since the TA insisted that no structural changes could be made to the stations. Noorda returned to Milano to have prototype signs mocked up. These were shipped to New York where addition-al presentation boards were created. Then, according to architec-

26. Details of what occurred during Unimark's first contract with the NYCTA have been assembled from a variety of oral and printed sources. Massimo Vignelli to the author, 29 April 2008, 6 August 2008 and 10 August 2008; Bob Noorda to the author, 30 May 2008; Jan Conradi to the author, 26 July 2008, 31 July 2008, 1 August 2008 and 5 August 2008; Blake (1967), p. 108; Unimark International, "Segnaletica–Signs projects," *Casabella: rivista di architettura e urbanistica* 339/340 (August/September 1969), p. 56; Emilio Ambasz et al, *design: Vignelli*. (New York: Rizzoli International Publications, Inc., 1981), p. 19; Germano Celant, Mildred Constantine, David Revere McFadden and Joseph Rykwert, *design: Vignelli*. (New York: Rizzoli International Publications, Inc., 1990), p. 94; Lauwen, *Bob Noorda*; Conradi, *Unimark International*, pp. 150–153. It is likely that Unimark's sign system for the NYCTA did not appear in the special "Mass Transportation" issue of *Industrial Design* (November 1966) because it was still being presented as the issue went to press.

Along with the signage proposals, Unimark presented a new logo for the NYCTA to replace the one that Sundberg-Ferar had done. They intended it to be used for signs, trains and printed matter. It was a dark circle with a horizontal band met by an upward arrow reversed out. Lahr says that it was not accepted but provides no further details. Most likely it was because the existing logo was still new—though it was soon replaced by the two-toned **M**. John Lahr, "The Cities: New York Is New York—Alas," *Print* XXII:II (March/April 1968), p. 51, figs. 1 and 5.

tural critic Peter Blake, Vignelli and Noorda made their presentation, were "thanked and, apparently, forgotten". [26]

The TA was glad to have Unimark's advice, but nothing more. They did not have enough money to pay Unimark to create a complete manual of design recommendations or even an explanation of the modular system; and they failed to ask for a working document. Instead they sought to carry out the proposals themselves using their in-house sign shop. The result was, in Vignelli's words, "the biggest mess in the world". The Transit Authority's Bergen Street Sign Shop ignored the modular system, misinterpreted the black stripe at the top of the drawings (which indicated the metal channel housing holding the signs) as a design element, rendered the type by hand rather than photomechanically, and did not space the letters to Vignelli's satisfaction (figs. 96, 144). "It had never occurred to us that they would carry out the proposals in their own shop," Vignelli said a year later, "We were able to give them a little instruction, but not enough. Whenever we inquired how the project was going, they were very optimistic. We weren't even allowed to inspect it." The new signs were often installed on top of old ones, creating more confusion in the subway system. The whole clash between the "signpainters"—as Vignelli called them—of the Bergen Street Sign Shop and designers at Unimark reflected fundamentally different expectations between craftsmen and designers. The former were intent on making signs while the latter were interested in sign systems. [27]

81

82

80 Advertisement for Pirelli Cinturato [belted] tires, c.1962. Design by Bob Noorda. Set in Helvetica Medium.

81 Poster for Piccolo Teatro di Milano 1964–1965 season schedule, 1964. Design by Massimo Vignelli. Set in Helvetica Medium.

82 Poster for Le baruffe chiozotte by Carlo Goldoni at Teatro Piccolo di Milano, 1964. Design by Massimo Vignelli. Note Vignelli's use of a black band at the top. Set in Helvetica Medium.

27. Most of the descriptions about the difficulties involved in the TA's initial implementation of the Unimark sign system come from Lahr (1968), pp. 50–54. Lahr's article was part of a special issue of *Print* dedicated to "Graphic Design in the Human Environment". *Print* editor Martin Fox, who conceived the idea for the issue, says that planning for it began six to eight months prior to publication, indicating that Vignelli's comments were made in summer 1967. Additional details have been provided by Massimo Vignelli. Massimo Vignelli, to author, 29 April 2008, 6 August 2008—"Signs were done by the TA in their workshops, we had no access (only once and we were horrified by the process). Old sign painters with a very skeptical attitude toward our signage."—and 10 August 2008. Noorda and Vignelli did not fully explain the modular sign system because they assumed that

that would be part of a second phase of work for the NYCTA. Looking at the diagrams of the signs it is easy to see how the Bergen Street Shop could have made the mistake of thinking the black stripe was a design element and not a structural one. In the years since, many others—heavily influenced by Vignelli's use of bold black bands in his work for the Piccolo Teatro di Milano, Stendig, the United States National Park Service, Fodor's Travel Guides, The Fort Worth Art Museum, *Skyline*, the Institute for Architecture and Urban Studies, and IDCNY among others—have assumed the same thing. And Noorda used black bands in some of the secondary signage for the Milano Metro. See Celant et al, *design: Vignelli* and Bob Noorda, "Studies for Signs and Indicator Board in the Milan Underground—Studi per la segnaletica della

Metropolitana Milanese–Etudes pour la signalisation du Metropolitain Milanais," *Pagina* no. 4 (Gennaio 1964), pp. 12–13. The sign shop's unacceptable spacing was partly due to Unimark's failure to provide spacing guidelines. Jan Conradi to author, 5 August 2008. The other evidence of the sign shop's "incompetence" besides the presence of the black stripe and poor letterspacing was the sometimes crude quality of handcut stencils they provided to the porcelain enamel signmakers. There is a surprising lack of photographic documentation of the problematic 1967 NYCTA signs. Neither Bob Noorda nor Massimo Vignelli has any photographs of signs from the entire period that Unimark worked for the NYCTA. The MTA Archives have one. One appears in the *New York Post*, November 27, 1967 in connection with the Chrystie Street Connection opening and

another is in "The Cities: New York Is New York—Alas," p. 52. The photographs of New York City subway signage included in Lauwen, *Bob Noorda* are a fabrication since they show white letters on a black ground.

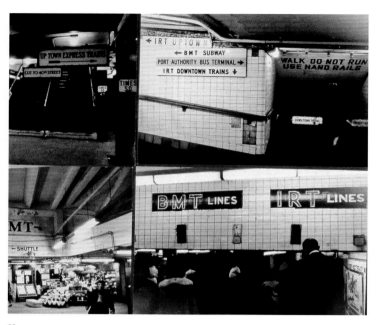

83

83 **Signage. Times Square station, 1966.**
Photographs and collage by Bob Noorda.

84 **Study of subway traffic flow at
Times Square station.** Drawing
by Bob Noorda, 1966.

85 (opposite page) **Study of subway
traffic flow at Grand Central station.**
Drawing by Bob Noorda, 1966.

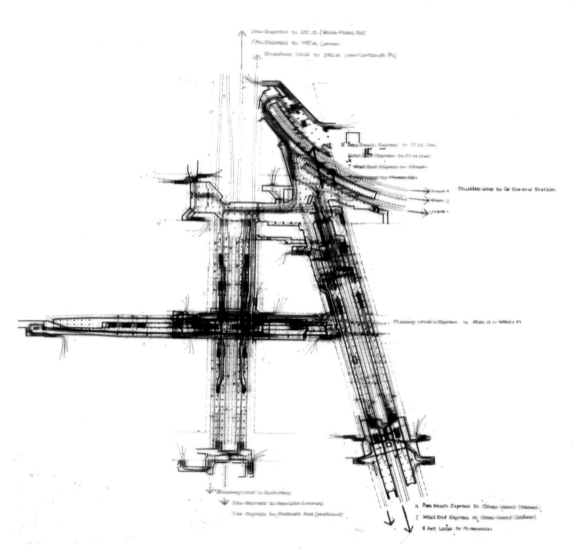

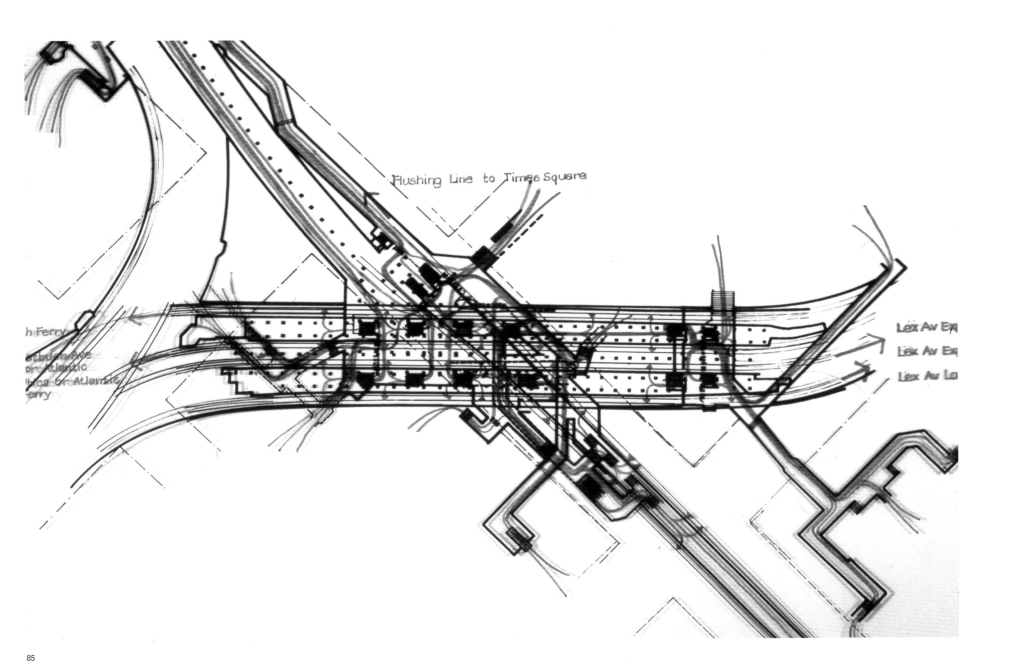

Flushing Line to Times Square

h Ferry

tibulan Ave
on Atlantic
ica or Atlantic
Ferry

Lex Av Ex
Lex Av Ex
Lex Av Lo

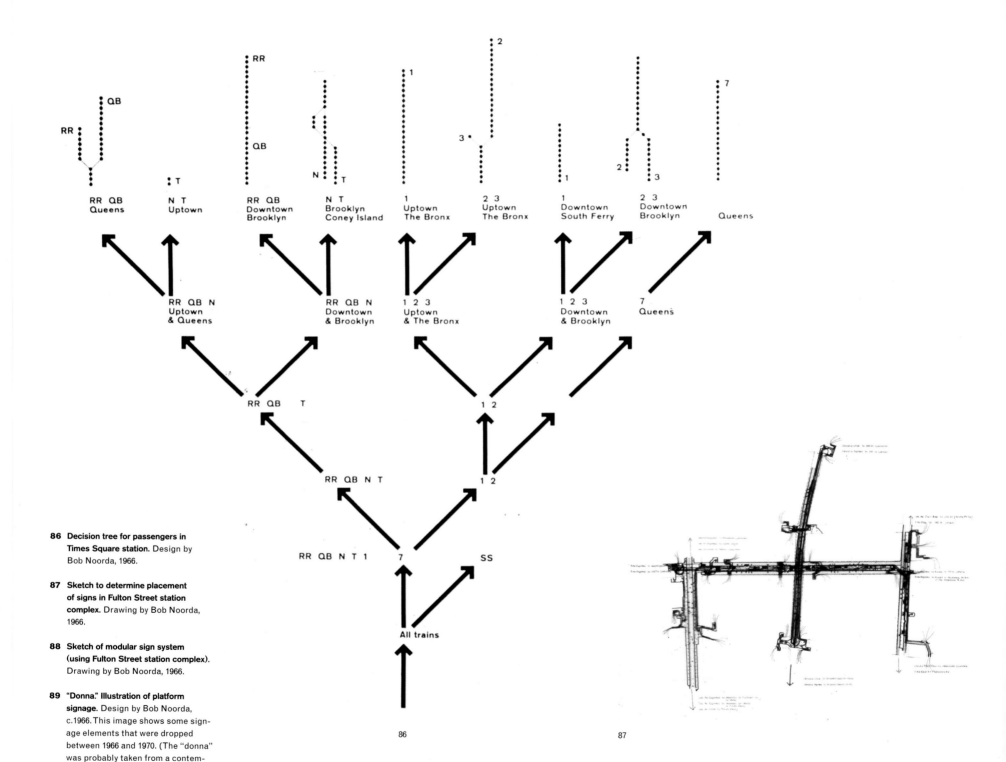

RR QB
Queens

N T
Uptown

RR QB
Downtown
Brooklyn

N T
Brooklyn
Coney Island

1
Uptown
The Bronx

2 3
Uptown
The Bronx

1
Downtown
South Ferry

2 3
Downtown
Brooklyn

Queens

RR QB N
Uptown
& Queens

RR QB N
Downtown
& Brooklyn

1 2 3
Uptown
& The Bronx

1 2 3
Downtown
& Brooklyn

7
Queens

RR QB T

1 2

RR QB N T

1 2

RR QB N T 1   7   SS

All trains

86

87

86 **Decision tree for passengers in Times Square station.** Design by Bob Noorda, 1966.

87 **Sketch to determine placement of signs in Fulton Street station complex.** Drawing by Bob Noorda, 1966.

88 **Sketch of modular sign system (using Fulton Street station complex).** Drawing by Bob Noorda, 1966.

89 **"Donna." Illustration of platform signage.** Design by Bob Noorda, c.1966. This image shows some signage elements that were dropped between 1966 and 1970. (The "donna" was probably taken from a contemporary advertisement. The color was added digitally in 2005.)

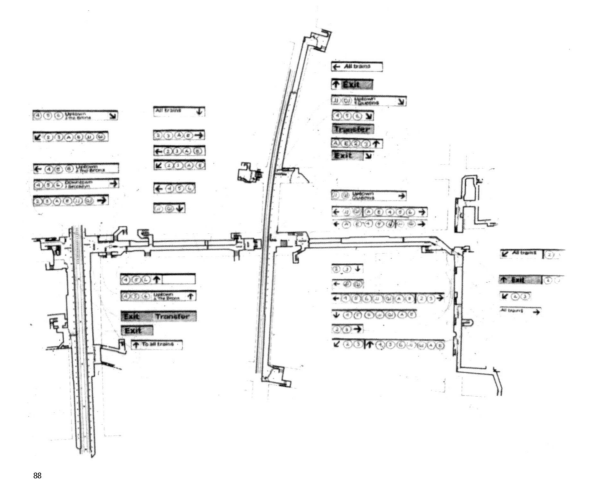

88

89

Lack of money was the principal explanation for the TA's refusal to allow Unimark to oversee the implementation of their signage recommendations, but several other factors were probably at work as well: bureaucratic inertia, labor union rules, and outside political forces. Certainly TA management would have been wary of antagonizing the Transport Workers Union and Amalgamated Transit Union in the wake of the twelve-day transit strike that brought New York City to a halt in January 1966. [28]

The Chrystie Street Connection, the largest overhaul of the New York City subway system since unification in 1940, was opened on November 26, 1967. The Connection linked the former IND Sixth Avenue Line east of Broadway-Lafayette with the BMT Nassau Street Line via the Manhattan Bridge. It was the first true integration of the IND and BMT and resulted in the creation of a new station at Grand Street, eight new routes and several new free transfer points. The massive changeover was accompanied by a set of new maps overseen by Prof. Goldstein and the first Unimark signs, both of which incorporated new color-coding and naming for all of the subway lines. [29]

The "big switch" was announced well in advance by the NYCTA and several days beforehand newspaper columns explained the changes in detail. Despite this, the opening of the Chrystie Street Connection did not go smoothly. Under the headline "Riders Burn as TA Pulls the Switch" the *New York Post* described the confusion and chaos that reigned at several of the affected stations, especially in Brooklyn. Passengers were unable to quickly absorb the new train routes and designations as well as the introduction of free transfer points. Confusion was not limited to the subway passengers. "A mild panic set in at the Atlantic Av. station when TA officials arrived early to find old signs still hanging," the *Post* wrote, "They quickly ordered the old signs and maps covered with newspapers before the rush set in." Atlantic Avenue was one of the stations where free transfers between the IND and the IRT were being instituted for the first time. However, despite the presence of Unimark-designed red, gray and blue metal "Transfer Exit" signs directing them to the Lexington Avenue and Seventh Avenue Lines, passengers did not fully grasp their meaning and the TA was forced to add "handlettered cardboard signs" announcing free transfers. [30]

90

28. For details of the subway strike see wikipedia.org/wiki/1966_New_York_City_transit_strike. Unimark wanted to carry out the program, but "the whole thing had suddenly been stopped" Vignelli recounted. He blamed things on the TA's fear of moving too quickly and alienating riders. In his disappointment he lamented: "You give them the possibility of a tool and they use it the wrong way. It's like giving a man an electric light bulb, and then he keeps right on striking matches in the dark." Lahr (1968), pp. 54 and 56.

29. Information about the Chrystie Street Connection, its impact on the subway system, and its role in introducing new maps and signage comes from the following sources: New York City Transit Authority. *Annual Report 1966–1967*,

pp. 14–15; New York City Transit Authority. *Annual Report 1967–1968*, pp. 4–5; and nycsubway.org. The new maps are described in some detail in note 31. During the "big switch" the TA told the *New York Times* that it had already put up "940 new permanent signs in 482 stations". Seth King, "City Hall Parley on Subways," *New York Times*, November 22, 1967. This statement is at odds with the 1967–1968 NYCTA annual report which claimed that 3000 signs in 100 stations had been erected by July 1968. New York City Transit Authority. *Annual Report 1967–1968*, p. 5. The likely truth is that the TA had installed 940 signs in 100 or so stations—meaning those on the IND and BMT lines affected by the changeover—out of the 482 in the entire subway system by the end of November 1967; and that the remaining 2000 plus were

added between then and July 1968. The sharp increase in the number of signs is plausible given the reaction of Transportation Commissioner John Gilhooley—a potential mayoral candidate in 1968—to the Chrystie Street Connection opening turmoil: "All the signs will be properly lettered even if we have to write them on." He guaranteed that TA employees would work through the night to make all of the necessary new signs. Anthony Mancini and Jean Crafton, "Note to Straphangers—No, It's Not a Noose," *New York Post*, November 28, 1967. The original 940 signs were apparently erected only on the platforms and nowhere else in the stations. See Lahr, p. 52 and fig. 10 which appears to show a sign at Whitehall Street (then a stop for both the EE and RR trains).

30. This account of the problems surrounding the Chrystie Street Connection changeover come from the following contemporary sources: "Subway Suits Are Rejected," *New York Daily News*, November 25, 1967; Lester Abelman, "Subways: Straps and Maps," *New York Daily News*, November 26, 1967; Lester Abelman, "Confusion Day on Subways," *New York Daily News*, November 27, 1967; Edwin Ross, Frank Mazzi and Richard Henry, "Subways Are for Weeping & Tears Are Bitter" and "TA Acts to Clear the Flubway Tracks," *New York Daily News*, November 28, 1967; Anthony Mancini and Jean Crafton. "Oh, Those Subways" and "Riders Burn as TA Pulls the Switch," *New York Post*, November 26, 1967; Anthony Mancini and Jean Crafton, "Note to Straphangers—No, It's Not a Noose," *New York Post*, November 28, 1967; "The Subway:

One Tough Brake after Another," *New York Post*, November 29, 1967; Ted Poston, "Mayor Blasts TA Foulup." *New York Post*, November 30, 1967; Seth King, "City Hall Parley on Subways," *New York Times*, November 22, 1967; Eugene Perlmutter, "BM—IND Changes Bewilder Many," *New York Times*, November 27, 1967; John H. Fenton, "Imported Ideas Improve Boston Subways," *New York Times,* November 27, 1967; "Rerouted Subways a Little Late, Lost." *Newsday*, November 27, 1967; and Blake (1967), p. 108. A citizens group sued unsuccessfully to stop the Chrystie Street Connection from opening and Mayor John V. Lindsay futilely tried to delay it until March 1, 1968 when the NYCTA was due to be absorbed into the MTA. Before the introduction of the MetroCard in 1995 not all transfer points within the subway

Goldstein's suite of maps—a large wall map for the platforms, a mini-map for the new routes, individual strip maps for each route, and a new overall system map—and Unimark's signs failed to prevent commuter confusion because they were not fully supported by the route designators on the trains. According to the *New York Post* and the *Daily News*, many trains still had their old route numbers and letters. The schematic maps themselves may also have been at fault, if one is to believe Blake. "The new maps and diagrams were quite stunning in composition and in color... but, unfortunately, they failed to communicate," he wrote in *New York Magazine* in April 1968. He described them as "a battlefield filled with typographers and color-experts locked in mortal combat". Unimark's signs escaped criticism but it was clear there were not enough of them. They were only installed on the platforms and not throughout the stations as Vignelli had urged (figs. 92–94, 137, 141, 169, 283). "Flubway"—as the *Daily News* dubbed it—made clear what the NYCTA already knew. It needed to do more to make the subway system navigable. Merely installing a few new signs was not the same as implementing a coordinated sign system. [31]

91

system were free. They required a second token, thus explaining the importance of signs announcing free transfers as part of the Chrystie Street Connection opening.

31. Blake (1967), p. 108; Edwin Ross, Frank Mazzi and Richard Henry, "Subways Are for Weeping & Tears Are Bitter" and "TA Acts to Clear the Flubway Tracks," *New York Daily News*, November 28, 1967. The suite of new maps followed Prof. Goldstein's 1965 recommendations: "System maps should be placed in convenient locations and well lighted. Strip maps of all trains stopping at a platform should be provided at regular intervals along the platform. Consideration should be given to the addition of an auxiliary map at station exits, which would be a street map of New York City with the

superposition of the subway lines stopping at that particular station." Goldstein (1965), p. 34. With one exception, the overall system map incorporated all of Prof. Goldstein's Map 4 ideas from his 1965 report. (See note 22.) The lone exception was the use of familiar typefaces—a mix of Standard, Trade Gothic and Helvetica—rather than "Navy Aeronautical Medical Equipment Laboratory Letters and Numerals, (MIL-C-18012)" for the map's lettering. The mini-map for the new routes—B, D, F, EE, QB, QJ, RJ, and RR—anticipates the Vignelli map of 1972 in its colorfulness and abstraction. It appears to be set in Univers and Trade Gothic. The overall map, mini-map and strip maps are viewable at nycsubway.org/maps/historical.html#1960. Despite the problems of the Chrystie Street Connection opening, the NYCTA

was proud of its new signs. "Unimark International, graphic arts specialists whose work includes serving as consultants for the signage system of the Milan, Italy subway, assisted the Authority in developing the new signage system for New York City subways." New York City Transit Authority. *Annual Report 1966–1967*, p. 15. "A new signage system, designed to better guide travelers to their destinations at 484 subway stations, was developed in consultation with Unimark International, graphic art specialists. By the end of the fiscal year, 3,000 new signs had been installed at 100 stations and old ones removed to reduce visual clutter. Headway was being made also in installing new color-coded signs in subway cars." New York City Transit Authority. *Annual Report 1967–1968*, p. 5.

The number of stations in the New York City subway system has fluctuated over the years as underutilized ones have been closed and new ones built. In 1968 new stations at 148th Street and Lenox Avenue (no. 3) and 57th Street and Sixth Avenue (Q) were opened. (See the Chronology for details of the opening and closing of individual subway stations.)

90 **Curb Your Dog sign, 1967.** Design by Walter Kacik & Associates for Department of Sanitation, City of New York. From "The Cities: New York is New York—Alas." *Print* XXII:II (March/April 1968), p. 55.

91 **New York City Department of Sanitation truck, 1967.** Design by Walter Kacik & Associates. From "The Cities: New York is New York—Alas." *Print* XXII:II (March/April 1968), p. 56. The simplified agency name is set in lowercase Helvetica Medium.

A month before the Chrystie Street Connection opened the NYCTA publicly announced that it had hired Unimark to "devise a new system of signage". The announcement was part of a presentation on the New York City subway by Daniel T. Scannell (1913–2000), one of the three NYCTA commissioners, at "Transportation Graphics: Where Am I Going? How Do I Get There?", a symposium held October 23 at the Museum of Modern Art. Among the other speakers at the symposium, organized by Mildred Constantine, were Jock Kinneir, Peter Chermayeff and Noorda. If the NYCTA was not already aware of the gap between its own transportation signage and that for British Rail, the Boston T and the Milano Metro, they certainly were after the close of the symposium. In fact, Arlington Street, the first of Boston's renovated T stations had finally opened that month to much publicity and praise. Ironically, the *New York Times* waited until November 28 to profile the station, placing the article next to one detailing the problems caused by the "big switch" in New York. That must have really stung the NYCTA. [32]

92–93

32. The "Transportation Graphics: Where Am I Going? How Do I Get There?" symposium at the Museum of Modern Art included the following speakers and topics: Lowell K. Bridwell of the Federal Highway Administration on highway signage, Jock Kinneir on British Rail, architect Pierre Bourgeau on Expo '67 and the nascent Montreal Métro, Henry A. Barnes (Commissioner, Department of Traffic, New York City) on street signs and traffic signs, Will Burtin on signage for the University Circle neighborhood in Cleveland, Jonathan Barnett (Principal Urban Designer, New York City Planning Department) on the 53rd Street experimental sign project by Unimark, Donald Appleyard on highway systems, Peter Chermayeff on the renovation of the Boston T, Bob Noorda on the Metropolitana Milanese sign system, Charles M. Haar (Assistant Secretary, Department of

Housing and Urban Development), Harmon H. Goldstone (Commissioner, New York City Planning Commission) on the 1964 NYCTA map competition, and Daniel T. Scannell of the New York City Transit Authority on the New York subway system. The results were published in edited form in *Dot Zero* 5, the magazine that Unimark and paper manufacturer Finch, Pruyn & Co. jointly published. Mildred Constantine, ed., "Transportation Graphics." *Dot Zero* 5 (Fall 1968). The Noorda, Burtin and Scannell sessions are missing from the Museum of Modern Art tapes of the symposium. Noorda's notes are in the Bob Noorda Archives. It is curious that Scannell and not Massimo Vignelli spoke about the situation in New York. Scannell made no reference to the work that Unimark had done in 1966 for the NYCTA, focusing instead on plans for

renovating stations. (One of the accompanying drawings for the proposed makeover of the 49th Street and Seventh Avenue station by Johnson/Burgee Associates shows a Unimark-style sign.) Presumably, Vignelli was asked to participate but declined on the grounds that the Unimark sign recommendations had not been properly carried out by the TA and thus were not fit to be publicized. Scannell was probably asked to speak in his stead since the local situation could not be ignored at such a major conference. Vignelli does not recall why he was absent from the MoMA symposium but believes this scenario is plausible. Massimo Vignelli to author, 6 August 2008. For information on Scannell see "Daniel T. Scannell Dies at 87." *New York Times*, February 25, 2000.

33. Exactly when Unimark received the contract from the NYCTA to prepare a graphics manual is unclear. No documents survive but Massimo Vignelli believes it was early 1968. The events of fall 1967 suggest that it may have occurred then or that, at the very least, the NYCTA was already aware it needed to rehire the design firm. Massimo Vignelli to author, 29 April 2008; Steven V. Roberts, "Subway Stations to Be Redesigned," *New York Times*, September 30, 1967; Hope MacLeod, "The View from the Subway," *New York Post*, October 16, 1967; Steven V. Roberts, "Mayor Hires Consultants to Study Street Design," *New York Times*, November 14, 1967. As important as the completion of the Chrystie Street Connection was to the future of the subway system, it was not the only significant change that occurred that year. In July the TA extended service to the

Far Rockaways and in September it unveiled ambitious plans to renovate its stations. The latter was to begin with a test design of the 49th Street and Seventh Avenue station that would introduce new lighting, new turnstiles, a "greater use of color, more legible signs and maps", glass and stainless steel, quarry tile and terrazzo flooring. New York City Transit Authority. *Annual Report 1966–1967*, p. 13. The station was not completed until 1973, but in the interim the NYCTA needed to develop signage guidelines. Of the flame red glazed tiles used in the finished station, architect Philip Johnson said: "Cheer is the word. Like a big shopping center." Edward C. Burks, "Subways' Colored Tile Gets Cover Up Job," *New York Times*, February 21, 1970. Coincidentally or not Unimark began a hiring push in August 1967 that included not only graphic

It is unclear whether Scannell's announcement at the MoMA symposium that the NYCTA had hired Unimark referred to the first contract or to the second contract the design firm had with the agency. Certainly by early 1968—if not fall 1967—Unimark had been rehired to prepare a comprehensive set of guidelines covering the design, fabrication and installation of signs for the subway system. The MoMA symposium coupled with the Chrystie Street Connection fiasco made it clear to the commissioners that they could not continue to do things the old way. In December 1967 the TA undertook a comprehensive survey of the subway system to determine how many signs it needed and where they should be posted. This marked the first about-face from the way the agency had been doing business. Previously, it had ignored Unimark's broader ideas about signage. As Vignelli recalls, "We designed the system to standardize the production and accelerate the implementation. No way. They were still doing all the signs individually, one here another there without a precise implementation plan. I wanted to do one line at a time, they were doing a station here and there, just like they have done since the beginning of the subways." It is doubtful that the TA adopted Vignelli's line-by-line approach, but they certainly sped up the pace of installation in the wake of the events of November 26, 1967. By the end of June 1968, they were boasting that "3,000 new signs had been installed at 100 stations and old ones removed to reduce visual clutter". [33]

94

designers but draftsmen-renderers with experience in signage. See classified advertisements in the *New York Times*, August 6–13, 1967.

Information on the TA's December 1967 survey is from New York City Transit Authority, *New York City Transit Authority Graphics Standards Manual.* (New York: Unimark International, 1970), p. 71 and Massimo Vignelli to author, 6 August 2008. Vignelli's comments regarding the differences between Unimark and the NYCTA over the implementation of the signs is from Massimo Vignelli to author, 6 May 2008. See also Germano Celant, Mildred Constantine, David Revere McFadden and Joseph Rykwert, *design: Vignelli.* (New York: Rizzoli International Publications, Inc.), 1990, p. 94: "Previously, signs had been made [by the TA] to order. Ours were

designed to be prefabricated and assembled like movable type to form sentences—an incredibly easy way to solve a problem for a program characterized by inefficiency and as old as the subway itself." The number of signs installed by the TA in 1967 and 1968 is noted in New York City Transit Authority. *Annual Report 1967–1968*, p. 5. The number of signs may seem exaggerated, especially given the small number of stations, but if signs were installed at every one of the decision points that Noorda had determined twenty to thirty would have been needed for each ordinary station (that is, a station such as Houston Street serving only one line and having only four exits, one at each corner) and over 100 for stations such as Times Square where multiple lines converge. Also see note 29.

There is no way to assess the boast of how many new (i.e. Unimark) signs had been installed by the middle of 1968 or even by the time the graphics standards manual was readied in 1970. Photographs of Unimark signs between 1969 and 1979 show them principally on the BMT Broadway Brooklyn Local (KK) and the IRT White Plains Road, BMT Broadway, BMT Brighton, IND 6th Avenue and IND 8th Avenue lines.

92–94 Porcelain enamel station and route signs 1967–1968. These photographs show Unimark signs erected between the time of the firm's initial contract for a signage system and their subsequent contract for a standards manual.

92 Grand Street (B/D), November 26, 1967. Photograph from the *New York Times*. Unimark signs in use with older signs at the opening of the Chrystie Street Connection.

93 Celebration of the opening of the new IND 57th Street terminal, June 26, 1968. Among the 300 guests were (left to right) Christopher Marschhausen (Superintendent, Employee Services), unknown, T.G. Isle, Harold McLaughlin (Assistant General Superintendent, NYCTA)

and Len Ingalls (Spokesman for the NYCTA). Despite the early appearance of Unimark signage the columns have older porcelain enamel station signs. Note that the "picnic" was catered by The Brasserie, located in The Seagram Building, former home to Unimark International.

94 Modular porcelain enamel Unimark route sign. 59th Street–Lexington Avenue (N/R/W), April 18, 1968. Note the older directional sign at the left.

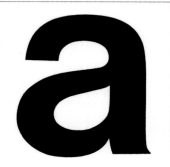

abcdefghijklmnopqrstuvwxyzß& ABCDEFGHIJKLMNOPQRSTUVWXYZ 1234567890

abcdefghijklmnopqrstuvwxyzabcdefghijklmnopqrstuvwxyzabcdegß&
ABCDEFGHIJKLMNOPQRSTUVWXYZABCDEFGH 1234567890

abcdefghijklmnopqrstuvwxyzabcdefghijklmnopqrstuvwxyzß&
ABCDEFGHIJKLMNOPQRSTUVWXYZABC 1234567890

abcdefghijklmnopqrstuvwxyzabcdefgß& ABCDEF
GHIJKLMNOPQRSTUVWXYZABC 1234567890

abcdefghijklmnopqrstuvwxyzabcdegß&
ABCDEFGHIJKLMNOPQRSTUVWXYZ
ÆŒÇØ$$£.,-([§†!?*«'„/ 1234567890

Helvetica

As a lineal design the new Helvetica sans-serif is the result of careful research and much practical experience. The basic form of every single letter was designed and cut with the utmost precision, with special consideration of its juxtaposition to other letters in the case of close leading. Quite apart from delicately adjusted alterations in the spaces occupied by the letters, in the thickness of the strokes and the diminishing of apparently parallel contours, one of the most striking innovations is the almost perfectly horizontal position of the curved segments of the letters e, c, and s and of the capitals C and S as well as the curving form of the downward stroke of the capital R. This lends the type a greater homogeneity and compactness in comparison with other sans-serif types, and in a close-set passage the effect is more regular and smooth.

Helvetica sans-serif light is available in 4-24 pt, the medium is obtainable in 6-48 pt and the bold is available in sizes 6-24 pt. The type is also available for the composing machine and film type setting. The sans-serif type has proved to be the most useful of all types after the chief group of roman faces. Today, in contrast to earlier times, when it was used solely for commercial printing, it is often preferred for general purposes, and when correctly and skilfully handled (with regard to size and leading) it is able to impart information legibly and agreeably. Sans-serif, with its clear and precise character, the restriction of its forms to essentials and very slight variations in thickness, is a particularly appropriate type face for this program.

Typography

As the medium through which information is communicated, typography must work functionally. The idea must be expressed in easily legible type.

The specifier should know and accept the technical possibilities of modern typography and, instead of striving for ornamental effects, be able to see the plan as a formal conception. This economic, time-saving and practical method of composition is consonant with our image of technical perfection and clarity and has led to the following postulates:

a) The arbitrary, fortuitous and individual composition of typographical elements should be replaced by an objective design in accordance with typographical principles.

b) The primary requirement is an unadorned typographical form clearly serving the needs of communication.

Used in this way, typography becomes functional, objective and informative in the logical composition of letters to form words and of words to form sentences, in the arrangement of sentences according to their contents and, finally, in the organization of the contents according to its inner coherence. Typography of this kind is informative because all its groups of sentences are clearly laid out for good legibility and the message can thus be easily read and readily understood. Apart from considerations of principle and practice, the rules-of-thumb below can be of help in specifying typography in collateral literature and advertising.

1/ Never combine different type families
2/ Never use different forms of the same family, e.g. the sans-serif, in the same piece of composition.
3/ Do not use a lot of different type sizes, but make sure those used are

clearly distinguishable.
4/ Try to achieve a compact effect in the type arrangement (type area).
5/ Never attempt to set a word apart in the text by spacing its letters: instead set it in bold or extra bold type or isolate it.
6/ Attempt to relate the picture and copy, i.e. the type matter should be arranged in relation to the photograph or drawing employed so that there is a link with the picture that compels attention and is visually and aesthetically satisfying. Type matter and picture become a harmonious composition.
7/ The spaces between the lines should be chosen so that it leaves a space between the descender height of one line and the ascender height of the next line without, however, creating the impression that they are isolated lines. The compactness of the composition must be preserved so that

the typography is easily read and remains aesthetically effective.
8/ The distance between words should be uniform; white interspaces of varying size give rise to a form of composition that is disturbing to the eye and difficult to read.
9/ As figures are equivalent to capitals, it may be necessary, so as not to disrupt the appearance of the composition, to set the figures a size smaller than the rest of the type, particularly when a large number of figures have to be accommodated.

opposite page:
a and s lower case characters in Helvetica medium and s in Helvetica light.

this page:
Full type specimen of Helvetica medium with ligatures, signs and figures

95

The detailed survey carried out by the TA in December 1967 was a necessary follow-up to Noorda's mid-1966 investigations and an essential prelude to Unimark's subsequent formulation of comprehensive signage guidelines. Noorda had looked only at critical subway stations—those with the most traffic in the system— but now the TA needed to examine the entire system (or at least those stations affected by the Chrystie Street Connection route changes). During 1968 and 1969 Unimark worked on the guidelines while juggling work for their corporate clients. *The New York City Transit Authority Graphics Standards Manual* was finally issued in 1970 (fig. 97). It included Noorda's traffic-flow research of mid-1966, the TA's station December 1967 survey results, and some of the original design and fabrication specifications presented to the TA in fall 1966. But it also built upon those specifications to include precise manufacturing instructions, explicit spacing guidelines, a glossary of terms, semantic rules for the information to be included on signs, examples of mandatory signs as well as informational and directional ones, and suggestions for a line map intended for use inside subway cars and a directory to aid riders seeking the best way to get from point A to point B via the subway. It also replaced Goldstein's Munsell Color System colors for the route disks with equivalent ones from the Pantone Matching System. [34]

34. Although issued in 1970, there is evidence the manual was completed by mid–1969. See Unimark International. "Segnaletica–Signs projects," *Casabella: rivista di architettura e urbanistica* 339/340 (August/September 1969), pp. 56–57. The spacing guidelines closely mimicked those Noorda had created for the Milano Metro. The mandatory signs were primarily prohibitive: "No littering–No smoking–No spitting", "Do not lean over the edge of platform, enter upon or cross tracks", etc. The inside line maps were not produced until nearly two decades later. The directory has never been produced (**112**). Intriguingly, the NYCTA had tested out something similar to it called the Directomat in the early 1950s (**111**). An undated photograph of the device in the MTA Archives has this note on its reverse: "Finding one's way around the 237.98 [sic] route-miles of the

New York subway system is easier now that this 'directomat' has been installed at Times Square. A passenger just pushes a numbered button beside the name of his destination, and written directions come out, telling him where to go." The directory, glossary and semantics instructions were presumably Vignelli's idea. *New York City Transit Authority Graphics Standards Manual* (1970), pp. 9–10, 75, 76, 87–170 and 171–172. Some of the illustrations in the manual were reused from the 1966 presentation. Others were altered. For instance, the illustration on p. 70 of the woman standing next to the modular platform signs no longer has the strip map at the right that appeared in earlier versions. A vertical route map that was originally proposed has also vanished. Their fate is unknown. See Lahr (1968), p. 51, figs. 3 and 4. The PMS colors for the lines were:

PMS 130 yellow (no. 6, N), PMS 165 orange (no. 1, no. 7, D, EE), PMS 185 red (no. 2, HH, QB), PMS 239 magenta (no. 4, AA, F), PMS 300 (A, KK), PMS 312 light blue (no. 3, no. 8, E, M), PMS 354 green (CC, GG, RR, SS), and black (no. 5, B, LL, QJ). It should be noted that all of the diagrams in the manual are in black and white. The PMS colors for the disks are described in the captions and full page color swatches are included. *New York City Transit Authority Graphics Standards Manual.* (1970), pp. 11–45. Thus, depictions of the signs with colored disks are later fabrications. See Ventura, *Bob Noorda Design*, pp. 46–49 and Noorda and Dondina (2009), p. 29. (The latter incorrectly dates the manual to 1973.) Peter Van Delft played a principal role, alongside Noorda and Vignelli, in the creation of the manual.

35. *New York City Transit Authority Graphics Standards Manual.* (1970), pp. 4–10, 61, 168–169. The justification for choosing Standard Medium is especially curious in light of Noorda's rejection of it in favor of a custom typeface for the Milano Metro signage. However, a similar custom face for the NYCTA was obviously out of the question due to the limited nature of the first Unimark contract. And once some signs using Standard Medium had been installed in stations there was no possibility of turning back. The black bar created by the sign shop in 1967 had become similarly ensconced.

As if in response to the confusion engendered by the "big switch", the first page of the manual emphatically insisted that "...there must be no overlapping of old and new signs. All signs erected previous to this program should be removed." It was a brave statement, but not a practical one given both the extensive nature of the New York City subway system—at that time it consisted of 484 stations—and the NYCTA's financial situation. The manual specified modular signs—in sections of 1, 2, 4 and 8 feet in length—with black type on a white background. Three types of signs were prescribed: 1. station identification, exit and transfer signs (with a cap height of 9 inches); 2. directional signs (with a cap height of 4¼ inches); and 3. informational and small temporary signs (with a cap height of 1⅜ inches). Wordspacing, letterspacing, leading and the number of lines per sign were carefully detailed. The typeface was Standard Medium (fig. 100). "Research has shown that the most 'appropriate' typeface for this purpose [a quickly and easily read sign] is a regular sans serif," the manual stated, "Of the various weights of sans serif available, Standard Medium has been found to offer the easiest legibility from any angle, whether the passenger is standing, walking or riding." The inadvertent black band at the top of the signs was now accepted as part of their look: "The 1⅝" black band at the type of the panel represents a structural device to which the panels are fastened.

Whenever the panel requires a different structure, the black band should be part of the graphics on the sign." The signs were still porcelain enamel, but the reproduction of elements was to be "by photographic means only" via silkscreening with die-cut film. The exception was temporary signs that were to be made with vinyl adhesive letters. These requirements were clearly a response to the Bergen Street Sign Shop's use of handcut stencils for making porcelain enamel signs and the type of makeshift signs the TA had resorted to during the Chrystie Street Connection opening. [35]

Unimark's choice of Standard Medium comes as a shock given Vignelli's reputation—burnished by his passionate testimony in *Helvetica: A Documentary Film*—as a life-long proponent of Helvetica. Furthermore, he has stated on several occasions that he wanted to use Helvetica for the New York City subway signage but that "it was not available." Why not? [36]

95 Double-page spread from Varian corporate identity manual by Unimark showing correct type and typographic usage. From *Dot Zero* 1 (1966), p. 16. The typeface is Helvetica Medium: "As a linear design the new Helvetica sans-serif is the result of careful research and much practical experience. The basic form for every single letter was designed and cut with the utmost precision, with special consideration of its juxtaposition to other letters in the case of close leading. Quite apart from delicately adjusted alterations in the spaces occupied by the letters, in the thickness of the strokes and the diminishing of apparently parallel contours, one of the most striking innovations is the almost perfectly horizontal position of the curved segments of the letters e, c and s and of the capitals c and s as well as the curving form of the downward stroke of the capital r. This lends the type a greater homogeneity and compactness in comparison with other sans-serif types, and in a close-set passage the effect is more regular and smooth."

96 Sign at unidentified station, 1969. The first paragraph is a handpainted attempt at Standard Medium while the second and third parageaphs are set in a handcut stencil version of Standard Medium that has been silkscreened.

36. Vignelli's explanation for why Unimark chose Standard over Helvetica has been repeated on several occasions, though never elaborated upon. See Wim Crouwel and Massimo Vignelli interview by Alice Twemlow, "Modernism on Two Planes: A Conversation with Wim Crouwel and Massimo Vignelli," AIGA–NY. New York, 25 October 2007; Massimo Vignelli to author, 29 April 2008 and 6 May 2008; and *Helvetica: A Documentary Film*. The irony about the *New York City Transit Authority Graphics Standards Manual* is that its text is set in Helvetica! Furthermore, the two diagrams explaining The Inside Line Map are set in Helvetica Medium and Light even though the text above specifically states, "For better distinction between type showing express stops and local stops we have chosen 48 pt. Standard medium and light."

(The illustration for The Outside Identification Sign on the same page is in Standard, however.) See *New York City Transit Authority Graphics Standards Manual*. (1970), p. 74.

Jan Conradi says that Unimark wanted to specify Helvetica but that the TA sign shop insisted on Standard. She provides no documentation. See Conradi (2010), p. 152. Noorda, in conversation with Francesco Dondina, detailed the drawbacks of Helvetica but did not explain why Standard was chosen. See Noorda and Dondina (2009), p. 30.

To travel to stations on the Rockaway Peninsula or Broad Channel

When paying fare buy a special refund ticket for 20¢

When exiting at Rockaway Peninsula stations or Broad Channel surrender the ticket and obtain 20¢ refund from the railroad clerk

96

New York City Transit Authority

Graphics Standards Manual

M

Letter spacing

The illustration shows three examples of letter spacing.

The first line is an example of space units found between letters of opposed and similar visual character.

The second and third lines show the space unit counts found in typical words used in the subway system. The chart on page 10 shows all possible letter and number combinations and their space unit counts. The size and positions of the space units in relation to the three alphabet sizes are found on pages 88-170.

Letter spacing

A modular system has been devised, which offers consistent spacing for letters and words for the three sizes of type. This unit system must be scrupulously adhered to at all times as this will preclude any inconsistency, regardless of where or when any given sign is being manufactured.

On those rare occasions where environmental considerations necessitate a deviation from the standard, all reductions in size must be done photographically so as to preserve the most desirable proportions. Moreover, fractional reductions and the creation of 'odd' sizes must be avoided.

Because typefaces tend to become distorted when enlarged many times their actual size, the following chart is provided to help determine proper letter-spacing for the 'Standard Medium' typefaces.

To find the proper spacing for any word, select the preceding letter in the left-hand column and the following letter from the top column. The box that corresponds to each column contains the exact number of space units that is to separate the two letters.

The sizes of the space units have been predetermined. They have been drawn in position on the right and left side of each letter and number of the three sizes of alphabet on pages 88-170. Space units must be added to or subtracted from these units in the same relationship to the letters as they appear in the manual, otherwise the chart will not function properly.

Capital letters appear only in the left-hand (preceding letter) column since style is always to be upper and lower case.

Word spacing
All word spaces are to be equal one-half the height of the capital letter.

	asg kl	bhi oq	cde ft	j	mn pr.,	u	vwy	x	z		1	2	3?	4	5	689 0c	7
ahmn	2	3	2	1	0	3	3	-1	1	2	[1] 1	1	1	1	2	2	1
bceops	1	2	1	0	-1	2	2	-1	-1	0	[2] 1	1	0	-3	0	0	-1
fr	0	2	0	1	-2	2	2	0	0	0	[38$] 0	0	1	1	1	1	-1
kx	-1	1	-2	1	0	1	1	0	0	1	[4] -3	-1	1	1	1	1	-3
tz	1	2	0	1	0	2	2	1	1	2	[5] -1	1	1	1	1	1	0
vwy p	-1	1	-1	1	-3	1	1	0	-1	0	[6] 1	0	1	1	1	1	0
AKLX	0	1	-1	-2	0	1	0	-4	0	1	[7] 0	-1	-1	-6	-3	-1	1
BCDOS	1	2	1	1	-1	2	2	-1	0	0	[90] 1	1	1	1	0	1	-1
E	1	2	0	-1	0	2	1	-2	0	1							
F	-3	2	-2	-1	-2	-1	-1	-2	-3	-3							
GHIJMNU dgijlqu;!	2	3	2	2	0	3	3	1	1	2							
QR	0	1	-1	0	0	1	0	-1	0	1							
TY	-5	1	-5	-1	-3	-4	-4	-4	-5	-5							
VW	-3	1	-3	0	-3	-1	-1	-2	-3	-3							
Z	1	2	0	0	0	2	1	0	0	2							

Type face

It is vital that all signs be read easily and understood quickly. This demands the consistent use of a distinctive type face throughout the entire system.

Research has shown that the most 'appropriate' type face for this purpose is a regular sans serif. Of the various weights of sans serif available, Standard Medium has been found to offer the easiest legibility from any angle, whether the passenger is standing, walking or riding.

The specific size type to be used will vary according to the three basic sign categories:*
1. For Station Identification, Exit and Transfer signs the largest type face, X height 9"
2. For Direction signs, X height 4¼"
3. For Information Signs, X height 1⅜"

Tables showing the alphabet follow below:

*Note: X height has been used as a point of reference and represents the height of upper case X in the Standard Medium alphabet.

ABCDEFGHIJKLMN
OPQRSTUVWXYZ
abcdefghijklmn
opqrstuvwxyz ( ) & ? !
1234567890 ., : ; - _ ' ' /

97–109, 112 *New York City Transit Authority Graphics Standards Manual* **(New York: Unimark International, 1970).** Designed by Unimark International. The modularity, layout and typography of the sign system shown in illustrations (**103–106**) derive from Noorda's 1966 sketches (**88**).

97 (opposite page) Binder cover. *New York City Transit Authority Graphics Standards Manual* **(1970).** Designed by Unimark International.

98 "Letter spacing." *New York City Transit Authority Graphics Standards Manual* **(1970), p. 9.**

99 "Letter spacing." *New York City Transit Authority Graphics Standards Manual* **(1970), p. 10.**

100 "Type face." *New York City Transit Authority Graphics Standards Manual* **(1970), p. 4.** The typeface is Standard (Akzidenz Grotesk). "Research has shown that the most 'appropriate' type face for this purpose is a regular sans serif. Of the various weights of sans serif available, Standard Medium has been found to offer the easiest legibility from any angle [see Noorda's Milano research], whether the passenger is standing, walking or riding."

101 "Diagram of the Information Tree."
New York City Transit Authority
Graphics Standards Manual (1970),
p. 2. This is a simplified version of
the 1966 Noorda diagram **(85)**.

102 "Diagram of basic sign distribution."
New York City Transit Authority
Graphics Standards Manual (1970),
p. 3.

103 "Sign plate modulation." *New York*
City Transit Authority Graphics
Standards Manual (1970), p. 61.

104 "Special conditions of station
identification signage." *New York*
City Transit Authority Graphics
Standards Manual (1970), p. 63.

105 "Criteria and examples of Exit
and Transfer signage." *New York*
City Transit Authority Graphics
Standards Manual (1970), p. 64.

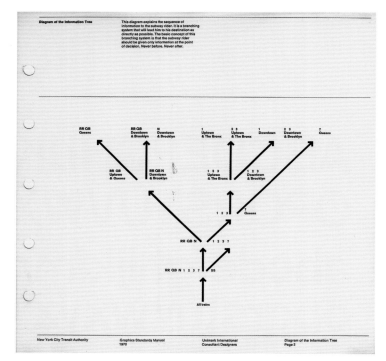

101

102

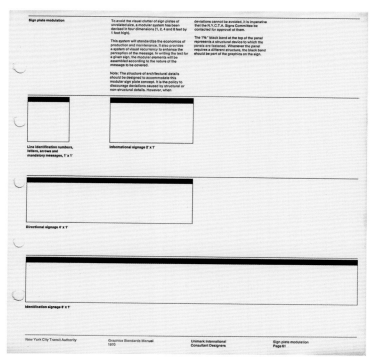

103

104

Criteria and examples of Exit and Transfer signage

To insure that these signs are especially noticeable, they are positioned at right angles to the track. White on red, PMS Warm Red, for exit. Black on yellow, PMS 109, for transfer.
The importance of these signs also warrants the use of X height 9″ Identification type.
Exit signs should be on a 2′ x 1′ module. Transfer signs should be on a 4′ x 1′ module.
When directional arrows and colored discs are used with these signs, the arrow will precede them: the colored discs will always follow them. When both transfer and exit appear on one sign, using one arrow, Transfer is to the left, Exit to the right.
Here again, any necessary reduction in size for environmental reasons must only be executed photographically and by no other method, to insure consistent spacing relationship.

Note: It is vital that the Exit sign on the platform be positioned in close contact to the stairs, leading up.

To avoid misinterpretation of the straight-ahead arrow on the platform, it is important that the transfer sign be positioned so that there will be no confusion between the Exit sign and the Transfer information.

The traveler disembarking from a train will receive his exit information in context and at the point of decision. In the case of a transfer, the position and frequency of the transfer sign should be such that the straight-ahead arrow and the message direct the traveler along the platform to the stairs where a transfer sign is positioned in close proximity to these stairs.

New York City Transit Authority

Graphics Standards Manual
1970

Unimark International
Consultant Designers

Criteria and examples of Exit and Transfer signage
Page 64

106 "Directional Signs on platforms." *New York City Transit Authority Graphics Standards Manual* (1970), p. 70. Note the loss of the route map from Noorda's 1966 diagram. **(89)**

107 "Mandatory Signs." *New York City Transit Authority Graphics Standards Manual* (1970), p. 80.

108 "Line map in the train." *New York City Transit Authority Graphics Standards Manual* (1970), p. 74. The detail also shows "The Outside Identification Sign" intended for the sides of train cars. This was never implemented but the in-car line map eventually was in the 1990s.

109 "Sign Glossary and Semantics." *New York City Transit Authority Graphics Standards Manual* (1970), p. 171.

106

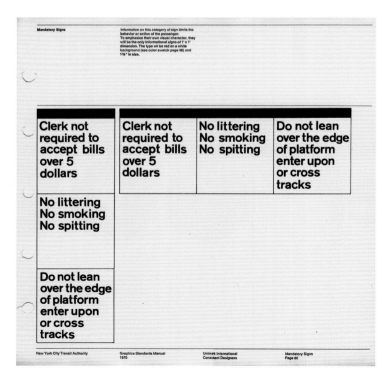

107

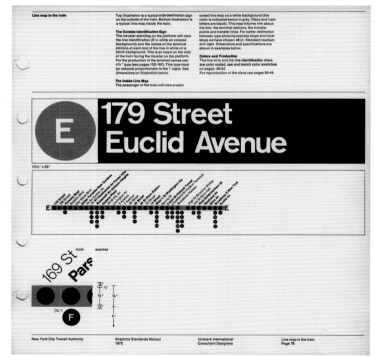

108

Sign glossary and semantics must be carefully considered as a strict discipline established in order to be consistent throughout the entire signing system. Many different terms have been used in the past, causing confusion and hesitation. It is the policy that the copy writer of sign messages should use positive language, for example: open 10 am—8 pm instead of closed 8 pm—10 am. The purpose of this glossary is to establish a long-range policy and standard.

Abbreviations
When names, rather than numbered streets or avenues, appear for station identification abbreviations Av, St, Blvd, are always used. In the case of numbered streets or avenues, no abbreviations are used. However, for train information signs, use the abbreviations: Av, St, Blvd. In addition, days of the week are abbreviated: Sun, Mon, Tue, Wed, Thu, Fri, Sat. East and West are abbreviated E and W. When other abbreviations are used in the total signing system, it is the policy to conform to the basic rules of the English language. Punctuation should be avoided. It should be used only when necessary to clarify the meaning of the copy. However, when used, it should conform to the standard rules of the English language.

Arrows
Used as first left hand module of all directional signs. The arrow always appears to the left of disc(s) and/or copy to which it refers. See directional signs page 59.

Discs
This is a bullet of the appropriate color with the line letter or number designation in white. Bullets are arranged in alphabetical order, left to right, followed by numbers in numerical order.

Directional Signs
The nature of the system is such that we have two types of directional signs. We have the directional sign that leads the passenger to a certain point; second we have the combination directional—train information. This second category is called the train information sign; it is located on the platform parallel to the track.
1. Directional signs consist of (left to right) arrow(s), directional inscription, disc(s).
Examples:

2. The directional inscription is the extreme left hand module on the train information sign. In boroughs other than Manhattan, the directional sign indicates only 'Manhattan' for service going in that direction. For service in the opposite direction, the terminal is shown.
Examples:
Northbound platforms on the D QJ line in Brooklyn will show 'Manhattan'
Southbound platforms on the D line in the Bronx will show 'Manhattan' (For services, such as GG, which do not go to Manhattan, the borough to which service is heading will be shown).
In Manhattan the sign reads 'Uptown' or 'Downtown' and the Borough of destination

other than Manhattan, if any, where appropriate. Borough(s) of destination may be omitted 1) if there are two, 2) if service is part-time. Uptown and downtown are not used on crosstown lines. Examples:

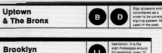

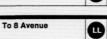

Entrance
'in' is used at controls (turnstiles) to indicate the way to trains.

Exit
'out' is used at controls on two-way turnstiles. 'Exit' is used in all other places to indicate the way out. When the passenger has a choice of two stairways at the exit, the name of the cross street (as opposed to the street in which the line is located) is in the primary or top position.
Examples:

Informational Copy
This is the detailed information about the service(s) operating; it is placed immediately to the right of the appropriate disc(s) on the train information sign.
Example: see page 176.

Mon—Fri
This is used to describe limited service. It is placed before the hours of operation.
Example:

Mon—Fri
7 am to 8:10 pm

Part-time service (Also see Rush Hours)
When shown on train information sign, it is normally accompanied by travel instructions for the hours when the part-time service is not operating. When part-time service varies according to the day of the week, show a common time, when practicable, by using the latest starting time and the earliest ending time when it will not create a passenger hardship.
Examples use:

Uptown   **5** To E 180 St or Dyre Av
             7:40 am to 9:15 pm
             Other times take **4** to 149 St,
             Change to **2**

rather than:

Uptown   **5** To E 180 St or Dyre Av
             Mon-Fri 6:05 am to 9:50 pm
             Sat 6:25 am to 9:15 pm
             Sun 7:40 am to 9:30 pm
             Other times take **4** to 149 St,
             Change to **2**

Routing
When two or more services, using various routings, go to the same terminal or locality, the route is shown on the train information sign:
Examples:

via 8 Av   via 7 Av-Broadway
via Queens Blvd   via Av of the Americas
via Brighton   via McDonald Av
via West End   via Broadway
via Sea Beach   via Lexington Av
via Broadway Brooklyn

Rush Hours
Generally, rush-hour services are briefly explained in an extreme righthand module of the train information sign which is headed 'Rush-hour Service(s) Mon-Fri:' (see train information sign for examples). The policy is to avoid showing actual times on the train information sign when not necessary. For example, at 34 St and Avenue of the Americas, the B train runs at all times at the same platform (although not always on the same track) thus precluding the necessity for showing actual times. The result is a reduction in visual clutter. The passenger merely watches both tracks if he is not sure if it is 'rush-hour' or not.

Street Entrance Signs (Elevated Structure)
The sign on the elevated structure will be visible to the passenger at street level when he ascends the stairs. It includes the station name and discs of service. In the event the entrance leads to trains going in only one direction, the same sign will include that information.
Examples: See page 89.

Street Entrance Signs (Underground Structure)
These are signs on the railing facing descending passengers, and on the opposite side of this railing. It includes the station name and discs of service. In the event the entrance leads to trains going in only one direction, the same sign will include that information.
Examples:

Sign on side railings have downward pointing arrow and 'Subway'.
Examples:

See pages 86-88.

Train Information Sign
This is mounted parallel to track, facing passengers on platform. Normally, these are divided into three basic sections (each one on a separate module so that changes can be made readily) which are, left to right:

New York City Transit Authority   Graphics Standards Manual   Unimark ternational   Sign Glossary and Semantics
1970   Consulta Designers   Page 171

109

47

The Directory is designed to help a passenger find his "Destination" and "How to get there" quickly and easily. Each station will have its own directory listing all other stations alphabetically and numerically. Each station name will be followed by the color disc designating the trains that stop there. If there is no direct train, transfer information will follow the station name. This directory will be placed at all important points in the subway station both inside and outside the turnstiles.

The following illustrations show the entire directory, with a grid, and an example of a section of it:

Directory from Grand Central

Destination	How to get there	Destination	How to get there	Destination	How to get there	Destination	How to get there
Alabama Av							
Allerton Av							
Aqueduct							
Astoria Blvd-Hoyt Av							
Atlantic Av							
Avenue H							
Avenue I							
Avenue J							
Avenue M							
Avenue N							
Avenue P							
Avenue U E 16 St							
Avenue U McDonald Av							
Avenue U W T 9 St							
Avenue X							
Bay 50 St							
Bay Parkway							
Bay Ridge Av							
Baychester							
B							

New York City Transit Authority

Graphic Standards Manual
1970

Unimark International
Consultant Designers

The Directory
Page 75

Destination

How to get there

Destination		How to get there
Alabama Av		⑥ Downtown to Fulton St. Transfer to ⓆⒿ Queens
Allerton Av		⑤ Uptown & Bronx
Aqueduct		④⑤⑥ Downtown to Fulton St./Broadway. Transfer to Ⓐ Ⓔ Far Rockaway & Brooklyn
Astoria Blvd-Hoyt Av		④⑤⑥ Uptown to 59 St. Lexington Av. Transfer to ⓇⓇ Queens
Atlantic Av		④⑤ Downtown & Brooklyn
Avenue H		⑥ Downtown to Bleecker St. Transfer to Ⓓ Downtown & Brooklyn
Avenue I		⑥ Downtown to Bleecker St. Transfer to Ⓕ Downtown & Brooklyn
Avenue J		⑥ Downtown to Bleecker St. Transfer to Ⓓ Downtown & Brooklyn
Avenue M		⑥ Downtown to Bleecker St. Transfer to Ⓓ Downtown & Brooklyn
Avenue N		⑥ Downtown to Bleecker St. Transfer to Ⓕ Downtown & Brooklyn
Avenue P		⑥ Downtown to Bleecker St. Transfer to Ⓕ Downtown & Brooklyn
Avenue U E 16 St		⑥ Downtown to Bleecker St. Transfer to Ⓓ Downtown & Brooklyn
Avenue U McDonald Av		⑥ Downtown to Bleecker St. Transfer to Ⓕ Downtown & Brooklyn
Avenue U W 7 St		④⑤⑥ Downtown to 14 St. Union Sq. Transfer to Ⓝ Downtown & Brooklyn
Avenue X		⑥ Downtown to Bleecker St. Transfer to Ⓕ Downtown & Brooklyn
Bay 50 St		⑥ Downtown to Bleecker St. Transfer to Ⓑ Downtown & Brooklyn
Bay Parkway Avenue O		④⑤⑥ Downtown to 14 St. Union Sq. Transfer to Ⓝ Downtown & Brooklyn
Bay Parkway 86 St		⑥ Downtown to Bleecker St. Transfer to Ⓑ Downtown & Brooklyn
Bay Ridge Av		④⑤⑥ Downtown to 14 St. Union Sq. Transfer to ⓇⓇ Downtown & Brooklyn
Baychester Av		⑤ Uptown & Bronx
Beach 25 St-Wavecrest		④⑤⑥ Downtown to Fulton St. Transfer to Ⓐ Ⓔ Far Rockaway & Brooklyn
Beach 36 St-Edgemere		④⑤⑥ Downtown to Fulton St. Transfer to Ⓐ Ⓔ Far Rockaway Brooklyn

110 Porcelain enamel entrance sign at John Street and Nassau Street. **Fulton Street (4/5), c.1966?.** Note the white on gray coloration and the inclusion of the arrow. This may be one of the signs made in the wake of the 1966 Unimark contract by the TA's Bergen Street sign shop without Vignelli's supervision. (1968)

111 **"Directomat" Times Square station (1/2/3/S), April 30, 1956.** The Directomat, invented by urban planner Dr. Max M. Tamir and built by electrical engineer Murray Schiffman, was intended to remove the guesswork from subway travel. "All the traveler has to do," wrote the *New York Times*, "is press the desired button and, in a matter of four to twelve seconds, the required information is printed on a slip of paper and ejected from a slot."

112 **"The Directory."** *New York City Transit Authority Graphics Standards Manual* **(1970), p. 75 and gatefold.** The Directory, a chart indicating how to get from one station in the system to another, was conceived by Massimo Vignelli. It was intended to be displayed at each station, but was never implemented.

helvetica

helvetica

THE MYTH OF THE HELVETICA JUGGERNAUT

Helvetica celebrated its 50th anniversary with a movie, an exhibition at the Museum of Modern, and a book. All of the excitement seems to have blinded people to the reality of its history in the United States. In the 1960s European types were imported and distributed in the United States by two companies: Amsterdam Continental and Bauer Alphabets. The latter was owned by the Bauersche Giesserei of Frankfurt am Main and had been in business in New York since the late 1920s when it was responsible for introducing Futura to the American market. Amsterdam Continental, owned by Lettergieterij Amsterdam (also known as the foundry of N. Tetterode), was established in 1948. It imported types from Berthold, Stempel, Klingspor, Haas and Nebiolo as well as those from its parent company. Exactly when Amsterdam Continental began importing Standard is unclear but it appears on several record album covers as early as 1957. From 1960 on the company heavily promoted it to the graphic design community (fig. 127). Bauer countered by touting Folio, a neo-grotesque designed by Konrad Bauer and Walter Baum. American Type Founders (ATF) began importing Adrian Frutiger's Univers in late 1960 and in 1961 it became available on monotype machines. Mergenthaler Linotype belatedly responded to the foreign invasion in 1963 with advertisements for Trade Gothic. ATF made no special attempts to sell its popular News Gothic and Franklin Gothic types, probably because none was needed. These were the rivals that Helvetica faced (fig. 114). [**37**]

113 **(opposite page) Helvetica type specimen, front detail. D. Stempel AG, 1963.** Inserted in *Print* XVII:6 (November/December 1963).

37. For information on Lettergieterij Amsterdam and its subsidiary see Jan Middendorp, *Dutch Type.* (Rotterdam: 010 Publishers, 2004), p. 86. The introduction of Univers can be tracked in advertisements. See *Print* XIV:5 (September/October 1960) and *Print* XIV:6 (November/December 1960); and Emil O. Biemann, "Univers." *Print* XV:1 (January/February 1961), pp. 32–36. Advertisements for Folio are constant throughout the 1960s in *Print*. Mergenthaler Linotype's "retaliatory" advertisement for Trade Gothic appears in *Print* XVII:6 (November/December 1963), the same issue that has the special Helvetica insert described in the text.

Mortimer Leach, *Lettering in the Graphic Arts* (New York: Reinhold Publishing Corporation, 1960) p. 14 lists the popular new typefaces at the end of the 1950s as: Consort, Melior, Palatino, Torino, Craw Clarendon, Studio, Rondo, and Libra.

ABCDEFGHIJKLMNOPQRSTUVWXYZ&abc
defghijklmnopqrstuvwxyz1234567890$.,
''-:;!?''''

24 POINT NEWS GOTHIC BOLD, ATF

ABCDEFGHIJKLMNOPQRSTUVWXYZ
&abcdefghijklmnopqrstuvwxyz12345
67890$.,-,:;!?

24 POINT FRANKLIN GOTHIC, LUDLOW

ABCDEFGHIJKLMNOPQRSTU
VWXYZ&abcdefghijklmnopqrstu
vwxyz1234567890$.,:;-'!?

36 POINT VENUS BOLD, BAUER

ABCDEFGHIJKLMNOPQRRSTUVWXYZ&abc
defghijklmnopqrstuvwxyz1234567890$.,'-:;!?""

24 POINT FOLIO MEDIUM, BAUER

ABCDEFGHIJKLMNOPQRSTUVWXY
Z&abcdefghijklmnopqrstuvwxyz1234
567890!?$.,:;)''

24 POINT (large) UNIVERS 65, ATF

114

ABCDEFGHIJK
LMNOPQRSTU
VWXYZ&abcd
efghijklmnopq
rstuvwxyz123
4567890$.,'"-:;!
?'"""

115

115 Standard Medium. *From Type and Typography: The Designer's Type Book* by Ben Rosen (1963), p. 167.

116 Book cover. *Conflict and Creativity: Control of the Mind,* Part 2 edited by Seymour M. Farber and Roger H.L. Wilson (New York: McGraw-Hill Paperbacks, 1963). Design by Rudolph de Harak. Set in Standard Medium.

116

Helvetica began life as Neue Haas Grotesk, a new interpretation of a 19th century grotesque (principally Akzidenz Grotesk) conceived by Eduard Hoffmann and executed by Max Miedinger for the Haas'sche Schriftgiesserei (Haas type foundry) in Munchenstein, Switzerland in 1957 (figs. 117-119). Three years later it was licensed by D. Stempel AG of Frankfurt (which owned shares in Haas) and renamed Helvetica. Stempel manufactured the face in foundry type and its partner German Linotype made it available in matrices—but only in *mager* (light) and *halbfett* (medium) weights. Other weights followed in the next few years. This is one reason that Noorda was unable to find the right weight of Helvetica for the Milano Metro signage in 1962. [**38**]

117

38. Coincidentally, Neue Haas Grotesk was released the same year as both Folio and Univers. Walter Greisner, "The History of the Most Successful Sans Serif," *Linotype Matrix* vol. 4, no. 3 (Winter 2008): 64–79; Erich Alb to author, 2 May 2008 and 15 May 2008. It is commonly believed that Helvetica is simply a revision of Akzidenz Grotesk but the story is more complicated than that as indicated in *Helvetica: A Documentary Film.* In the film Alfred Hoffmann explains how his father Eduard Hoffmann had the idea for a new, more consistent grotesque in the 1940s and that he asked Max Miedinger to translate his thoughts into workable type drawings. The elder Hoffmann made sketches for Miedinger to follow and discussed his ideas with him verbally. See *Helvetica Forever: Story of a Typeface* edited by Victor Malsy and Lars Müller (Baden: Lars Müller Publishers 2009) pp. 71–97 for

Hlevetica*, a scrapbook maintained by Eduard Hoffmann from 16 November 1956 to 21 July 1965 that details the genesis and development of Helvetica (**117–119**). Berthold's Akzidenz Grotesk is a family cobbled together in 1908 from several 19th c. grotesques, including Royal Grotesk issued by the foundry of Ferdinand Theinhardt in 1880. Many of the problems with the family lay in discrepancies among its sizes and weights. In trying to resolve them Hoffmann took ideas for the ideal shapes he wanted in the new face from other grotesques (e.g. Schelter Grotesk) besides Akzidenz Grotesk. Erich Alb to author, 12 March 2005.

117–119 Pages from Helvetica*, a scrapbook kept by Eduard Hoffmann (1956–1965) chronicling the development of Neue Haas Grotesk which subsequently was renamed Helvetica.

117 Entries for August 1957 to 27 November 1957. Helvetica*, pp. 22–23.

118 Entries for 11 November 1956. Helvetica*, p. 1.

119 Entries for 8–18 April 1957. Helvetica*, pp. 10–11.

118

Versal G   Würde noch nicht geändert

[ ]   eckige Klammern zu fett.

t   sollte etwas mehr nach unten gezogen werden, steht optisch (unten) zu hoch über der Fußlinie, speziell zwischen 2 runden Buchstaben, siehe Osten

E   etwas zu breit

r   scheint auf meinen Abzügen nicht dünner   dito

x   Ändern zu mager (5-Zacken)

§   immer noch ein wenig oben nach links fallen

W   äusserer rechter Balken mehr senkrecht

S   fällt oben noch ganz wenig nach links, also oben Haken abdrehen nach rechts

U   unten rechts innen runder wie links

M   finde ich nun gut. Falls die beiden Schrägbalken fetter werden, erscheint das M zu fett und fällt bestimmt aus dem Rahmen.

8. April 57   Miedinger   (← ein süsser)

doch, aber zu wenig.

doch, aber zu wenig

Unterredung mit M. Miedinger.   8. April 57.   17 ³⁰ h.

für Graveur: t   tiefer stellen
für Glaspreis: §   drehen nach rechts
                 S   "   "
E.H. ——   Meiner Verenica M (innerdig fetter, äussen dünner).
          a   inwendig etwas lichter links.
          s   Gemeine S finde ich gut.

— 9. APR. 1957

10

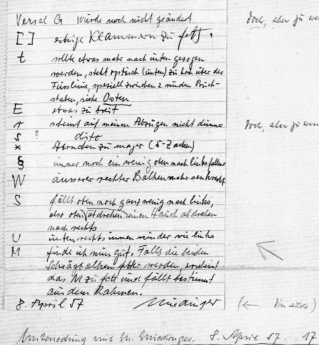

G = gut
E = "
M = "
S = "
U = "
W = "
a = "
r = "
s = etwas drehen
t = gut
Ziffer 9 = unten innen zu fett
§ = gut
x = "
ß   ß = ein wenig?
v = dünner.
[ ] = gut

23. IV.   mit M. Miedinger
E   alle 3 Balken 1. kürzen.
9   innen etwas heller.
§   nochmals drehen
s   "   "
ß   = gut.
M   = gut !!
F   etwas schmäler
U   " dünner

ABCDEFGHIJKLMNOPQR
ABCDEFGHIJKLMNOPQR
STUVWXYZ
STUVWXYZ
abcdefghijklmnopqrstuvwxyz
abcdefghijklmnopqrstuvwxyz
1234567890 & ß
1234567890 & ß

18. IV. 57

Aarau Baden Cibourg Dolder
Eismeer Fischbach Grandson
Hagneck Inkwil Jongny Kunst
Lajoux Mumpf Nortfrux Osten
Paccots Quinto Romoos Sulz
Thurquelle Urigen Villeneuve
Winkel Xaver Yverdon Zurich
1234567890 Der Schießplatz
PETER & GLOOR DORNACH
CHEMISCHE FARBENFABRIK
XAVIER UMBRICH ZWINGEN
.,-:;!?'()[]§†*«»„"—/£$JARDIN

18. IV. 57

11

In the days of metal type, graphic designers were forced to use whatever typefaces their local printers or type houses had in stock. There was no typographic candy store as there is today. And printers and type houses only bought new typefaces when they thought there would be sufficient demand for them or they filled a specific stylistic niche. Buying a typeface meant buying a range of sizes and thus metal type took up a lot of space. Imported type was even more expensive—it meant shipping lead across the Atlantic—and had the further disadvantage of having to be specially manufactured for use with American printing presses. A new typeface often meant an investment of a thousand dollars or more.

From the designers' perspective a new typeface intended for a wide range of applications had to be available in both foundry and composition versions, the former for display use and the latter for text setting. Only a handful of sans serifs met this criteria in the early 1960s: Futura, News Gothic, Franklin Gothic, Standard and Univers. Designers were often forced to mix and match different text and display sans serifs—for example Futura and Spartan or News Gothic and Trade Gothic. [39]

Helvetica joined this select group in 1963 when Stempel adapted it for the pica-point system and German Linotype prepared matrices for export. To announce Helvetica's availability for American consumption, the foundry inserted a special double-sided, red and black advertisement in the November/December 1963 issue of *Print* touting the face for "its spare simplicity, its utter legibility, its uniformity and its flawless color" (figs. 113, 121–122). Despite this, Helvetica was slow to catch on in the United States. One reason was that German Linotype mats did not align with American ones. This problem was resolved when Mergenthaler Linotype in Brooklyn began manufacturing Helvetica in February 1964. They released the 10 pt version first and the remaining sizes by early 1965. At the same time, the Visual Graphics Corporation (VGC), manufacturers of the Typositor which set display phototype, offered faces "similar to" Helvetica. Linofilm Helvetica, a text phototype version of the font, was begun by Mergenthaler in 1965 but not completed until 1967. [40]

120 Helvetica*: einige Gedanken über eine neue Schrift. Type specimen cover. (Haas'schen Schriftgiesserei, 1962).

Helvetica*

Einige Gedanken über eine neue Schrift

120

39. Matthew Carter has confirmed the "considerable investment" for a printer or type house in installing a range of sizes of a typeface. Matthew Carter to author, 5 May 2008. Details of the availability and use of Futura, Spartan, News Gothic and Trade Gothic in the United States can be found in Mac McGrew, *American Metal Typefaces of the Twentieth Century*. 2nd, rev. ed. (New Castle, Delaware: Oak Knoll Books, 1993), pp. 47, 231, 287, 311. After Helvetica's introduction to the United States it was often combined with Standard (**189, 190**).

40. D. Stempel, "Helvetica," *Print* XVII:6 (November/December 1963), insert; Matthew Carter to author, 5 May 2008; and Mike Parker to author, 30 April 2008. Helvetica's lag time in the United States is evident in the changes between the two editions of Ben Rosen's *Type and Typography*

(1963), a standard book for several decades. Standard is included in the first edition but not Helvetica. The latter was finally added as a supplement to the second edition (1976). See Ben Rosen, *Type and Typography: The Designer's Type Book*. (New York: Reinhold Publishing Corp., 1963) and Ben Rosen, *Type and Typography: The Designer's Type Book*. rev. ed. (New York: Van Nostrand Reinhold, 1976). Also see Henry Wolf, "Foreword." *#1 Handbook by Haber: Helvetica*. (New York: Haber Typographers, [November] 1971): "...Helvetica is a major event. It is right for today, therefore in the conventional sense 'modern'. But it is also timeless because it fulfills the basic demands of a typeface: readability, clarity, versatility and beauty. Helvetica has become symbolic of the visual character of the country where it was born...." One of the first New York City

type houses to offer Helvetica was The Composing Room which claimed to have the face in late 1963. See the note on materials in *Print* XVII:6 (November/December 1963). The firm was also one of the first, along with Aaron Burns & Company, to have a film version of Helvetica. See Composing Room, Inc., *The CRT Typebook*. (New York: The Composing Room, Inc., 1965) and Aaron Burns & Company, *Typositor Typography*. (New York: Aaron Burns & Company [Rapid Typographers, Inc.], 1965). By 1973, the Visual Graphics Corporation was offering a legitimate version of Helvetica. See Visual Graphics Corporation, *The World Famous Photo Typositor Alphabet Library*. (Tamarac, Florida: Visual Graphics Corporation, 1973). The situation for British designers was similar to that for American ones as Helvetica was not

available in England in Linotype or foundry form until 1965. See the advertisement for Helvetica by Linotype & Machinery, Ltd. in *The Penrose Annual* 59 (1966) and note that the face does not appear in John R. Biggs, *Basic Typography*. (London: Faber and Faber, Ltd., 1968). It is unclear when transfer type versions of Helvetica became available in the United States. Colin Brignall of Letraset says that his company offered the face, under its original name of Neue Haas Grotesk, in late 1962 in England but not in America until 1966 or later. However, he thinks that Chartpak may have been selling it in the United States before Letraset did. Colin Brignall to author, 1 May 2008.

The goal of every Gothic type design — uniform color through exact balance of each letter form — is at last attained in Helvetica. Every letter and symbol in this exquisite and softly rounded Gothic stands in harmonious relation to every other. In body text and in display, in light face, in bold and in italics, absolute color consistency is maintained line by line and over the entire length of the page. The chronic illness of "holes" and "clumping" which results from certain letter combinations in other faces is overcome in Helvetica; and the meticulous uniformity of Helvetica assures that this desirable effect will prevail from size to size and from weight to weight. In using Helvetica designers will not be forced to the expedient of letter spacing or text manipulation to achieve evenness of tone.

In its spare simplicity, its utter legibility, its uniformity and its flawless color, Helvetica embodies and conveys an esthetic satisfaction which will outlast the vicissitudes of fashion. Regular, Italic, Medium and Bold; specimen sheets on request.

Sole importers and distributors:
**Amsterdam Continental Types
and Graphic Equipment, Inc.,
276 Park Avenue South, New York 10, N.Y.;
3319 West Magnolia Blvd., Burbank, Calif.**

Type faces: 12 pt. Helvetica   12 pt. Helvetica Italic   12 pt. Helvetica Medium

Printed in Germany

121/122 Helvetica type specimen, front and back covers. D. Stempel AG, 1963. Inserted in *Print* XVII:6 (November/December 1963).

121

122

By 1965 Helvetica began to appear in award-winning designs and advertising, principally from graphic designers working for Unimark and CCA in Chicago and at MIT (Massachusetts Institute of Technology) in Cambridge, Massachusetts (figs. 124–125). It took longer for designers in New York to embrace it. The ubiquity of Helvetica, which has been both lauded and lamented since, did not begin in the United States until 1969. Vignelli has often taken credit for the spread of Helvetica in this country. This may seem like braggadocio, but his claim has a very large grain of truth in it. [41]

Vignelli was already an enthusiastic advocate for Helvetica prior to his move to the United States. What he most loved about it was its lack of sidebearings. This enabled him to tightly pack letters together—as in his famous posters for the Teatro Piccolo in Milano—without having to cut up galley proofs (figs. 81–82). Vignelli shared his love of Helvetica with his colleagues at Unimark and it quickly became the firm's "house face". The "new sans serif" was especially prized for visual identity systems such as the one Unimark developed for Varian (fig. 95). Not only could Helvetica be set closely but it was available in a variety of sizes and weights and on a variety of typesetting systems. More importantly, compared to its sans serif rival Standard, it was considered more harmonious in design because the terminals of c, e, s, etc. were horizontal. [42]

41. This summary of Helvetica's diffusion in the United States is based on a survey of winning entries to competitions held by the American Institute of Graphic Arts (AIGA), Type Directors Club (TDC) and Art Directors Club (ADC) between 1963 and 1975 in conjunction with an examination of designs profiled in *Print* during that period as well advertisements in the magazine. One of the first major uses of Helvetica in New York was for new signage and graphics at Yankee Stadium in 1967. But the designers, Lou Dorfsman and Peter Palazzo, mixed it with Standard which they found looked better at large sizes. See *Print* XXI:V (September/October 1967). Palazzo: "To minimize this illusionary effect [of white type on a black background], we had to combine Standard Medium with the Helvetica, mix Helvetica Light and Medium, change the scale of

some letters, and shave the proportions of others." p. 25. Arnold Saks was one of the few New York City designers to use Helvetica. See the 1966 annual reports for Time, Inc. and Eastern Airlines in John Lahr, "James Ward and Arnold Saks: A Portfolio", *Print* XXI:VI (November/December 1967), pp. 34–35. Saks: "I'm more of a formalist. I'll use almost only one type face—Helvetica—until I get bored with it."

In August 1967 the New York City Sanitation Department made a big splash when it unveiled new white trucks with the name of the department set in lowercase Helvetica on the side. The design was the work of Walter Kacik of Walter Kacik Associates, a former employee of Unimark. A summary of the commission and its ultimate fate can be found in Lahr (1968), pp. 53–55; see also "Sanitation Department Changes

Aspect of Its Sprinkler Trucks but They're Still Cool." *New York Times*, August 8, 1967 and "Arrogance," *Communication Arts* vol. 13, no. 4 (1971), pp. 24–31 where the Sanitation truck was treated like a Playboy pinup. In 2007 Vignelli said: "Then in 1965 I came to the USA with UNIMARK and since we had offices in New York, Chicago, Detroit, Denver and San Francisco I placed orders for Helvetica from all those cities, and consequently spread the use of Helvetica across the USA." Massimo Vignelli email to Erich Alb, 25 August 2007. He also had a series of friendly debates with Rudolph de Harak, a proponent of Standard, over the relative merits of the two sans serifs. Massimo Vignelli interview by author, 29 April 2008; and Richard Poulin interview by author, 8 June 2009.

R. Roger Remington and Robert S.P. Fripp have claimed that it was Will Burtin who was most responsible for popularizing Helvetica in the United States, even titling one of the chapters in their monograph on him "Kalamazoo Wows Germany: Helvetica Finds New York". "When the Burtins returned to New York [from Switzerland] in the fall of 1958, they imported Helvetica [sic] with them." R. Roger Remington and Robert S.P. Fripp, *Design and Science: The Life and Work of Will Burtin.* (London and Burlington, Vermont: Lund Humphries, 2007), p. 84. This story is not documented and is not supported by work done by Burtin. In the monograph the earliest dated example of Helvetica in one of his designs is for *The Story of Mathematics for Young People: The Development of Mathematical Thought from the Finger-Counting of Primitive Man to the*

Electronic Computer by James T. Rogers (New York: Pantheon Books, 1966). (fig. 88) A photograph of Burtin in 1957 (fig. 60) is juxtaposed with an uncredited, undated advertisement for Helvetica (fig. 61). The implication is that the design is Burtin's. However, credit belongs to an anonymous employee at Haas'sche Schriftgiesserei AG who published it in 1968. See Victor Malsy and Lars Müller, eds., *Helvetica Forever: Geschichte einer Schrift.* (Baden: Lars Müller Publishers, 2008), p. 56. Elsewhere Remington and Fripp write that, "James Marston Fitch had a contract from the City of New York to improve urban esthetics, a task that included restoring city streetscapes and parks, including Central Park. Fitch, a pioneer and the leading practitioner of restoration architecture, asked Burtin to design new signage. Before long, new signs in Helvetica began

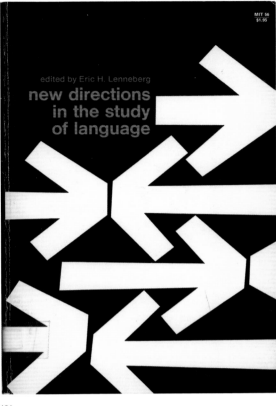

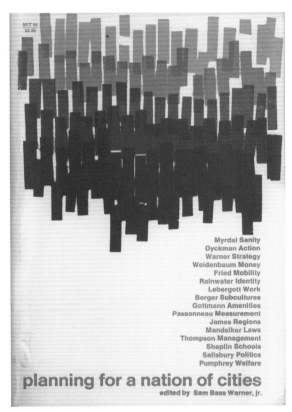

124

125

123 Helvetica type specimen. D. Stempel AG, 1968. Inserted into *Penrose Annual* 61 (1968). This is the first Helvetica advertisement to appear in the British printing trade. Note the asterisk which indicates that Helvetica Medium in foundry type is the same as Helvetica Bold from English Linotype. Similar discrepancies occurred in the United States.

124 Book cover. *New Directions in the Study of Language* edited by Eric H. Lenneberg (Cambridge, Massachusetts: The MIT Press, 1966). Designer unknown. Set in Helvetica Medium.

125 Book cover. *Planning for a Nation of Cities* edited by Sam Bass Warner (Cambridge, Massachusetts: The MIT Press, 1966). Designer unknown. Set in Helvetica Medium.

to appear all over the city. (The fact that 'Curb your dog' was the first to require the Burtin touch caused the maestro some chagrin!) Other cities followed New York's example." *Design and Science*, p. 127. This passage provides no date for Fitch's urban improvement project and the accompanying footnote says, in toto, "Burtin was impressed by the work of a Japanese design team led by Masaru Katzumie, some of whose iconic symbols for the 1964 Tokyo Olympics were later adopted into Japan's modern urban and traffic signage. Katzumie, or one of thirty young volunteer designers working with him on the Olympics, created the universal wheelchair symbol, among others. Katsumie [sic] made a visual presentation at Vision 65." *Design and Science*, p. 155. The "Curb your dog" sign was not done by Burtin, but by Walter Kacik. (**90**) There is no evidence of Fitch's

project nor Burtin's contribution to it. Fitch was appointed the preservation director of Central Park in August, 1974, two years after Burtin died. The post did not include the redesign of New York City's street signage. Since 1963 that has been the responsibility of the Department of Traffic. "We adopted a new type of reflectorized sign with six-inch character meeting national standards, and have been installing them with our own manpower at the rate of about 10,000 since 1964," wrote Commissioner Theodore Karagheuzoff in a letter to the *New York Times*, February 8, 1969. The street signs pictured in the *New York Times*, January 29, 1969 [the editorial that Karagheuzoff was responding to] do not use Helvetica—and today they still do not. However, Burtin did do a documented urban street sign system that used a modified version of Helvetica. It was for

the University Circle neighborhood in Cleveland in 1966–1968. See *Dot Zero* 5 (Fall 1968), p. 22. Documents, artwork and other material pertaining to the University Circle project are in the Will Burtin Collection in Special Collections, Wallace Library, Rochester Institute of Technology. See Containers 19.1–19.3, 19.4, 227.1–227.2, 239.1, 239. 2–240.2, 241.1, 243.1–245.2, and Box 262. The University Circle project is not mentioned in *Design and Science*.

42. On several occasions Vignelli has told the following anecdote about his eagerness to acquire and use Helvetica upon its release: "In 1960, when I went back to Milano, from my first exposure to the USA, I met the printer Nava, and [asked] him to go to Münchenstein to buy the Helvetica font from the Haas Foundry. A week later I met him again and asked if he got the type. So he told me the story that when he got to the border the customs officer asked him if he had anything to declare and he said NO. The problem was that the little FIAT loaded with all the lead was basically flat to the ground, which made the Customs Officer suspicious, and to make a long story short, he confiscated the type. The poor Nava returned to Milano empty handed. So I asked him what he would do now, so he told me he will go back but choose a less guarded pass. Finally he did

it and the type reached Milano, and we started to use it all the time. I had been waiting so long to have a typeface that would have almost no shoulder so that we could have a very tight kerning, and avoid to cut every letter by hand.... That was the real success of Helvetica, not the style. For style Akzidenz would have been good, but Helvetica allowed us to achieve the compact look we wanted in our design." Massimo Vignelli email to Erich Alb, 25 August 2007. Also see Wim Crouwel and Massimo Vignelli, interview by Alice Twemlow. "Modernism on Two Planes: A Conversation with Wim Crouwel and Massimo Vignelli." AIGA–NY. New York, 25 October 2007. That "compact look" is evident in Vignelli's celebrated posters for the Piccolo Teatro of Milano done in 1964/1965 (**81, 82**).

QRS
efgh
123

126

126 Key letters and figures for identifying Standard (Akzidenz Grotesk) Medium. The terminals of curved strokes in **C**, **G**, **S**, **c**, **e**, **s** and **3** are angled. **J** does not hook. The tail of **Q** lies outside the bowl and is slightly curved. **R** has a diagonal leg. **2** has a ski-slope spine.

127 Amsterdam Continental Types advertisement for Standard family, 1960. From *Print* XIV:3 (May/June 1960).

Hint

Besides reading crisp and even on the page, Standard has a great talent for solving problems. With sixteen faces in the family, it's the largest and most versatile modern sans serif family going. Each face works hard alone, all work well together. No wonder it's considered a contemporary classic among sans serifs.

Sole importers for the U.S.:
AMSTERDAM CONTINENTAL TYPES
276 Park Avenue South, New York 10, N.Y., 212 SP 7-498
3319 W. Magnolia Boulevard, Burbank, Cal., 213 VI 9-6319

STANDARD LIGHT
standard light
6, 8, 10, 12, 14, 18, 24

STANDARD
standard
6-S, 6-L, 8, 10, 12, 14, 18, 24-S, 24-L, 30, 36, 48

STANDARD ITALIC
standard italic
8, 10, 12, 14, 18, 24-S, 24-L, 30, 36

STANDARD MEDIUM
standard medium
6-S, 6-L, 8, 10, 12, 14, 18, 24-S, 24-L, 30, 42, 60, 72

STANDARD MEDIUM ITALIC
standard medium italic
8, 10, 12, 14, 18, 24-S, 24-L, 30, 42

STANDARD BOLD
standard bold
6, 8, 10, 12, 14, 18, 24-S, 24-L, 30, 42, 60, 72

STANDARD EXTRALIGHT EXTENDED
standard extralight extended
6-S, 6-L, 8, 10, 12, 14, 18, 24-S, 24-L, 30

STANDARD LIGHT EXTENDED
standard light extended
6-S, 6-L, 8, 10, 12, 14, 18, 24-S, 24-L, 30, 42

STANDARD EXTENDED
standard extended
6-S, 6-L, 8, 10, 12, 14, 18, 24-S, 24-L, 30, 42

STANDARD MEDIUM EXTENDED
standard medium extended
6, 8, 10, 12, 14, 18, 24-S, 24-L, 30, 42, 48, 60

STANDARD EXTRABOLD EXTENDED
standard extrabold extended
6, 8, 10, 12, 14, 18, 24-S, 24-L, 30, 42, 48, 60

STANDARD LIGHT CONDENSED
standard light condensed
6, 8, 10, 12, 14, 18, 24-S, 24-L

STANDARD CONDENSED
standard condensed
8, 10, 12, 14, 18, 24-S, 24-L, 30, 42, 48, 60

STANDARD MEDIUM CONDENSED
standard medium condensed
8, 10, 12, 14, 18, 24, 30, 36, 42, 60, 72

STANDARD BOLD CONDENSED
standard bold condensed
8, 10, 12, 14, 18, 24-S, 24-L, 30, 42, 60, 72

STANDARD EXTRABOLD CONDENSED
standard extrabold condensed
8, 10, 12, 14, 18, 24-S, 24-L, 30, 42, 48, 60

127

QRS
efgh
123

128

128 Key letters and figures for identifying **Helvetica Medium.** Terminals of curved strokes on **C, G, S, c, e, s, 2** and **3** are horizontal or nearly so. **J** ends in a hook. The tail of **Q** intrudes into the counter. **R** has a curved vertical leg.

129 Helvetica in photolettering. From *Type and Typography: The Designer's Type Book* (rev. ed.) by Ben Rosen (1976), p. 389. Note the presence of Helvetica Bold Roman which was subsequently renamed Helvetica Medium.

Helvetica Light Roman
Helvetica Light Italic
Helvetica Roman
Helvetica Italic
Helvetica Bold Roman
Helvetica Bold Italic
Helvetica Bold Roman No. 2
Helvetica Black Roman
Helvetica Black Italic
Helvetica Light Condensed Roman
Helvetica Light Condensed Italic
Helvetica Condensed Roman
Helvetica Condensed Italic
Helvetica Bold Condensed Roman
Helvetica Bold Condensed Italic
Helvetica Black Condensed Roman
Helvetica Black Condensed Italic
Helvetica Bold Outline
Helvetica Inserat Roman
Helvetica Inserat Italic
Helvetica Compressed
Helvetica Extra Compressed
Helvetica Ultra Compressed

A virtual signature of many outstanding designers, Helvetica has had universal acceptance in the past decade. Used in many variations, and as display copy or as text in combination with other display faces, this beautiful and versatile type demands room in this book.

An historical factor, with subtle, far reaching implications, occurred during the 1960's. Phototype and the earnest onset of automated computerized typesetting gathered the momentum that has, after 500 years, changed the typesetter's art forever. By the end of this decade, hot metal and foundry type may be on its way to becoming a kind of folk art.

Computerized, automated typesetting became possible because the electronic technology for it was at hand. That same technology also paved the way for information gathering in a new sense. Those characteristics that make high speed, quality typesetting possible, also opened the door on a range of potential for communication as yet only partially explored.

Remote input stations, international information banks accumulating data from routine typesetting chores, more efficient storage and recall of political, scientific, military, and financial information, and world wide instant dissemination of trends, experience and creative effort have suddenly burst on the scene. Formerly thought of as futuristic technology, these techniques are now well beyond the theoretic stage.

But the route to understanding type will probably always include a preliminary study of traditional wood and metal types, their origins and development for centuries.

Phototype, being unrestricted by the conditions governing the production and use of metal type will, in time, alter its design characteristics. But for the present, phototypesetting, like any evolving technology, carries over most of the characteristics of the faces from which it derives. In many cases the original drawings for alphabets were simply rephotographed and put on film.

Yet slight differences in visual character developed, especially in the spacing of individual characters of text settings. The use of light sensitive surfaces to pick up the specific weight and character of each face gave a more precise rendition of alphabets that previously had to go through the typographer's repro-proving process. The question of aesthetic superiority may be argued for years to come.

To the left, is an abbreviated one line series of currently available variations on Helvetica, set on Mergenthaler V.I.P. (Variable Input Phototypesetter) for both display and text settings. And on the following pages, a relatively full showing of four basic weights of Helvetica, set on the V.I.P., a piece of equipment that responds to a computer, or may be directly activated by punched tapes representing original copy. The V.I.P. in turn produces the printouts you see reproduced on the following pages.

389

129

BERGEN ST. SHOP

TINSMITHS · CARPENTERS · MASONS · IRONWORKERS · ELECTRICIANS · MATERIAL HANDLING · TRUCKING · MACHINISTS · OPERATORS · HEAVY EQUIPMENT · PAINTERS · SIGN FABRICATORS

MTA New York City Transit

EXCELLENCE THROUGH TEAMWORK

STANDARD, HELVETICA AND THE NEW YORK CITY SUBWAY SYSTEM

At the time the NYCTA awarded its first contract to Unimark in 1966, Helvetica was offered for sale in New York City as foundry type, linotype matrices, phototype and even transfer type. So why was it not "available" for the subway signage? The obstacle must have been tied to the Bergen Street Sign Shop, its outside vendors and the signmaking process.

In the late 1960s the workers at the Bergen Street Sign Shop painted signs by hand and silkscreened others as they had done for decades (fig. 131). They also prepared artwork for porcelain enamel signs but did not fabricate them. That task was handled by outside vendors, most likely Nelke Sign Manufacturing Corporation, the only enamel signmaker from the Vickers era that was still in business. [43]

Porcelain enamel signs are made by applying enamel in coats to iron or sheet metal and then heating it at a temperature of 800° after each coat. Dark colors are applied before light colors. There are two methods of doing a design: stencils or screenprinting. Stencils, made of either paper or metal, are the original method but since the 1960s screenprinting has been preferred. "In the stencil process," according to Geoffrey Clarke, "the colour is sprayed on the plate and, after drying, it is of the consistency of weak distemper. The stencils, cut to the appropriate design, are placed on the plate and the exposed colour is brushed away, leaving the design intact. The plate is then fired and the colour vitrified indelibly on the background." The process is repeated for color in the design using additional stencils. In the silkscreen method the designs are usually created photomechanically and thus have more detail. Porcelain enamel signs made by the stencil process require stencil cutters and "brushers" wth a high degree of skill. [44]

131

130 (opposite page) Bergen Street Shop roundel sign, post-1994. (2008)

131 Motivational sign from Bergen Street Shop. "do each Job Right the" is in Standard. (2008)

43. Nelke Sign Manufacturing Corporation was located at 115 Worth Street in Manhattan in 1967 but by the time the graphics standards manual had been completed they had moved to 12-07 44th Avenue in Long Island City. Both Baltimore Enamel and the Manhattan Dial Company are not listed in the New York City telephone books in those years and presumably had gone out of business. New York Telephone Company, Manhattan Telephone Directory: White Pages, 1966/1967 and 1969/1970. There are no known written accounts of the activities of the Bergen Street Sign Shop. This circumstantial discussion about the shop is based on the various accounts Massimo Vignelli has made of Unimark's difficulties with it as well as information about the process of preparing porcelain enamel signs at the

MTA in the late 1970s and afterwards gleaned from conversations with several individuals who worked for the MTA during those years. See especially Peter Joseph to the author, 12 August 2008, 13 August 2008 and 14 August 2008; and John Tauranac to the author, 6 August 2008. The discussion is also supported by visual evidence found in photographs of signs in the Archives of the New York Transit Museum, *Subway Style*, and Plumb (1965). My visit to the shop, summarized on p. 67, occurred after this essay was originally written.

44. This description of the porcelain enamel process (called vitreous enamel in England) is summarized from Geoffrey Clarke, "The plate that outlasts all others," *Penrose Annual* 64 (1971), p. 44. Clarke's account is nearly contemporaneous with Unimark's work for the NYCTA. Since then the porcelain enamel process has continued to evolve. See the websites of such manufacturers as Winsor Fireform, Enamel Signs, and Permar Systems, Inc. The latter has an excellent summary of the process, including a description of the photo-mechanical means used to reproduce lettering and images today: "The image is typically made by an art department by any suitable graphics program available to the art or hand typesetting technique. The image is eventually shot onto a film positive, and the film positive

placed on to a previously photo-sensitized, stretched screen, and exposed. The screen now has the image burned into it, and the image appears as openings in the screen mesh; with the unprinted background having the opaque coating." patentstorm. us. A description of the MTA's requirements for porcelain enamel signs in the late 1980s can be found in Metropolitan Transportation Authority, *Graphic Standards: Signage*. (New York: Michael Hertz Associates, 1988), n.p. This is a working draft of the 1989 manual. The specifications include steel thickness, coatings, firings, surface finish, color quality, and resistance to acids.

One of the reasons that Vignelli was unhappy with the TA's handling of Unimark's 1966 signage recommendations is that they were carried out by its own sign shop. The porcelain enamel signs were apparently made by the stencil method but without highly-skilled stencil cutters, leading to letters that were inexact and inconsistent. To make stencils of Standard at the large sizes recommended by Unimark it would have been necessary to either draw the "type" by eye or enlarge it using a Goodkin Lucigraph (a form of opaque projector) or Ludlow Typograph's Brightype process. Although there is evidence that some signs were painted by hand, the porcelain enamel ones must have been done through enlargement. Type enlarged via a Luci had to first be proofed which meant the letters were subject to being over- or underinked. Further inaccuracies were introduced during the tracing stage, depending upon the skill of the draftsman—unless a pantograph was employed. The Brightype process avoided those pitfalls.

Instead of inking the type after it was locked up, it was sprayed with black lacquer or lampblack. The printing surface was then wiped clean wth a rubber pad until it was shiny. Next, the reflective forme was photographed on a Brightype camera to create a photomechanical master. This film negative was used for the final enlargement. The letters were crisp and accurate. But they still had to be hand cut as stencils. Car identification numbers on several subway lines, most notably the number 1 and the D train, are still set in Standard and close examination of them shows flat spots in the curves indicating that they were made from hand-cut stencils. By insisting on silkscreening instead of stencils in the *Graphics Standards Manual*, Unimark was trying to avoid defects such as these that had previously made Vignelli furious. [45]

132

132 Silkscreen. Bergen Street Shop. The text, set in Helvetica Medium, is for a train car destination roll-up. (2008)

133 Silkscreened tin pan signs. Bergen Street Shop. All are set in Helvetica Medium. (2008)

45. Vignelli is not the only designer to have unhappy memories of the Bergen Sign Shop. Both Michael Hertz and Peter Joseph have also indicated that the work it turned out was often "sloppy" and "crappy". Michael Hertz interview with author, 25 August 2008. Information on the Brightype process comes from Rod McDonald interview with author, 19 July 2008 and L. W. Wallis, *A Concise Chronology of Typesetting Developments 1886–1996*. (London: The Wynken de Worde Society and Lund Humphries, 1988), p. 27. The Goodkin Lucigraph was not the only epidiscope used by designers at the time. Another was the Art-O-Graph. In addition to the car identification numbers (**135**) several other examples of signs made with Standard hand-cut stencils can be found throughout the system (**144, 145, 177, 178, 181, 184)** Also see the April 1969 sign regarding travel to stations on the Rockaway Peninsula where the smaller Standard type has been silkscreened from handcut stencils and the larger type has been handpainted (**96**). Photograph Z MISC4-(1573-1574), Archives of the New York Transit Museum.

134

134 **Silkscreened tin pan signs in storage. Bergen Street Shop.** All are set in Helvetica Medium. (2008)

135 **R62 car number (IRT no. 3 train from 240th Street yard).** The numerals are handcut Standard Medium. (2008)

135

What did the Bergen Street Sign Shop workers use as a source for creating their painted and hand-cut stencil versions of Standard? Did they work from proofs of type made in-house or ordered from outside type houses? Or from specimens of type taken from a book? It is very likely that a type house that had Standard in its repertoire may have been loath in 1966 to add Helvetica as well, given the costs involved and the fact that the two faces appear indistinguishable to most people. This would have been especially true for the larger foundry sizes of the face since they would have weighed more and thus cost more—and been less likely to be used by other customers. Similar considerations would have occurred to the sign shop regarding its typesetting capabilities. Even if the shop worked from a book instead, Helvetica would not have been an option since no American type book at the time included it. Ben Rosen's *Type and Typography* (1963), the principal specimen book in the 1960s, had 17 pages of Akzidenz Grotesk and Standard but the largest size of Standard Medium was 72 pt—large by the standards of foundry type but small from the perspective of transportation signage (fig. 129). [46]

The decision to use Standard instead of Helvetica may not have been as disappointing to Noorda as it was to Vignelli. While Vignelli was a strong believer in the virtues of Helvetica, Noorda was not as committed. His custom typeface for the Metropolitana Milanese was born out of dissatisfaction with both types. Although it is usually described as a modified version of Helvetica it can also be seen as a modified version of Akzidenz Grotesk (Standard).

Given how much the New York City subway sign system owes to Noorda's work in Milano it is very likely that the choice of Standard was his in 1966 and that Vignelli readily acquiesced because Helvetica was, for whatever technical reason, not "available" to the TA—and the sign "system" was more important to him than the specific face used. [47]

Noorda and Vignelli had an opportunity to change the NYCTA type to Helvetica when Unimark received its second contract but they stuck with Standard. Presumably, they were more focused on insuring that the signs were properly fabricated and installed than on which sans serif was used. Certainly, Vignelli had other opportunities to use Helvetica. In November 1967 the New York office of Unimark was hired by the New York City Planning Department to create a signage standards manual for all city agencies. To test out the signage, a prototype design for East 53rd Street—home to the Museum of Modern Art, CBS and the Seagram Building—was created. The goal was to coordinate the graphics with the street furniture—bus shelters, telephone booths, benches etc.—and lighting. At the same time architect Harry Weese tapped Vignelli to design the graphics for the new Washington Metro. Neither assignment involved Noorda. Both used Helvetica. Unimark showcased all three of these signage projects in the August/September 1969 issue of *Casabella*. The text praised Standard for its legibility—in words taken directly from the NYCTA *Graphics Standard Manual* then in preparation—but made no mention of Helvetica. [48]

Note although Vignelli, Hertz and other designers refer to it as the Bergen Street Sign Shop it is actually a signmaking department within the Bergen Street Shop, the facility which also handles carpentry, tinsmithing and other fabrication needs for the NYCTA. I visited the facility on 22 November 2008 as part of a tour organized by the New York Transit Museum. None of the signmakers working there today were around before the early 1990s so there is no one who remembers the Unimark program. The signmakers no longer have much responsibility for determining the look of a sign. (The exception is plastic and metal signs which are made by the carpentry staff using a Hermes Gravograph engraving machine.) They quit cutting stencils by hand in the late 1980s when computer-aided machines* became available. Now artwork is prepared on a computer by the Graphics Unit and sent to them to execute.

*Gerber Scientific Products entered the signmaking business in 1983 with the introduction of the Signmaker III, Graphix 3. They touted it as "the world's first low-cost, easy-to-use, automated lettering system for letters up to 12"." In 1987 they released the GerberScanner which was capable of automatic digitizing. This is most likely the computer-aided machine that ended the practice of hand-cutting stencils. See http://www.gspinc.com/default.asp?contentID=79. Also see *GSP Type Styles*. (**205, 208**)

46. Michael Bosniak says that the TA's maintenance shops had "full typesetting, screen-printing and metal fabrication capabilities", but he provided no details about its equipment or the faces at its disposal. See *Type and Typography* (1963), pp. 167–184 for showings of Standard (as foundry type) and Akzidenz Grotesk (as Linotype matrices). The second edition of *Type and Typography* (1976) includes Helvetica as a supplement. The size of the available type was critical in Vignelli's opinion. Massimo Vignelli to author, 15 August 2008. Erich Alb says that stencil versions of Helvetica intended for commercial signmaking existed in Switzerland in the early 1960s but Weingartner AG, the company he cites, was not in business until 1971. Vignelli says that he and Noorda never considered preparing stencils for Standard (or Helvetica) for the sign shop to use. He assumed that the artwork for the signs would be made by photosilkscreening since that was "the state of the art". Massimo Vignelli to author, 10 August 2008.

47. Bob Noorda was not as passionate and excited about Helvetica as Vignelli was at the time. Bob Noorda to author, 30 May 2008. However, Noorda later changed his mind, specifying Helvetica for the signage systems of both the Metro São Paulo do Brazil (1974) and the Metropolitana di Napoli (1993). Ventura, *Bob Noorda Design*, pp. 52–55; Unimark International, "Segna-letica–Signs projects," *Casabella: rivista di architettura* 339/340 (August/September 1969), p. 56; and *Transit Maps of the World*. 2nd rev. ed., pp. 99 and 112. It should be noted that the spacing guides in the 1970 NYCTA *Graphics Standards Manual* are taken directly from those for the Milano Metro.

48. Information on the 53rd Street Project comes from Steven V. Roberts, "Mayor Hires Consultants to Study Street Design." *New York Times*, November 14, 1967; and Jonathan Barnett in "Transportation Graphics," *Dot Zero* 5 (Fall 1968), pp. 23–25. The Washington Metro commission is shown in Germano Celant et al, *design: Vignelli*, p. 97. Both are in *Casabella* (1969), pp. 56–59; and at vignelli.com. Also see Zachary M. Schrag, *The Great Society Subway* (Baltimore and London: The Johns Hopkins University Press, 2006), p. 118: "Along with the name [Metro], Vignelli gave Metro: a capital M in the Helvetica typeface a symbol to be printed, embossed, and emblazoned on trains, stations, uniforms, and pylons throughout the region." The Washington, DC Metro did not open until 1976.

THE FATE OF THE UNIMARK SYSTEM

The Metropolitan Transportation Authority (MTA) was created in March 1968. The new agency replaced the Metropolitan Commuter Transportation Authority (MCTA) which had been formed three years earlier to oversee the commuter railroads, including the Long Island Rail Road and the New York, New Haven & Hartford Railroad. The MTA added the NYCTA, the Manhattan and Bronx Surface Transit Operating Authority (MaBSTOA, a subsidiary of the NYCTA created in 1962 to oversee bus routes), and the Triborough Bridge and Tunnel Authority (TBTA) to the mix. From the moment the MTA was born, the Rockefeller administration began making grandiose plans to modernize and coordinate the metropolitan transportation system. A $2.6 billion program was announced that February to expand the subway system with a Second Avenue line, a new Bronx line, an extension of one of the Queens lines, and the development of a "novel Transportation Center in the 48th Street area". (A LIRR spur to JFK Airport was also proposed.) A few months later the "Fund for Better Subway Stations", headed by real estate developer Peter Sharp, announced plans to upgrade and beautify stations in conjunction with the

TA. On its own the NYCTA had already, a year earlier, set forth a station renovation program with 49th Street as a test station. All of this activity should have boded well for the Unimark signage system. [49].

Vignelli hoped that the *Graphics Standards Manual* would lead to a more rational implementation of signs within the New York City subway system. But that did not happen. This was due to two factors: 1. the sheer size of the New York subway system, and 2. the financial woes that overtook both the MTA and the city of New York in the early 1970s, culminating in the city's rescue from bankruptcy in 1975. The 1968 "Program for Action" was largely abandoned by the end of 1975. During the gestation of the *Graphics Standards Manual* the NYCTA installed signs on an ad hoc basis and it continued to do so throughout the 1970s. "In many stations," Paul Goldberger wrote in the *New York Times* in 1979, "the signs are so confusing that one is tempted to wish they were not there at all—a wish that is, in fact, granted in numerous other stations and on all too many of the subway cars themselves.

---

136 (opposite page) Unimark sign at 59th Street—Columbus Circle (A/B/C/D). (1970)

49. This summary of the MTA's ambitious transportation plans is taken from Richard Witkin, "MTA Takes Over Transit Network," *New York Times*, March 2, 1968; Sylvan Fox, "Lindsay Names 2 to M.T.A. Board," *New York Times*, March 8, 1968; Metropolitan Transportation Authority, *Transportation Progress: An Interim Report Number One*, December 1968; and Metropolitan Transportation Authority. *1968 Annual Report*. The MTA took over the Staten Island operations of the Baltimore & Ohio Railroad in 1971, leading to the creation of Staten Island Rapid Transit. In 1972 it took over the Hudson and Harlem lines of the Penn Central (the successor to the New York Central Railroad) south of Poughkeepsie. These lines were combined with the New Haven Line as Metro-North in 1983. Today, Metro-North also includes a Pascack Line and a Port Jervis Line.

See american-rails.com/metro-north-railroad.html. Although the MTA allegedly took over "unified policy direction and control" of the formerly independent agencies in 1968, the reality was that it mainly functioned as a financial umbrella for them while leaving operational decisions in their hands. Internecine friction between the "corporate" MTA, a state agency, and the "blue-collar" NYCTA, a city agency, was constant. John Tauranac interview with author, 14 August 2008 and Peter Joseph interview with author, 15 August 2008. The two-toned **M** was introduced in 1968 as an emblem for the entire MTA (**189**). It supplanted the lowercase red and blue **ta** created by Sundberg-Ferar for the NYCTA.

137 Porcelain enamel route sign. Jay Street/Boro Hall (A/C/G), February 4, 1971. Black-on-white Unimark signs in Standard Medium.

138 Porcelain enamel station sign. Allerton Avenue (2), 1973. Photograph by Jack Stewart. From Jack Stewart. *Graffiti Kings: New York City Mass Transit Art of the 1970s.* (New York: Melcher Media, Harry N. Abrams, Inc., 2009), p. 29

139 Graffiti-covered exterior of subway car, 1971. Photograph by Jack Stewart. From Jack Stewart. *Graffiti Kings: New York City Mass Transit Art of the 1970s.* (New York: Melcher Media, Harry N. Abrams, Inc., 2009), p. 54.

140 Graffiti-scarred interior of subway car, 1973. Photograph by Jon Naar. Note the 1972 Vignelli subway map at the right.

141 Porcelain enamel Unimark station sign. 57th Street (B/Q). (1976). Note that the train is a no. 7 because it was part of a fan trip! This station was opened in 1968 as part of the Chrystie Street Connection and it is possible that this sign was erected that early (**94**).

137–139

70

And the system is so complex that one might feel signs make very little difference—a rider may as easily find his destination by taking a chance as by any sort of careful planning." His description is borne out by contemporary photographs that show stations with a mix of Unimark and older signs or without any Unimark signs at all even though it was over a decade since the NYCTA had first hired Vignelli and Noorda to bring order to a chaotic system (figs. 136, 141, 146, 147, 169). [50]

The early 1970s were the years when the subway system was probably at its lowest ebb, along with the city itself. "Dank, overcrowded, underlit and terrifyingly labyrinthian, the New York subway at its best suggests nothing less depressing than a public lavatory; at its worst, it's a vision of purgatory." was one contemporary description. The early 1970s were also the years when modern graffiti was born. As cars "bombed" on the outside and "tagged" on the inside rolled through the city, the subway woes and the graffiti explosion became intertwined in the public consciousness (figs. 139, 140). "If nothing else," Patricia Conway wrote in *Print*, "the subway graffiti are a testimony to the monumental failure of TA officials and their design consultants to make the system legible." She went on to lambaste the transit agency for spending millions of dollars on anti-graffiti efforts rather than on capital improvements such as "repairing inoperative doors, replacing burnt-out lights, securing rickety seats and maintaining or improving directional signs". [51]

140

50. A good overview of the situation of the New York City subway system in the 1970s is Mark S. Feinman, "The New York Transit Authority in the 1970s," at nyc.subway.org/ articles/history–nycta.1970s.html. 2002. For New York City's decline see Jason Epstein, "The Last Days of New York," *The New York Review of Books* vol. 23, no. 2 (February 19, 1976). Also see Stanley Abercrombie, "New York's Subway," in *Subways*, edited by Peter Blake. (New York: Cooper-Hewitt Museum, 1977) who said the Unimark signs were still not consistently applied; and the annual reports of the Metropolitan Transportation Authority from 1969 to 1976. "Work continued on the new sign system designed to guide passengers throughout the subway system," is the only reference during these years to the Unimark signs. Metropolitan Transportation Authority. *1969 Annual Report*, p. 23. Paul Goldberger,

"Design Notebook: At Last, A Usable Subway Map," *New York Times*, August 2, 1979. Although photographs are scarce, dated examples of the white Unimark signs in use between 1968 and 1980 can be found in the MTA Archives (1968 and 1971–1977) and online at nycsubway.org. (1969, 1970 and 1972). The 1968 sign in the MTA Archives—"Subway" in white on gray with a black arrow on white—is at an entrance to the Fulton Street station on the IRT Lexington Avenue Line. Undated examples of white Unimark signs are in the MTA Archives (1970s and 1995), the collection of Dr. Stuart Gitlow (1977) and the collection of John Tauranac (1982–1985) (**110**). An example at Stillwell Avenue (Coney Island) is visible in Walter Hill's 1979 film *The Warriors*.

51. Patricia Conway, "Subway Graffiti: The Message from Underground," *Print* XXVI: III (May/June 1973), pp. 25–32. Although Conway praised the graffiti artists for making the subways less dreary she also admitted that the tags inside the cars obliterating the maps and the windows were a problem for riders. Conway was married to a former Unimark employee and wrote extensively on mass transportation subjects from the mid-1960s on. The definitive history of the origins and early years of graffiti in New York City is Jack Stewart, *Graffiti Kings: New York City Mass Transit Art of the 1970s*. (New York: Melcher Media–Harry N. Abrams, Inc., 2009).

141

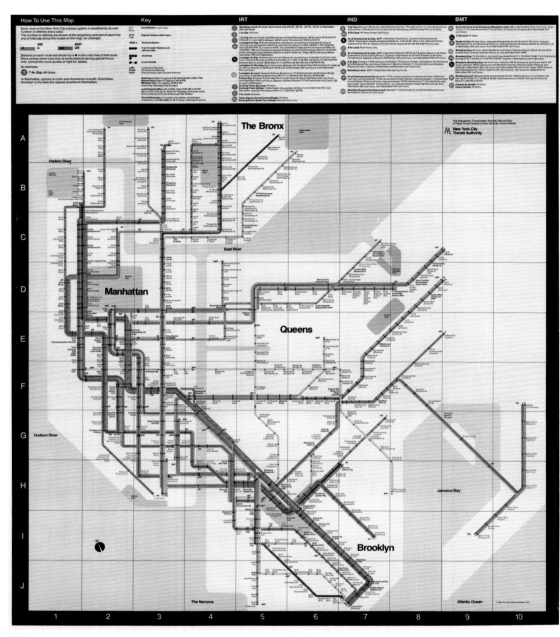

142

But change was already underway by 1975 when Fred Wilkinson, Director of Consumer Affairs at the TA, convened a committee to devise a new map for the subway system to replace the one that Massimo Vignelli had designed only four years earlier (fig. 142). While the citizen members of the committee were focused on creating a more geographically accurate map, the transit agency itself was interested in showing partial-time service on eleven lines. To do this, it was decided to add diamonds to the existing circles designating lines. John Tauranac, the committee's chairman, also wanted the existing system of parallel lines for routes sharing the same track to be replaced by trunk lines. This posed a color-coding problem—which meant a financial problem as well—that was not solved until Len Ingalls came up with the idea of basing colors on the "flagship" line where multiple lines ran in tandem. Ingalls' solution meant that there would have to be a change in the color coding of the routes. The proposed changes in the map had far-reaching ramifications: they meant that the station signage would have to be updated to insure that the two were synchronized. [52]

By 1979—the subway system's Diamond Jubilee year—the MTA had finally begun to get some Federal financial assistance and the subway's prospects were starting to slowly turn around. That summer, in an attempt to encourage more ridership "an overall

52. This account is based on conversations with John Tauranac, Peter Joseph and Arline Bronzaft; and on Dave Hogarty's interview with Michael Hertz. John Tauranac interview with author, 14 August 2008, Peter Joseph interview with author, 15 August 2008 and Arline Bronzaft interview with author, 19 August 2008; and Dave Hogarty, "Michael Hertz, Designer of the NYC Subway Map." at gothamist.com/2007/08/03/michael_hertz_d.php. Psychologist Bronzaft, one of the citizen members of the commission, was one of the first critics of the Vignelli map. She and Stephen Dobrow wanted a geographically accurate map as a means of encouraging New Yorkers and visitors to use the subway system at a time when both it and the city were plagued by high levels of crime. They believed that a map with clearly marked neighborhoods, parks and landmarks would make riders feel more secure than the abstracted Vignelli map. Their theories were supported by research. See Arline L. Bronzaft, Stephen B. Dobrow and Timothy J. O'Hanlon, "Spatial Orientation in a Subway System," *Environment and Behavior* vol. 8, no. 4 (December 1976), pp. 575–594; and Arline L. Bronzaft and Stephen B. Dobrow., "Improving Transit Information Systems," *Journal of Environmental Systems* vol. 13, no. 4 (1983–1984), pp. 365–376. The color-coding problem caused by the idea of using trunk lines was recognized by Tauranac from the outset, but the TA management was unwilling to address it, knowing full well that it would cause a financial burden. They were finally moved to act by the intervention of Phyllis Cerf Wagner, chairman of the MTA's esthetics committee—and wife of former mayor Robert F. Wagner. See John Tauranac to author, 27 August 2008.

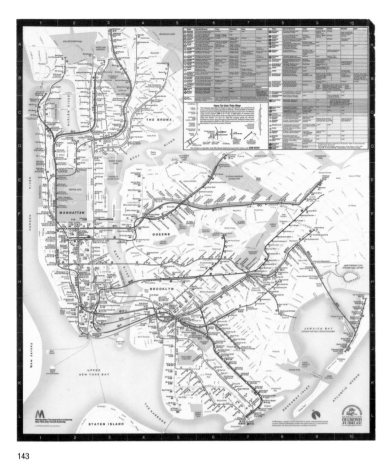

143

program aimed at easing passenger travel around New York City" was introduced. The 1978 MTA annual report, anticipating the program's inception, described it thusly: "The program includes color-coding of lines by their track routes; new station signage that conforms to the color-code; and a new pocket-sized geographical subway map. In addition, as roll signs are replaced, they will indicate route and destinations, as well as the color-code." The program, the fruit of events set in place by the Tauranac committee several years earlier, was expected to take up to 36 months to complete. [**53**]

The real news to most people was the replacement of the controversial Vignelli-designed schematic map by a geographically-based one executed by Michael Hertz and his staff (fig. 143). However, in light of the problems that occurred during the opening of the Chrystie Street Connection, the intention of color-coding all train roll signs was equally important; and so too was the news about the station signage. The new signs differed markedly from the ones that Unimark had designed in 1966 and codified in 1970 (figs. 152–155, 168–170). Not only did they have diamonds as well as disks as route markers and new colors for both, but they were black with white type. The errant black band at the top had been replaced by a thin white line, demarcating the (non-existent) location of the gap between sign and housing. But the typeface was still Standard Medium. [**54**]

142 **New York Subway Guide, 1972. Designed by Vignelli Associates. Printed in 12 colors.** The map was executed by Joan Charysyn. Note the difference in route colors compared to today (e.g. 7 was orange, 4 was magenta) as well as the presence of double-letter route designations. Set in Helvetica and Helvetica Medium. Subsequent editions designed by the MTA staff used fewer colors (with tints) and were set in Trade Gothic.

143 *New York City Subway Map,* 1979. Poster version. Designed and executed by Michael Hertz Associates.

53. Metropolitan Transportation Authority. *1978 Annual Report*, pp. 6 and 10. The timeframe was optimistic as the new roll-ups and signs needed to be installed in 6200 subway cars and 460 stations (down from the number cited in the 1960s). The MTA estimated 18,000 signs were going to be needed.

54. The roots of the Hertz map go back to November 1975 when "public dissatisfaction with the Vignelli map prompted the New York City Transit Authority to organize a committee to study the problem of designing a better map". (Also see note 52 for Arline Bronzaft and Stephen Dobrow's role.) Hertz's first attempt appeared in John Tauranac's *Seeing New York: The Official MTA Travel Guide* (1976); the second in February 1978 when a full-scale map was introduced at the Cityana Gallery

on East 53rd Street. During the year it was subjected to public criticism—encouraged by the MTA—including a debate at Cooper Union on April 20, 1978. The 1978 map incorporated Tauranac's idea of trunk lines but every line was red with the color-coding relegated to the disks and diamonds. Paul Goldberger, design critic at the *New York Times*, said it had the "appearance of a plate of spaghetti dropped on a map of the city". The red lines were replaced in the 1979 map by color-coded lines following Ingalls' idea of having flagship lines. Hogarty at gothamist.com (2007); Paul Goldberger, "Design Notebook," *New York Times*, February 9, 1978; "The New York Subway Map Debate," *Skyline* no. 1 (April 1, 1978), p. 6; and Paul Goldberger, "Design Notebook: At Last, A Usable Subway Map," *New York Times*, August 2, 1979. An example of the criticism the Vignelli

map engendered is Patricia Conway's comment: "True, the graffitists have obliterated most of the system maps, but the maps are practically unreadable anyway." Conway (1973), p. 32. There is much debate about the authorship of the 1979 map but the 2007 Hertz interview with Hogarty appears to be the most reliable in allocating credit, including acknowledging the role of Hertz's colleague Nobu Siraisi. As to whether the Hertz map is "better" than the Vignelli map or vice-versa that is a topic still being hotly debated, both in print and online. But those taking sides should consider the map in light of the complex nature of the New York City subway system as well as its role as only one component in the system's navigational tools along with station and train car maps and station and train signage. Goldberger's verdict on the 1979 map was

that, when seen in conjunction with the new station signs, it exemplified "what graphic design is all about." The definitive account of the 1979 map will be part of Peter B. Lloyd's forthcoming (2011) history of New York City subway maps.

It should be noted that the map that was discontinued in 1979 was no longer the map that Massimo Vignelli designed in 1972. The basic design was still present, but it had been tinkered with for at least four years as the TA tried to adapt it to accommodate route and station changes. One casualty of these changes was that Helvetica was replaced by Trade Gothic for the station names beginning in 1974. See the various iterations of the Vignelli map at subway.com.ru. These maps were printed by Diamond National and it is possible—though it would have been surprising at

this late date—that the company did not have Helvetica. Michael Hertz interview with author, 25 August 2008. Joan Charysyn designed a commuter map for the MTA in 1973 (**184**) that mimicked the Vignelli map for the subway so well that decades later Vignelli was moved to say that it looked as if he had done it. Not surprisingly, she had worked on the 1972 subway map. Metropolitan Transportation Authority. *1974 Annual Report*, p. 30; Massimo Vignelli to author, 8 August 2008; Joan Charysyn to author, 21 October 2009.

The history of Harry Beck's map for the London Underground is told in detail in Ken Garland, *Mr. Beck's Underground Map: A History*. (Middlesex: Capital Transport Publishing, 1994).

Electric service room

Do not re:
on escala
Please gr

144–145

The black/white inversion of the signs has been attributed by Vignelli to TA worries about graffiti and by others to concern over simple grime. Although Vignelli's explanation is an attractive one, especially in light of the graffiti explosion that overtook the city and the subway system by 1973, the truth is that the TA made the change to increase the legibility of the signs and first contemplated doing so sometime in 1972. According to Michael Bosniak, Jacques Nevard, Director of Public Affairs at the MTA, and Len Ingalls requested that the "Transit Authority maintenance shop manufacture prototypes of the 'drop-out' reverse lettering" for installation in three prototype stations in 1972/1973. This decision was made after several visual perception studies came to the attention of Nevard, but "there was a general consensus that the reversed lettering had greater legibility in the bowels of the subway system and it was adopted without any formality."
R. Raleigh D'Adamo, head of the Office of Inspection & Review at the MTA from 1970 to 1975, says that the idea of changing the signs originated with him as an offshoot of a decision to change

the background colors of the route designators on the trains. "I triggered it because of my hobby interest in letterpress printing and graphics," he says. "I wrote a memo about it and attached a technical article on legibility of texts against different backgrounds. The test itself was done by the TA—I don't recall who was present at the 47-50 Street station, but it could well have been Jacques and Len. A new sign of bullet [route designation circle] against a black background was prepared and installed in the south end of an empty train which was positioned in one of the pocket tracks at the then 57th St /6 Avenue terminal. A regular train was alerted in advance that it would be part of a test. At the proper time, the operations department directed the empty train to leave 57 St and advance south to 47th St and both trains were directed to watch for each other and enter the station together and slowly. The TA team and I stood in mid-platform. At a certain point as both trains slowly entered, they were then directed (by hand signals as I recall) to stop—opposite each other. Hence, the team had the opportunity to observe (as passengers would) both

144–146 Miscellaneous surviving signs in the Unimark black-on-white style set in Standard Medium, early 1970s.

144 Porcelain enamel door sign. Rockaway Parkway (L). The letters have been handcut. (2008)

145 Warning sign, 1970s. Court Street (M/R). Set in handcut Standard Medium. (2009)

146 Porcelain enamel route sign. Coney Island/Stillwell Avenue ((D/F//N/Q), 1977. Photo by Stuart Gitlow. Modular black-on-white Unimark signs in Standard Medium. Note route signs showing M and QB routes which no longer run to Coney Island.

146

147 Porcelain enamel station sign and modular exit and transfer signs. **Atlantic Avenue (2/3/4/5/), October 22, 1975.** The exit sign is in white on red while the tranfer sign is black on yellow. The arrow and "LIRR" modules flanking trhe exit module confirm that the shift from black-on-white to white-on-black signs was already in progress by 1975.

148 Porcelain enamel station sign. **Canal Street (N/Q/R/W), May 7, 1975.** Note the station name in Chinese.

147–148

Brooklyn **4** **5** **Exit** B'way & Bowling Green ↑ Straight ahead ←

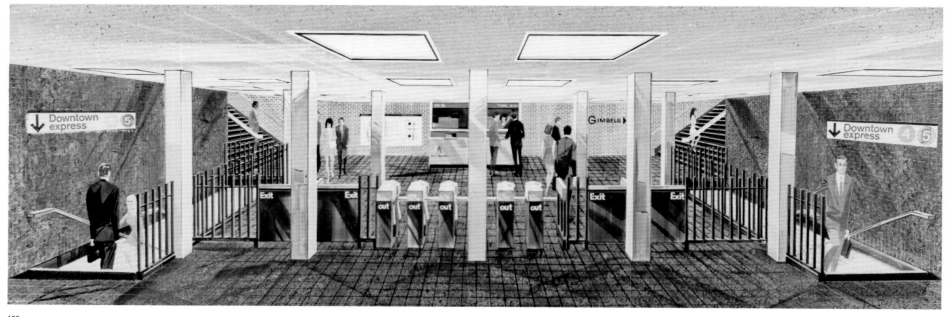

55. Stanley Abercombie echoed Conway in 1977 when he called the graffiti the "unofficial graphics" of the subway. Abercrombie (1977). Despite the wealth of photographs of 1970s graffiti in the subways and on the trains, only a few show graffitied signs; **(138)** and Patricia Conway's 1973 account of graffiti in the system cites station walls, train exteriors, train windows and maps as targets but not signs. Similarly, contemporary newspaper accounts of graffiti in the system are focused entirely on walls and trains. See Edward C. Burks, "Subways' Colored Tile Gets Cover Up Job," *New York Times*, February 21, 1970; Conway (1973), pp. 25–32; Metropolitan Transportation Authority. *1974 Annual Report*; Paul Goldberger, "Design Notebook," *New York Times*, May 3, 1979; Martha Cooper and Henry Chalfant, *Subway Art*. (New York: Holt, Rinehart and

Winston: An Owl Book, 1984); Henry Chalfant and James Prigoff, *Spraycan Art*. (London: Thames and Hudson, Ltd., 1987); *Graffiti Kings*; and Massimo Vignelli interview with author, 29 April 2008. Michael Bosniak, Howard York, Peter Joseph and John Tauranac have all stated that legibility concerns were the driving force behind the shift from black on white to white on black. Howard York to author, 3 August 2008; John Tauranac to author, 6 August 2008; Peter Joseph interview with author, 15 August 2008; and Michael Bosniak to author, 18 August 2008. The details of the story are from Michael Bosniak. R. Raleigh D'Adamo's account of the origins of the background color switch is from R. Raleigh D'Adamo to author, 22 August 2008 and 23 August 2008. D'Adamo says his interest in the train route designators came about because he was asked to check the

accuracy and quality of the Vignelli map. He does not recall the legibility study that concluded that white letters on a black background were more legible than the opposite, though he thinks the article was brought to his attention by book designer Sam Antupit. The article may have been one of several on television graphics and highway signage published in *The Journal of Typographic Research* (now *Visible Language*) during its early years: Rudi Bass, "The Development of CBS News 36," *The Journal of Typographic Research* vol. 1, no. 4 (1967); Donald Shurtleff, "Relative Legibility of Leroy and Lincoln/MITRE Fonts on Television," *The Journal of Typographic Research* vol. 3, no. 1 (1969); and John Lees and Melvin Farman, "An Investigation of the Design and Performance of Traffic Control Devices," *The Journal of Typographic Research* vol. 4, no. 1 (1970). Another

possibility is D. Shurtleff, B. Botha and M. Young, "Studies of Display Symbol Legibility: Part IV. The Effects of Brightness, Letter Spacing, Symbol Background Relation and Surround Brightness on the Legibility of Capital Letters," (May 1966). Michael Hertz mentions another reason that a black background was preferable to a white one for the train route designators: steel dust from the wheels dirtied them. John Montemarano, current Director of Transit Station Signage, recalls a memo to this effect. Michael Hertz interview with author, 25 August 2008; John Montemarano interview with author, 18 June 2009. Vignelli, who was never contacted about the change, says that Ingalls "was our man at the TA. He was a real believer in our project, and until he was there everything was going well. After he left, it was a disaster." He does not recall Jacques

Nevard, which suggests that it was Nevard who made the decision. Nevard apparently outranked Ingalls, though their titles were similar. Massimo Vignelli to author, 6 August 2008 and 18 August 2008. The decision to create the prototype signs may have been tied to route changes that were planned in September 1972 and implemented in January 1973. (A white on black sign set in Standard Medium in the 42nd Street/8th Avenue station is pictured in the Metropolitan Transportation Authority *1976 Annual Report*, p. 7.) Nevard told the *New York Times* that the "Transit Authority said it planned to have new maps of the entire system, which will reflect all of the revisions, ready for distribution to riders and for posting in subway cars and stations by mid-December." Did new maps mean new signs? "Subway Changes Set for Jan. 2 Praised," trains as they were entering the station, and then to observe them for a few moments as the two trains were standing still. It took no time at all for all to agree that the sign with the black background was clearly the more legible. It followed like night and day and without any discussion that I can recall, that all other signage should be against a black background instead of white." The test that D'Adamo describes may have been one of those that Bosniak recalls, suggesting that these recollections are in accord with one another. Vignelli was never involved in the decision. [55]

The switchover was codified in 1980 via a revised edition of the 1970 *Graphics Standards Manual*—photocopied at a reduced size and bound with black tape—created by Ralph DeMasi, a staff architect. Changes to the Unimark sign program were made by whiting-out specs and writing in new ones, by adding notes in the margins, by creating new diagrams from old ones (with Standard Medium rendered by hand), and by inserting entirely new pages of artwork. The revised manual was a work-in-progress not a polished document. Among the changes included in it were: an increase in the size of the smallest letters from 1⅜" to 1½"; the addition of diamonds to mark part-time trains—those that ran only in the day, at night, on weekends or at rush hour; symbols for the new "The Train to The Plane", a train dedicated to serving JFK Airport, and for buses; an expanded color code with ten hues instead of seven; new names for seven of the routes; new artwork for the route designations with larger type; the use of black instead of white for the type in the yellow disks and diamonds; new turnstile designs; new types of signs (e.g. to indicate escalators); new symbols to mark bathrooms and handicapped access; and map panels for the station platforms. Throughout, there are reminders that "all lettering [is] to be white on black background"; and the thin white stripe is introduced in the section on "typical Column Signage". Amidst these changes is note no. 2 on p. 9: "When letter 'J' appears in discs or diamonds—use Helvetica Style 'J'." This was the first official appearance of Helvetica in the sign system. [56]

149 **Illuminated directional sign. Bowling Green (4/5), c.1979.** (2008)
Illuminated or back-lit signs are rare in the subway system. Most exist at the terminuses of some lines (e.g. Dyre Avenue (5) to indicate "Next train" but there are also some that survive at Newkirk Avenue (B/Q)

150 **Architectural drawing. 86th St–Lexington Av Station Modernization of Control Areas, c.1977–1978.** Designed by Transit Authority Architects. Note the Unimark-style signs at left and right.

151 **Exit sign, c.1974. Bowling Green (4/5).** (2008)

151

New York Times, November 25, 1972. The visual perception studies that influenced Nevard and Ingalls have not been identified. They may have been reacting instead to Arline Bronzaft and Stephen Dobrow's research on the effectiveness of the Vignelli map done which included negative comments on the mix of signs in the system: "A further problem for the user of the subway system is the tendency of the Metropolitan Transit [sic] Authority (MTA) not to remove obsolete signs from the subway stations." See Bronzaft et al (1976), pp. 578, 591–592. Joan Charysyn says she worked on prototype signs for five stations c.1973 while at Unimark. Joan Charysyn to author, 22 October 2009.

The decision to use white letters on a black background may have also unconsciously stemmed from an illustration

on p. 76 of the 1970 signage manual devoted to signage for the trains (not the stations). The "insert on the side of the train facing the traveler on the platform"—illustrated with a sign for the E train going from 179 Street to Euclid Avenue—shows the route in white on a colored disk (grey in the manual) with a white background and the destination lettering, to the right, in Standard Medium reversed out of a black background. It should be noted that George Salomon suggested in 1957 that signage should be either white on black or black on white depending upon "legibility experiments under subway conditions". See Salomon [1957]. Also, the original signage Noorda created for the Milano Metro used reversed-out letters, but against a red background rather than a black one.

56. DeMasi, Ralph, *New York City Transit Authority Graphics Standards Manual Revision*. (New York: New York City Transit Authority, 1980). According to Peter Joseph, DeMasi collated loose sheets bearing revisions that had been made over several years—probably extending back to 1975 or 1976—so he should not be seen as the sole "author" of the altered manual. The diamonds were for part-time service on the 4, 5, 6, 7, B, C, D, J, N, Q and R lines; the short-lived JFK Express—championed by Phyllis Cerf Wagner (1913–2006, widow of Random House co-founder Bennett Cerf and wife of former Mayor Robert F. Wagner), head of the MTA's esthetics committee—was a special version of the A train; and the bus symbol was for connecting points to surface transportation. Under the new route designations double-letter names were replaced by single-letter ones:

the AA became the K, the CC the C, the GG the G, the LL the L, the QB the Q, the RR the R, and the various shuttles the S. Among the additional mandatory signs was "Please No Littering Smoking Spitting Radio Playing", a response to the boom-box craze. (The "Please" part of the sign was later dropped.) (One of these signs, along with a decal-modified white Unimark sign, can be seen at Bowling Green station c. 1980 in *Subway Style*, p. 126; the date of 1968 refers to the turnstile in the photograph.) The Map Panel consisted of a subway map, a bus map and a "Local Area Map" (the neighborhood map proposed by Vignelli as part of his map program in 1972 but not realized until 1983 by Hertz). The introduction of the "Helvetica Style 'J'" was a by-product of the new Hertz map and the addition of the diamond route mark: the

hook on Helvetica's J is more pronounced than the one on Standard and thus more legible at small sizes. Peter Joseph interview with author, 15 August 2008; Paul Goldberger, "Design Notebook." *New York Times*, May 3, 1979. During the process of designing the map, Wagner brought in graphic designer Rudolph de Harak to oversee the work that Hertz was doing. He recommended using an X suffix with the existing circles to indicate express trains rather than the diamond shape. Although his idea already existed for express bus designators, it was not feasible for the trains since the letters would have had to have been smaller to fit within the circle. That would have seriously compromised legibility, especially on the maps. Michael Hertz interview with author, 25 August 2008 (**179**).

152–158 Station signs set in Standard Medium (often handcut) but now in white on a black background—except for Hoyt Street—and with a white stripe in place of the black bar, c.1973–1988.

152 Porcelain enamel station sign. 62nd Street (D/M). Note the absence of the white stripe which was typical of the earliest white-on-black station name signs. (2008)

153 Porcelain enamel station sign. Avenue P (F). (2009)

154 Porcelain enamel entrance sign with vinyl root decals. Junius Street (3/4). (2010)

155 Porcelain enamel station sign. Rector Street (R/W), 1970s. This is the only remaining sign in Standard Medium among a group of stations on the BMT Broadway and Fourth Avenue lines that were renovated with large colored tiles in the 1970s. Regarding the disappearing mosaics, a TA spokesman said at the time, "We didn't consider these things had any great artistic merit anyhow." (2008)

156 Porcelain enamel station sign. Unusual variant of the Unimark-style sign in white on ox-blood red. Hoyt Street (2/3), c.1979. The IRT Hoyt Street station was renovated as part of the creation of the Fulton Street Mall, an eight-block stretch of Fulton Street which was converted to pedestrian and bus use between 1977 and 1984. Also see (**196**). (2006)

157 Porcelain enamel column sign. Cypress Avenue (6). Note that the hyphenation follows the guidelines established in the 1970 NYCTA manual. (2008)

158 Porcelain enamel column sign. St. Lawrence Avenue (6). The girder columns in several elevated stations are very narrow, making hyphenation of names not only indispensable but difficult. (2008)

152–154

157–158

155–156

159

159–164 *New York City Transit Authority Graphics Standards Manual Revisions* **(New York: New York City Transit Authority, 1980). Compiled by Ralph DeMasi.** The *New York City Transit Authority Graphics Standards Manual Revisions* existed only in photocopied form. It officially introduced the white stripe.

159 "Color coding." *New York City Transit Authority Graphics Standards Manual Revisions* (1980), p. 9. Color coding was revised in response to changes in route naming in 1979. Note the introduction of diamonds to accompany discs. "Note #2— when letter 'J' appears in discs or diamonds—use Helvetica style 'J' " (**179**).

160 Cover, *New York City Transit Authority Graphics Standards Manual Revisions* (1980).

161

162

163

164

161 "Examples of sign plate modulation." *New York City Transit Authority Graphics Standards Manual Revisions* (1980), p. 19. "To avoid visual confusion and clutter only the Standard sign plates should be used for each category of sign. Any other device like painting on tiles, walls, light fixtures, etc. is a violation of the standards."

162 "Station identification." *New York City Transit Authority Graphics Standards Manual Revisions* (1980), p. 25. Note the use of the apostrophe. This may have been done on the impetus of John Tauranac. It can still be seen at Bowling Green (4/5) and Ft. Hamilton Parkway (F).

163 "Special conditions of station identification signage." *New York City Transit Authority Graphics Standards Manual Revisions* (1980), p. 20. Note the hand rendering of the lettering.

164 "Escalator signs." *New York City Transit Authority Graphics Standards Manual Revisions* (1980), p. 29.

Now you can take The Train to The Plane.

Now you can get from Manhattan to JFK Airport, or back, in just over an hour, on the new JFK Express, "The Train to The Plane." It costs only $4.00, and operates approximately every 20 minutes, 5:30 a.m. to 12:30 a.m., every day of the year. The JFK Express travels from 57th at Avenue of the Americas, making six stops in Manhattan and one in downtown Brooklyn. It's economical and dependable, no matter what the weather! For more information, call (212)858-7272.

Metropolitan Transportation Authority

The JFK Express
The Train to The Plane©
© 1980 Metropolitan Transportation Authority.

165

Although the decision to change the figure/ground relationship of the signs was made c.1973 and announced publicly in 1979, it took awhile for the new signs to be implemented—just as it had taken years for the original Unimark signs to be introduced. Some signs were installed as early as 1975 (figs. 147 and 169) but large-scale installation did not begin until after 1978 when the TA began a program of station renovation under the guidance of in-house architect Paul Katz. But when the "We're Changing" campaign was unveiled in 1979 the accompanying photographs and posters showed white Unimark signs being amended with route decals bearing the new color coding and the new diamonds. These decals had a black background instead of a white or clear one, an indication that they were intended to eventually be used with white on black signs (figs. 166–167, 169–171). They were a stopgap measure—the brainchild of Len Ingalls who called them "pasties"—to solve the problem of quickly and economically coordinating the introduction of the new Hertz map with the signage in the stations. [57]

The MTA had expected to complete the entire color-coding program in thirty-six months, but its plans fell woefully short. The Hertz map was issued as promised in 1979, but in 1982 the MTA announced that it had just begun to update the station signage the year before (!) and that it had not yet begun changing the train scroll signs. It expected to have new signs in 78 stations by the end of the year. The situation with the scroll signs was more dire. *The New York Times* reported that they were so out-of-date that the destination signs for the AA train said Hudson Terminal (rather than the World Trade Center which had replaced it over a decade earlier) and for some no. 7 trains they said the World's Fair! (Things were even worse than the *Times* realized since the AA had been renamed the K.) However, by the end of the 1980s —thanks to an improving economy in New York City and a series of five-year capital programs dedicated to modernizing the stations— the revised Unimark signs managed to finally permeate most of the subway system. [58]

57. Michael Bosniak of the MTA Public Affairs Department told Philip Coppola in November 1978 "that they would soon send a team of personnel through the system on a station-to-station hunt for extraneous signs. Some stops were overloaded with directional placards which tended more to confuse than enlighten newcomers to the subway. Obsolete signs would be removed." Bosniak was especially upset that many of the signs covered the mosaic nameplates. *Silver Connections.* vol. II., pp. 1–2. Coppola's account is supported by Peter Joseph who says that he and Michael Hertz were part of an effort to root out all old signs in stations within "zones" (sections of a given line)—including the black on white Unimark ones—and replace them with the white on black ones. Peter Joseph interview with author, 15 August 2008. This process must not have been

complete even as late as 1988 since there is this statement in the working copy of the 1989 graphic standards manual: "Vinyl decals are sometimes used to update porcelain enamel signs or to provide temporary information which will be removed. These decals should always be prepared with a background color to match that of an existing sign. For older signs with white backgrounds, never apply a decal with a black background." The working copy also contained a section devoted to the "Removal of Existing Signs" which decreed that the old ones should be given to the New York Transit Museum. See Metropolitan Transportation Authority, *Graphic Standards: Signage.* (New York: Michael Hertz Associates, 1988), n.p. The poster in the 1978 MTA annual report was by Nancy Stahl. Metropolitan Transportation Authority. *1978 Annual Report*, pp. 6 and 10;

John Tauranac interview with author, 14 August 2008. Information about the origins of the decals comes from John Tauranac and Peter Joseph. John Tauranac interview with author, 9 August 2008 and Peter Joseph interview with author, 15 August 2008. The decals met with the approval of Paul Goldberger: "New signs on the station tracks carry through the diamond theme from the map: they also indicate the new, far more rational color-coding system." Paul Goldberger, "Design Notebook: At Last, A Usable Subway Map," *New York Times*, August 2, 1979. The only station where directional Unimark signs still exist is Bowling Green, though ancillary ones for doors to mechanical rooms, yard entrances, etc. can be found in the far reaches of the subway system. According to Michael Hertz the application of the decals was not carried

out smoothly. He recounts instances of decals being pasted over decals as lines were changed and then changed back. Michael Hertz interview with author, 25 August 2008.

Michael Hertz recalls that the architecture department of the TA, led by Paul Katz, did a rough estimate of the cost of replacing entire signs in order to coordinate them with the 1979 map color coding changes and it would have been $27 million. This was based on the fact that porcelain enamel signs cost $80 per square foot to make at that time. Thus, the decal idea made financial sense. Michael Hertz interview with author, 25 August 2008.

58. In 1981, Vignelli told *Graphis* that, "The project has so far been implemented in part." He was referring to the 1970 signage

manual specifications and made no reference to the change from black-on-white to white-on-black signs. Walter Herdeg, ed., *Archigraphia: Architectural and Environmental Graphics.* (Zurich: Graphis, 1981), p. 106. Glenn Fowler, "Subway Signs Often Sidetrack Riders," *New York Times*, March 14, 1982. The discrepancy in dates between 1979 and 1981 regarding the introduction of the "new" signs can be explained in several ways: 1. the "new" 1978/1979 signs may have been the decal-modified white Unimark signs while the "new" 1981/1982 signs were the complete white-on-black ones from the DeMasi manual; or 2. although some white on black signs may have been installed prior to 1981, their numbers were so few that the MTA was embarrassed by the lack of progress and preferred to publicly announce a new start date for their introduction; or

165 Advertisement for JFK Express. Back
cover of Culture Bus Loop I booklet
(rev. ed.), 1980. The JFK Express
("The Train to The Plane") was
introduced in September 1978. Its
graphic style included the use of
Helvetica Medium and Helvetica
Thin.

166 Installing a decal on a Unimark-style
sign at an unidentified BMT Broadway
line station, c.1979.
From Metropolitan Transportation
Authority. 1978 Annual Report, p. 10.

167 "We're Changing" MTA poster
(originally in color) heralding
route designation changes, 1979.
Illustration by Nancy Stahl. From
Metropolitan Transportation
Authority. 1978 Annual Report,
p. 11. Set in Trade Gothic.

WE'RE CHANGING,

Starting next week, there will be some changes in the subway.
The first thing you'll notice will be changes in the colors of the
signs in the stations. Then, the color of train signs will change.
And, a new subway map, showing the new color system, will be
introduced this summer.
When the new color coding system is complete, it will be
easier and simpler to get around in the subways. But it can't
happen overnight, because there are over 18,000 route signs,
6,200 subway cars, and 460 stations to change.
It's all part of a new program over the next 24 to 36
months to improve the subway...

AND WE WANT YOU
TO BE THE FIRST TO KNOW.

3. a combination of both. The April 1980
transit strike might have disrupted the installation of the new signs for awhile, but the
delay between 1979 and 1981 was probably
due more to the financial struggles of the
NYCTA. The first of a series of 5-year
capital programs for the MTA was begun
in 1982 and continued throughout the 1980s
under the chairmanship of Richard Kiley.
In the opinion of Peter Joseph they were
responsible for the final spread of the
white on black signs throughout the subway system. See Metropolitan Transportation Authority. 1984 Annual Report; Metropolitan Transportation Authority. 1987
Annual Report; and Peter Joseph interview
with author, 15 August 2008. New route roll
curtains were introduced to the trains
c.1983, replacing the c.1970 ones by Trans-
Lite, Inc. which had white letters within
a white ring on a colored background.

Subway Style, p. 225. (The Coney Island roll
curtain shown is from the 1990s since it is
set in a mix of Standard and Helvetica.)

Prior to the issuance of the Hertz map,
Helvetica was already in the system as the
typeface for the Train to the Plane (announced in 1978 and introduced in 1979) (165).
See the photograph in the Metropolitan Transportation Authority 1977 Annual Report
[issued in 1978], p. 26 which also shows
pre-Unimark signs on columns in the 57th
Street/6th Avenue station.

The modernization of the subway system's
stations in the 1980s occurred in fits and
starts as a perusal of newspaper articles
attests. In 1982 the MTA promised it would
modernize 50 stations; in 1985 the TA set
a goal of having 90 stations completed by
the end of the year and a total of 201 done

by the end 1986; but in 1990 it was reported
that only 55 had been completed. See
Michael Oreskes, "Analysts Expect
M.T.A.'s Projects to Aid Economy," New
York Times, November 28, 1982; "Excerpts
from the Bellamy Paper on Transit Issues,"
New York Times, July 30, 1985; Deirdre
Carmody, "To Gunn, City's Transit Is
Better, But Not Best," New York Times,
November 25, 1985; and Calvin Sims,
"Plans and Costs Expand to Fix Subway
Stations," New York Times, June 9, 1990.
The slow pace of the introduction of the
original Unimark signs and the modified
white-on-black ones is visible in several
movies made during those years, most
notably The Taking of Pelham 1-2-3 (1974),
Saturday Night Fever (1977) and The
Warriors (1979).

242 St Van Cortlandt Park

168 (opposite page) Porcelain enamel station sign. 242nd Street–Van Cortlandt Park (1). (2007)

169 Black porcelain enamel platform sign with white route module. Times Square (1) local track, March 18, 1975. Note the c.1920 station name sign still in place .

170 Porcelain enamel route sign. Times Square, c.1982. The sign is a mix of inverted Unimark-style modules and Unimark modules with (QB and RR) and without (N) route designation decals. The S route designation decal probably replaced an SS one.

171 Porcelain enamel platform sign. Columbus Circle (A/D) express track, c.1982. Note the experimental stylized strip map on the girder column, reminiscent of the line map Noorda included in the 1966 proposal (89), was the idea of John Tauranac.

172 Porcelain enamel trash sign. Jay Street–Boro Hall (A/C/F), c.1985. The trash symbol (201) was modified by Michael Hertz Associates from the 1981 AIGA version developed for the United States Department of Transportation. Note the Unimark sign for the A train at right.

169–172

173

173–175, 182 *New York City Transit Authority Graphics Standards Manual Supplement* **(New York: Michael Hertz Associates, 1984).** The 1984 *Graphics Standards Manual Supplement* was prepared and designed by Michael Hertz Associates. It only existed in photocopied form.

In 1984 Michael Hertz Associates was hired as "signage consultants to the architecture department of the TA". Hertz's work on the 1979 subway map had little bearing on the firm's selection as the contract was won through a competitive bidding process. The firm prepared a second revision of the 1970 *Graphics Standards Manual* for the NYCTA. The supplement that Hertz and his associate Peter Joseph created was more professional than the DeMasi version, though it too existed only in a photocopied, tape-bound form. The text was entirely typeset as were all the examples of signage. The supplement codified the major changes of the 1980 revised manual by providing high quality artwork for the new service disks and diamonds, route names and colors, and ancillary symbols. It also included guidelines for door signs and Off Hour Waiting Area signs. Although there was no mention of any change in the official typeface some of the sample illustrations used Helvetica instead of Standard. Whether actual signs were prepared with Helvetica as a result is unclear, but Helvetica-ization was around the corner. [59]

The process for preparing artwork for porcelain enamel signs was more professional by the time Michael Hertz Associates began working on the subway signage than it was when Unimark was first hired. This is Joseph's description of it: "The design, so to speak, consisted of a plan showing sign locations indicated by a number. These numbers corresponded to a schedule with message, sign size and sign type (pan-formed, flat, etc.). The contractor [e.g., Michael Hertz Associates] was required to submit full-size shop drawings of each sign to the TA for approval. These shop drawings were in turn sent to a PE [porcelain enamel] manufacturer to produce either stencils or screens... from which the actual signs were fabricated." The Bergen Street Shop was no longer involved in the process. [60]

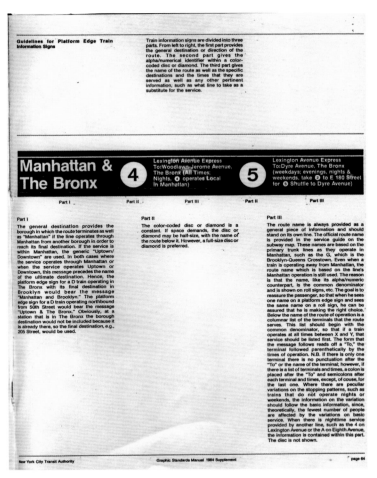

59. New York City Transit Authority, *New York City Transit Authority Graphics Standards Manual Supplement*. (New York City: Michael Hertz Associates, 1984). Helvetica appears in the illustrations for the sections on Intermodal (bus) information p. 48, Door signs p. 50, and Off Hour Waiting Area p. 55. Despite the use of Helvetica in the manual diagram, the first signs for the Off Hour Waiting Areas were set in Standard as indicated by an example in the New York Transit Museum. Peter Joseph says that these signs were not designed by Michael Hertz Associates but done in-house. Their installation was not coordinated with what he and Hertz were doing and some ended up on top of or in front of white-on-black signs including some that marked exits. Peter Joseph

interview with author, 15 August 2008. Hertz and Joseph were responsible for inclusion of the Helvetica **J** in the 1980 revised manual. The bus, bathroom (**172**) and handicapped symbols were taken from the American Institute of Graphic Arts, *Symbol Signs*. (New York: Hastings House and American Institute of Graphic Arts, 1981). The trash symbol (**189**), added later, was modified at the request of TA management. Peter Joseph, interview with the author, 15 August 2008. The new artwork was needed because contractors had been misinterpreting the diagrams in the 1980 revised manual. For example, photographs from c.1982 show Helvetica Medium used for no. 7 signage at Times Square.

60. Peter Joseph to author, 14 August 2008. See also *Graphic Standards: Signage.* (1988), n.p.

173 Cover, *New York City Transit Authority Graphics Standards Manual Supplement* (1984).

174 "Guidelines for platform edge train information signs." *New York City Transit Authority Graphics Standards Manual Supplement* (1984), p. 64.

175 "Off Hour Waiting Area sign." *New York City Transit Authority Graphics Standards Manual Supplement* (1984), p. 58. The "Off Hour Waiting Area" signs were created in response to continued high levels of crime in the subway system in the early 1980s. They were placed near token booths.

176–181,183 Examples of Standard Medium in use, c.1973–1989. The erratically leaning letters and bouncing baseline in these signs may be due to the use of press type (e.g. Letraset Instant Lettering sheets) in preparing the signs for silkscreening in the porcelain enamel process.

176 Porcelain enamel telephone sign. Beach 105th Street **(A/S)**. (2009)

177 Vinyl restroom door sign. York Street **(F)**. It was common practice in the 1970s to place new Unimark-style signs on top of existing signs, including mosaics. Paul Katz, MTA architect, tried to put a stop to this practice in 1978. (2008)

178 Remnants of vinyl decal sign. Beach 105th Street **(A/S)**. (2009)

179 Route roll-up sign. F train, c.1980. The type is Standard Medium except for the Helvetica Medium **J** in Jamaica. (2010)

180 Stainless steel station entrance sign. 68th Street–Hunter College **(6)**, c.1986. The station name is Standard Medium while the script "Subway" is by an unidentified artist. (2010)

181 Illuminated destination sign. Kings Highway **(F)**. Painted Standard Medium. (2010)

182 "Toilet signs (half size)." *New York City Transit Authority Graphics Standards Manual Supplement* (1984), p. 46.

183 Porcelain enamel toilet sign. Forest Hills–71st Avenue **(E/F/G/R/V)**, c.1984. Note: the type is Helvetica Medium. (2008)

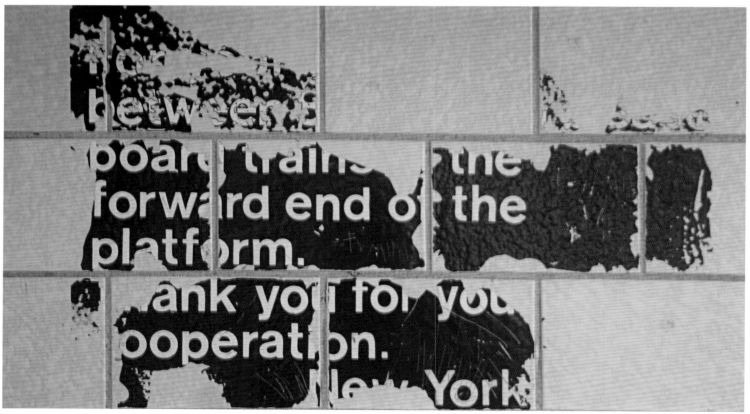

176–178

179–181

Men

Women

3⅝"

9"

Men

182–183

PORTER

Station Dept
Porters Room

STATION DEPT 212-712-4236

WATER METER

HELVETICA INFILTRATES THE NEW YORK CITY SUBWAY SYSTEM

The myth that Helvetica was the type of the New York City subway system began with Leslie Savan's 1976 *Village Voice* article, "This Typeface Is Changing Your Life." Savan tried to explain the sudden pervasiveness of the sans serif typeface in the 1970s, focusing her attention on Vignelli and Lippincott & Margulies. "Since 1967," she wrote, "the MTA has been gradually standardizing its graphics from about a dozen typefaces to a combination of Helvetica and Standard Medium. (The two are almost identical, but the latter was more available to the MTA.)." She incorrectly credited the transit agency's "graphic system" to Vignelli and Walter Kacik, making no mention of Noorda or Unimark, and she conflated the TA's signage with the MTA's printed matter. [61]

185

184 (opposite page) Porcelain enamel door sign. Liberty Avenue (A/C). (2008). Note the palimpsest of signs from handlettered porcelain enamel to Standard Medium vinyl to Helvetica Medium vinyl to Helvetica Medium in routed-out plastic.

185 "Visit Fort Hamilton Park" poster. Part of "MTA gets you there" advertising campaign, 1973. Designed by Howard York. Set in Standard Medium.

61. Leslie Savan, "This Typeface Is Changing Your Life," *Village Voice*, June 7, 1976. Reprinted in *Looking Closer 3: Classic Writings on Graphic Design* edited by Michael Bierut, Jessica Helfand, Steven Heller and Rick Poynor. (New York: Allworth Press, 1999), pp. 256–259. Savan focused on transportation systems and corporate identity programs as the chief culprits in the spread of Helvetica, but by 1974 the federal government also deserved some of the credit/blame. That year it initiated the Federal Design Improvement Program which led to graphic standards systems (including Helvetica) by John Massey and Massimo Vignelli for the Labor Department and National Parks Service respectively. Philip B. Meggs and Alston W. Purvis, *Meggs' History of Graphic Design*. 4th ed. (New York: John Wiley & Sons, Inc., 2006), pp. 412–413; "Second Federal Design Assembly" issue. *Design Quarterly* 94/95 (1975) and American Institute of Graphic Arts, *The Federal Design Response.* (New York: American Institute of Graphic Arts, 1977).

186–187

Savan's confusion was understandable. In 1973 an inter-agency marketing campaign entitled "MTA Gets You There" was launched by the MTA to boost ridership. The various printed materials—posters, brochures, maps, timetables—were intended to have a coordinated design yet some used Standard and some Helvetica. The most prominent of the latter was the controversial and now iconic 1972 subway map (fig. 142) designed by Vignelli. When asked recently why he had used Helvetica for the map when Standard was the typeface of the sign system, Vignelli replied that he simply "forgot" to do so. Given his devotion to Helvetica at the time, his answer rings true—especially since he set the explanatory text of the 1970 *Graphics Standards Manual* in it! [62]

When Vignelli designed the subway map he was no longer a member of Unimark International. He had left the firm the year before to establish Vignelli Associates in partnership with his wife Lella. In designing the map Vignelli did not have to worry about using any of the TA's in-house departments as Unimark had to do with the sign system. The artwork was created by his staff as a mechanical with type set by a type house of his own choosing. There were no reasons, technical or otherwise, not to use Helvetica. The transit agency did not complain because they had been using Helvetica here and there for various printed items since 1967. The "MTA Gets You There" campaign was only one instance of their mix and match sensibility. [63]

The subway map has led many—both within and without the design professions—to assume that Vignelli designed the NYCTA signage system on his own and that it used Helvetica. For example, interior designer Stanley Abercrombie, in an essay accompanying the 1977/1978 Cooper-Hewitt Museum exhibition "Subways", credited the signage to Vignelli and praised his use of a "clear, smart Helvetica face". Similarly, the website of the Design Museum in London, gushing over Helvetica, declares: "From the beautifully implemented New York Subway signage system by Vignelli to its usage on the lowly generic EXIT sign, the flexibility of the typeface seems to have no boundaries." Most astonishing of all, the authors of *Subway Style*—published by the New York Transit Museum of the Metropolitan Transportation Authority—insist that the manual stated the typeface for the signs was to be "exclusively Helvetica", photographic evidence to the contrary. [64]

62. Savan is not the only one who has been confused by Standard and Helvetica. Recently, Howard York, the designer of the award-winning 1973 "MTA Gets You There" poster series, asserted he set them in Helvetica, yet the typeface used is clearly Standard. Similarly, John Tauranac claims that Helvetica replaced Standard almost from the beginning because "the average sign manufacturer did not have it and was not willing to buy it, so they simply substituted Helvetica instead, and the TA/MTA went along with it. Helvetica became the standard, and, frankly, I don't think anybody ever knew the difference." He goes on to say that " I had the exalted title of Manager of Passenger Information from about 1981–1987, and I don't think I once saw a specification for Standard Medium." Yet, his view is contradicted by the physical

evidence of the signs as well as the various graphics standards manuals. Howard York to author, 11 August 2008 and John Tauranac to author, 6 August 2008. Vignelli's explanation for the use of Helvetica in the 1972 map comes from Massimo Vignelli interview with author, 29 April 2008. Part of Savan's confusion may also be due to the overlapping responsibilities of the MTA and the TA. For instance, several MTA employees worked at the TA in the 1970s.

63. There were several iterations of the Vignelli map between 1972 and 1979 (see note 54), not all of which were set in Helvetica or were carried out by him. This may have confused Savan further. Compare the 1972 and 1974 maps online at vignelli.com, columbia.edu/~brennan/

abandoned/bowling.html and subway.com.ru. The revisions to the Vignelli map may have been designed by the staff of Diamond National, the firm responsible for printing the TA maps from at least 1967 through 1979.

64. Abercrombie (1977); "50 Years of Helvetica" at designmuseum.org/exhibitions/2007/helvetica; and *Subway Style*, pp. 142–143. Also see the confusion online such as the comments at forgotten-ny.com/SUBWAYS/oldsubwaysigns/subwaysigns.html: "Also note the TA, then the MTA, had a fascination for a time with Standard Medium. Introduced by Massimo Vignelli's Unimark International design firm, the Helvetica-esque typefont was used from the 1960s into the 1980s, when it was replaced with the ubiquitous real

McCoy." Vignelli's activities involving the New York City subway system have been garbled by many. Within the design literature the following prominent texts all get one aspect or another wrong: Edward Booth-Clibborn and Daniele Baroni, *The Language of Graphics*. (New York: Harry N. Abrams, Inc., Publishers, 1980), p. 152 credits the signage entirely to Bob Noorda of Unimark International with no dates; James Craig and Bruce Barton, *Thirty Centuries of Graphic Design: An Illustrated Survey.* (New York: Watson-Guptill Publications, 1987), p. 202 credits the signage entirely to Vignelli, dates it to 1966, and calls it a "success"; Johanna Drucker, and Emily McVarish, *Graphic Design History: A Critical Guide.* (Upper Saddle River, NJ: Pearson Prentice-Hall, 2009), p. 262 credits the signage to Bob Noorda of Unimark

International, vaguely dates it to the 1960s but shows a post-2000 sign; Richard Hollis, *Swiss Graphic Design: The Origins and Growth of an International Style 1920–1965.* (New Haven: Yale University Press, 2006), p. 255 ignores Noorda and Unimark and dates the signs to 1965; Roxane Jubert, *Typography and Graphic Design from Antiquity to the Present.* (Paris: Flammarion, 2006), p. 364 says the signage was done in the 1970s and credits it entirely to Vignelli; and R. Roger Remington, *American Modernism: Graphic Design, 1920 to 1960.* (New Haven: Yale University Press, 2003), p. 162 credits the map to Vignelli as a member of Unimark and dates it to 1966 while making no mention of the signage.

16.

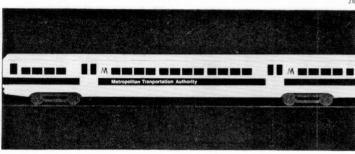

18.

19.

188

191

25 Fulton St.

26 Putnam Ave.

37 3rd Ave.

Platform C↑

Track 4

Hempstead

189–190

186 M41 Culture Loop bus, Metropolitan Museum of Art, 1973. MaBSTOA. Route designation set in Standard Medium.

187 Fulton Street bus. New York City Surface (**MaBSTOA**). Mid-1970s. Route destination set in Standard Medium.

188–190 Identity design by PMMA for Long Island Rail Road, c.1969. From Rose DeNeve. "Peter Muller-Munk: Design for the Urban Environment." *Print* XIV:III (1970), p. 63. PMMA is credited with introducing Helvetica to the LIRR and its bus operationss but these photographs indicate that it was mixed with Standard.

188 LIRR commuter train, locomotive and bus. Set in Helvetica Medium.

189 Long Island bus route signage. Set in Standard Medium.

190 LIRR platform signage. Set in Helvetica Medium.

191 Two-toned M logo. Token booth at Broad Channel (A). Logo designed by PMMA (Peter Muller-Munk Associates) for the Metropolitan Transportation Authority when it replaced the Metropolitan Commuter Transportation Authority, 1968. The PMMA designer may have been Kenneth Love. (2009)

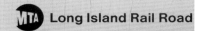

Douglaston

MTA Long Island Rail Road

Riverside

192–194

192 Douglaston. Long Island Rail Road station. Note the addition of the MTA logo after 1995. (2009)

193 Philipse Manor. Metro-North Hudson Line station. (1987).

194 Riverside, Connecticut. Metro-North New Haven Line station, 1970s. The type is Standard Medium. (2009)

195 MTA Commuter Rail System Map, 1974. Map side. Designed by Joan Charysyn while freelancing in between stints at Vignelli Associates and Unimark.

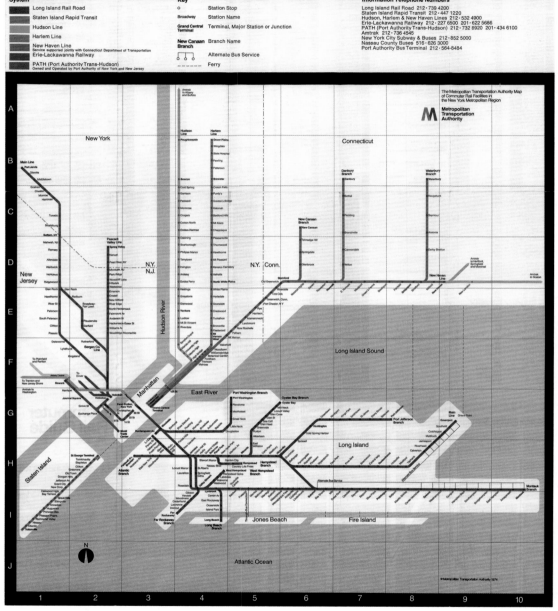

195

Helvetica finally became the official typeface for the New York City subway system signage in December 1989 when the MTA Marketing & Corporate Communications Division, the department in charge of its graphic standards, issued a new manual (fig. 203). The manual was prepared by Michael Hertz Associates at the request of Doris Halle. In the introduction to the *MTA Sign Manual New York City Transit Authority Long Island Rail Road Metro-North Commuter Railroad*, Richard Kiley, the MTA Chairman, called it "a first step toward the goal of unified, high-quality MTA-wide signs." It marked the first attempt by the MTA to establish a set of consistent graphic standards for all of its constituent agencies. Although it did not go into detail, it claimed to incorporate most of the 1970 *Graphics Standards Manual* "as well as modifications made over the years" and to "fine-tune some proven precedents." [65]

The 1989 MTA *Sign Manual* ratified the "modifications" made in the 1980 and 1984 interim revisions to the 1970 *Graphics Standards Manual*. Thus, Noorda's modular system no longer existed as physical components but only as graphical units. Signs were allowed to be a wider variety of lengths and there was a wider variety of fabrication options, including silkscreened vinyl adhesive backing for updates to the porcelain enamel signs. The thickness and position of the white stripe was officially defined. The colored disks from 1984 were modified to take into account the addition to the system of the 9, H, Z, 1/9 and J/Z trains. Diamonds were still in existence. The 1980 sizes of type were kept. But the typeface was no longer Standard Medium—with a few exceptions. [66]

The choice of typeface now reflected the complete MTA transportation system rather than the New York City subway by itself. The manual was a MTA product and not a NYCTA one. Helvetica Medium (with Helvetica Medium Italic) was chosen as the standard typeface for the NYCTA (including MaBSTOA and Staten Island Rapid Transit); Helvetica Medium and Helvetica Medium Condensed for the LIRR; and Helvetica Medium Italic for Metro-North. There was no mention made of replacing older signs. Standard remained as part of the old artwork for the roll designators, though a diagram was included for making new discs (with Helvetica) for future line designations (such as the V and W trains which ran from 2001 to 2010). Helvetica Medium Italic was added to describe the hours of operation for specific trains. The manual (fig. 206) cautioned that, "Any other form of Helvetica (e.g., condensed, regular, etc.) or other typefaces, are never to be used as a substitute for Helvetica Medium or Helvetica Medium Italic." This may have been a reference to the use in the early 1980s of Helvetica Ultra Compressed and Folio Bold Condensed (often mistaken for Helvetica Inserat) on some porcelain enamel column signs. [67]

196

65. Responsibility by Michael Hertz Associates for the preparation of the December 1989 MTA Sign Manual has been confirmed in conversation with Doris Halle and Peter Joseph. Peter Joseph interview with author, 15 August 2008. Doris Halle interview with author, 14 August 2008. Unlike the 1980 and 1984 versions of the manual, this was a professionally printed and assembled binder. A working draft was prepared between June and December 1988. See Metropolitan Transportation Authority. *Graphic Standards: Signage*. (New York: Michael Hertz Associates, 1988).

66. Work on the 1989 manual began in 1987 with a first draft issued in June 1988. Metropolitan Transportation Authority. *Graphic Standards: Signage*. (New York: Michael Hertz Associates, 1988). The draft

also has pages dated September 15, 1988, October 1988 and December 22, 1988. Peter Joseph interview with the author, 15 August 2008. See Metropolitan Transportation Authority. *MTA Sign Manual: New York City Transit Authority, Long Island Rail Road, Metro-North Commuter Railroad*, (New York: Metropolitan Transportation Authority, 1989), pp. 2.1–2.2, 2.25–226 and 4.1 for the specifications cited. The K train was discontinued in 1988; the H train is now the Rockaway Park Shuttle S; and the no. 9 train ran skip-stop service on the no. 1 tracks from 1989 to 2005. The exceptions were the route designators which continued to use Standard as did some roll-ups.

67. Metropolitan Transportation Authority. *MTA Sign Manual: New York City Transit Authority, Long Island Rail Road, Metro-North Commuter Railroad*. (New York: Metropolitan Transportation Authority, 1989), pp. 2.3–2.5, and 3.1–3.2. Peter Joseph does not recall whose idea it was to add Helvetica Medium Italic to the repertoire. Roll designators with Standard Medium are still visible in the system today on selected lines (e.g. the 1, 3, D, F, S trains). "Letters are not to be altered by shortening, mechanical condensing or other means," warned the 1988 working draft. Metropolitan Transportation Authority, *Graphic Standards: Signage*. (New York: Michael Hertz Associates, 1988). On one page is scrawled the note, "Mention NO Hel Cond". (Helvetica Ultra Compressed can still be seen at the Grant Avenue station and Folio Bold Condensed, nearly

identical to Helvetica Inserat, is still present at the Hoyt-Schermerhorn Streets station.) Also see Peter Joseph interview with the author, 15 August 2008.

As part of the 1992–1997 MTA capital program the Department of Transit Station Signs was created to consolidate all existing sign management. The impetus was to redo and modernize all existing subway signage. Fifty to 75 stations were refurbished per year. "It took about eight years to reinvigorate the subway system with new signage and a more modern way-finding system," said John Montemarano, the department's director. Louis M. Brill, "Taking the A-Train (or Any Other Train) in New York City Would Be Even Harder Without Directional Signage", p. 2 at signindustry.com/

196 Transit information kiosk. Fulton Street, 1978. Designed by Samuel Leibowitz. From *Archigraphia: Architectural and Environmental Graphics* (1981), p. 59. Set in Helvetica Medium. No longer in existence, the kiosk was 9'6" high and made of aluminum with the lettering silkscreened. The kiosk was created as part of the development of the Fulton Street Mall. Also see (156).

197

197–202 Examples of incorrect versions of Standard and Helvetica, c.1980s.

197 Porcelain enamel door sign. Fulton Street (4/5). Handcut Standard Medium with an **R** in Helvetica Medium. (2008)

198 Porcelain enamel prohibitory sign. East 189th Street (2/5), 1970s. Note the zero used in place of an **O**. (2009)

199 Porcelain enamel column sign. South Ferry (1), c.1986. Set in Folio Bold Condensed which is similar to Helvetica Inserat. No longer visible. (2008)

200 Trash receptacle. Jay Street–Borough Hall (A/C/F), c.1985. Set in Helvetica Medium and Regular.

201 Porcelain enamel girder column sign. Chambers Street (1/2/3), c.1988. Set in Neue Helvetica 65 (Medium). (2008)

202 Illuminated sign. 42nd Street–Port Authority (A/C/E), 1980s? Handcut Helvetica Medium. (2009)

188

199–200

201–202

203–204, 206–207, 209–15 *MTA–Graphic Standards Manual (NYCTA Signage) Outline* [Working Copy] (New York: Michael Hertz Associates, 1988). The working copy of The *MTA-Graphic Standards Manual (NYCTA Signage Outline)* was prepared and designed by Michael Hertz Associates between June and October, 1988. It only existed in photocopied form.

203 Title page. *MTA–Graphic Standards Manual (NYCTA Signage) Outline* [Working Copy] (1988). Annotations by Peter Joseph.

204 "Table of Contents." *MTA–Graphic Standards Manual (NYCTA Signage) Outline* [Working Copy] (1988). Annotations by Michael Hertz.

206 "Graphic Standards: Typography Alphabet." *MTA–Graphic Standards Manual (NYCTA Signage) Outline* [Working Copy] (1988), n.p. Annotations by Peter Joseph.

207 "Graphic Standards: Typography Technologies." *MTA–Graphic Standards Manual (NYCTA Signage) Outline* [Working Copy] (1988), n.p.

205, 208 Gerber Signmaker. Gerber Scientific Products (GSP) manufactured a computer-driven letter/stencil cutting system beginning in 1983. The MTA used it for producing all types of signs, including cut-out, applied vinyl letters for temporary signs and shop-drawings and stencils for porcelain enamel signs.

205 Cover of *GSP Type Styles* specimen book (Winter 1987).

208 Helvetica Medium specimen from *GSP Type Styles* (Winter 1987).

203

205

Metropolitan Transportation Authority

Graphic Standards: Signage

Table of Contents

9/15/88

June 1988

1. Chairman's Message
2. Introduction
3. Sign Types and Location
   System Overview
   Street Level Signs
   Fare Control Area Signs
   Mezzanine/Passageway Si
   Platform Signs
   Off-hour Waiting Area*
4. Sign Design
   Basic Module
   Typography
      Alphabet
      Letterspacing
      Letterspacing Chart
      Black/White Letters
      Sign-making technolo
   Text (syntax)
      Capitalization and A
      Station Names and Ab
      Destination/Directio
   Arrows
   Symbols
   Route Designators ("bul
   Colors
   Low Clearance Signs
5. Sign Layouts
   Exit
   Train Information
   Turnstile
   Door
   Escalator
   Prohibitory (No smoking..,)*
6. Sign Fabrication and Installation Details
   Type A (Single Steel Plate)
   Type B (Metal Gates)
   Type C (Pan-formed - Wall-mounted)
   Type D (Pan-formed - Hanging)
   Platform Edge Clearances)
   Vinyl Signs
      New
      Updates
   Illuminated Light Posts
7. Special Signs
   Institutional
   Temporary (Construction Signage)
   Elderly and Handicapped (E&H)
   Passenger Information Centers (PIC's)
8. Car Interior Graphics

204

Graphic Standards
Typography Text - Alphabet (Typography)

ABCDEFGHIJ KLMNOPQRS TUVWXYZ

abcdefghijkl mnopqrstuv wxyz

1234567890

$(&?!%'.,:;-)*

Helvetica Medium is the standard typeface for all graphics for the New York City Transit Authority. It is to be used for all permanent and temporary signage for stations, rolling stock, garages, yards and other facilities.

The alphabet shown is for reference only; it should not be reproduced. Typography for sign production may be obtained from a variety of commercial sources. Alphabets must match the weight of the characters illustrated on this page. Helvetica Condensed, Italic or other typefaces are not to be used.

* A listing of different sources of typography will be found on page —.

Letters are not to be altered by shortening, mechanical condensing or other means.

Graphic Standards
Typography Technologies

Most lettering for signage is now produced on typesetting equipment with built-in letterspacing capability (automatic kerning). In so far as the kerning is adjustable and the equipment is capable of exactly replicating the version of Helvetica Medium shown in this volume, such equipment can be used as a substitute for for the manual production of signs according to the chart on the preceding page. Some of the more common forms of typesetting equipment with comments on their applicability for sign-making and information on calibrating the automatic kerning functions are shown below.

TYPESETTING EQUIPMENT	COMMENT
DIGITAL/FILM TYPOGRAPHY	Used for smaller signs and type sizes and temporary notices.
Compugraphic	Should not be used for signs because their version of Helvetica Medium does not match the version shown in this manual.
Typositor	TV or Foundry spacing for negative, normal spacing for positive.
Linotronic	Same as Typositor; use Helvetica Bold to match.
TAPE-BASED LETTERING SYSTEMS	Useful for smaller signs and temporary notices.
Kroy	
Merlin	
COMPUTER-DRIVEN LETTER/ STENCIL CUTTING SYSTEMS	Used for producing all types of signs, including both cut-out, applied letters for temporary signs and shop-drawings and stencils for porcelain enamel signs.
Gerber Signmaker	
INDIVIDUAL SELF-ADHESIVE VINYL LETTERS (Various Brands)	Used directly for temporary signage for prodcing layouts for permanent signage. Manually spaced according to letterspacing chart on the preceding page.
FABRICATED OR CUT OUT LETTERS (METAL, PLASTIC OR OTHER MATERIALS)	For limited decorative applications; often produced from stencils. Individually applied letters must be spaced as per chart on the preceding page.

Helvetica Medium
abcdefghijklmnopqrstuvwxyz
ABCDEFGHIJKLM
NOPQRSTUVWXYZ
0123456789 ®!"#$%&'°()"+¢£:?-=;/,.

The registered trademark symbol is built into this Helvetica font. To draw or cut this symbol on your system, hold the accent key down and press the two key (2), then press SHIFT START.

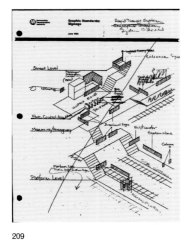

209

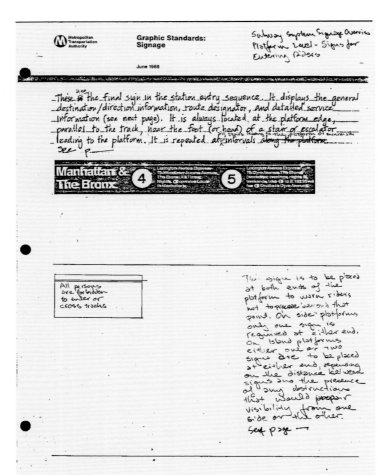

210

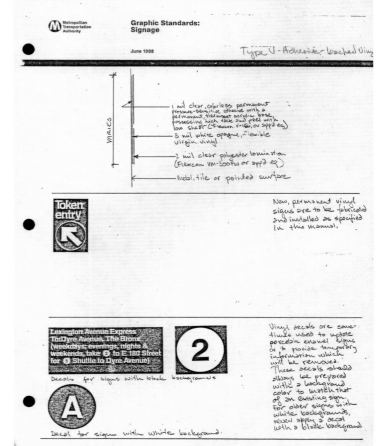

211

209 "Rapid Transit System: System Overview." MTA–Graphic Standards Manual (NYCTA Signage) Outline [Working Copy] (1988), n.p. Text by Peter Joseph and an unknown MTA architect.

210 "Subway System Signage Overview: Platform Level—Signs for Entering Riders." MTA–Graphic Standards Manual (NYCTA Signage) Outline [Working Copy] (1988). Text by Peter Joseph and an unknown MTA architect.

211 "Type V–Adhesive-backed Vinyl." MTA–Graphic Standards Manual (NYCTA Signage) Outline [Working Copy] (1988), n.p. Text by an unknown MTA architect. Note the existence of white-background decals as well as black-background ones.

212 "Car Interior Graphic Sign Layouts. Sign 5: Prohibitory Sign." MTA–Graphic Standards Manual (NYCTA Signage) Outline [Working Copy] (1988), n.p. This prohibitory sign was a response to the prevalence of "boom boxes" on subway trains in the early 1980s.

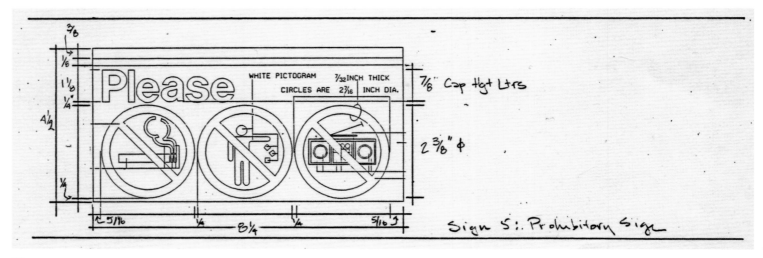

212

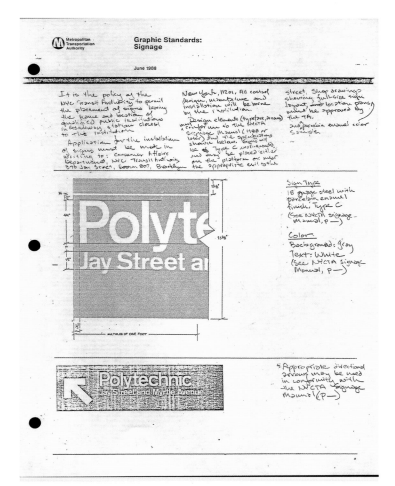

213

214

Metropolitan Transportation Authority — Graphic Standards: Signage — June 1988

Construction Methods

10E1.2 SHOP DRAWINGS.

The Contractor shall furnish shop drawings for approval, as required in Section 1C, for signs that shall show full-size inscriptions of lettering.

10E2.2 STEEL SIGN PLATES.

Steel plates shall be finished with porcelain enamel and shall be made of an approved low carbon, open-hearth steel, containing a low metalloid and copper content, and capable of retaining a non-metallic, inorganic, fused coating on both sides, gauge weight, gauge thickness and flatness of the uncoated sheet shall conform to the specifications prescribed in the latest edition of "Manufacturer's Standard Practice", issued by the American Iron and Steel Institute.

10E2.3 PORCELAIN ENAMEL.

(a) Porcelain enamel shall be impervious, inorganic glasses. All surfaces shall be prepared and porcelain enamel shall be applied by a recognized method and fired at temperatures which will fuse the enamel glass to the surface of the metal and which will expel any volatile matter. Steel plates shall be given one coat of grip enamel on both the front and back surfaces and on all edges and on the front surface one or more applications of cover coats of colors as directed. Each color shall be fired separately and shall be uniform and even. The back surface and all edges shall receive a protective porcelain enamel coating over the ground coating, and such additional coats as may be necessary to counteract stresses that may be placed upon the steel plates because of the thickness of the enamel coating on the front surfaces.

(b) The porcelain enamel surfaces shall be uniformly finished and shall be free from bubbles, holes, tits, or other blemishes and imperfections and surface defects. Enamel surfaces shall be full of gloss unless otherwise specified. The total thickness of coatings shall be not less than 0.015 inch nor more than 0.035 inch on each side of the sheet, except on parts bearing several colors and on corners and returns. Porcelain enamel finish of 8 square feet or less shall not be distorted more than 1/4 of an inch from a true plane after installation. All porcelain enamel shall be acid-resisting and shall show no variations in color when submitted to standard tests for staining. All tests shall conform to the Porcelain Enamel Institute Standard Tests for Special Properties and Classifications. In general, the panels shall be finished in a minimum of two colors. Colors shall be uniform and even in color and shade.

10E2.5 HARDWARE.

All bolts and screws shall be made of brass or bronze unless otherwise indicated.

Hangers, studs, clip angles and filler plates shall be galvanized steel, commercial stock, #10-20, unless otherwise indicated.

Gauge numbers shall be U.S. standard.

Contractor shall submit samples of hardware for approval which samples will be kept on file with the Authority.

Exposed fasteners shall be made tamper-proof by an approved method.

10E3.2 REMOVAL OF EXISTING SIGNS.

All Existing signs and hardware, including clips, screws, bolts and hangers, shall be removed as indicated on the Contract Drawings, or as directed by the Engineer. Removed signs shall be delivered to the Transit Authority Museum located at Schermerhorn Street, between Boerum Place and Court Street, Brooklyn, unless otherwise directed by the Engineer. Existing tile or terra-cotta signs are not to be removed.

213 "[Institutional signs]." *MTA–Graphic Standards Manual (NYCTA Signage) Outline* [Working Copy] (1988), **n.p.** Text by Peter Joseph. This is the first official statement of MTA policy regarding the creation of signs marking neighborhood institutions. White-on-gray institutional signs had been added ad hoc to the system since the mid-1970s. The new policy required that institutions pay for the signs!

214 "Construction Methods." *MTA–Graphic Standards Manual (NYCTA Signage) Outline* [Working Copy] (1988), **n.p.** Note the last paragraph which directs TA employees to deliver all removed signs to the Transit Museum.

215 Porcelain enamel institutional sign. Lawrence Street (M/R), c.1977. Note the different typeface and wording from the version in **(214)**. (2008)

215

Polytechnic — 333 Jay Street, at Myrtle Ave

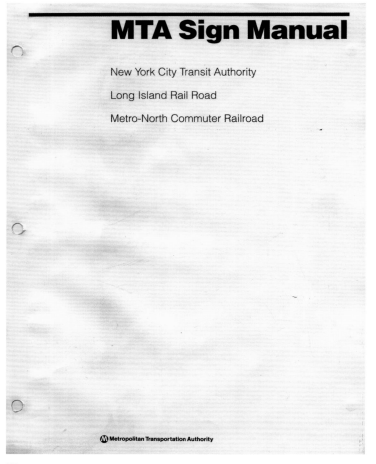

MTA Sign Manual

New York City Transit Authority

Long Island Rail Road

Metro-North Commuter Railroad

(M) Metropolitan Transportation Authority

216

Why did the MTA abandon Standard? At the time Helvetica's popularity was on the wane as its widespread use since the early 1970s had induced boredom and a backlash. Postmodernism had effectively exposed the subjective nature of the Modernist notion of neutral, rational and universal design and, in doing so, had undercut the principal reasons that many designers had given for choosing Helvetica over all other faces. [68]

The MTA's embrace of Helvetica may have been out of step with the times, but there were some compelling reasons for it. One, is that the new standards were intended to unify the MTA's operations. Some of its commuter rail lines were already using Helvetica for their signage. The industrial design firm Peter Muller-Munk Associates of Pittsburgh—designers of the NYCTA's two-toned M logo in 1968—had introduced it to the Long Island Rail Road (LIRR) in 1969 (figs. 188, 190–191). By the early 1980s the New Haven line was sporting white signs with red bands at the top and Helvetica. And by 1987 the Hudson and Harlem lines of Metro-North had white signs with green bands set in Helvetica Medium Italic. The heritage of these commuter lines was reflected in the 1989 *MTA Sign Manual*'s color-coding decisions: blue for LIRR and the Harlem and Pascack Valley lines of Metro-North; green for the Hudson line of Metro-North; red for the New Haven line of Metro-North; and orange for the Port Jervis line of Metro-North. The colored bands are all descendants of the errant black band the NYCTA created in 1966. [69]

216–218, 220–221 *MTA Sign Manual: New York City Transit Authority, Long Island Rail Road, Metro-North Commuter Railroad* (New York: Metropolitan Transportation Authority, 1989). Prepared and designed by Michael Hertz Associates.

68. See, for instance, Katherine McCoy, "How I Lost My Faith in Rational Functionalism," in the *AIGA Journal of Graphic Design* vol. 9, no. 1 (1990); Rick Poynor, "Introduction" to *Typography Now: The Next Wave* edited by Poynor and Edward Booth-Clibborn. (London: Booth-Clibborn Editions, 1991); and Keith Robertson, "Starting from Zero," in *Emigre* no. 19 (1991) all of which were gathered in Michael Bierut, William Drenttel, Steven Heller and D.K. Holland, eds., *Looking Closer: Critical Writings on Graphic Design*. (New York: Allworth Press and the American Institute of Graphic Arts, 1994), pp. 49–50 as "Rethinking Modernism, Revising Functionalism"; 77–80 as "Starting from Zero"; and 83–87 as "Type and Deconstruction in the Digital Era." Helvetica is rarely mentioned by name in these or other essays of the time but it is implicated, along with the grid, in the critique of Swiss Modernism. Postmodernism's rejection of Modernism was exacerbated in the design world by turmoil over the introduction of computers and digital type. Several typefaces emerged during this turbulent time that were direct refutations of Helvetica: Keedy Sans (Jeffery Keedy, 1989), Template Gothic (Barry Deck, 1990), Dead History (P. Scott Makela, 1990), Blur (Neville Brody, 1991), Remedy (Frank Heine, 1992), and Schmelvetica (Chester, 1994). Heine's Remedy was described explicitly as an antidote to the dominance of Helvetica. Erik Spiekermann's Meta (1985–1991) emerged as the new preferred sans, earning the dubious sobriquet "the Helvetica of the '90s". By the 1990s Helvetica was also being supplanted as the preferred typeface for transportation graphics by Frutiger, originally designed in 1974 for the airport at Paris-Roissy (now known as Charles De Gaulle Airport), its offspring (e.g. FF Transit used by the Berliners Verkehrsbetriebe (BVG)), and custom faces.

69. Peter Muller-Munk (1904–1967) was a leading American industrial designer whose firm branched out from the design of train cars to include signage and maps. See new.idsa.org. The LIRR graphic design program was led by Kenneth Love. Rose M. DeNeve, "Peter Muller-Munk: Design for the Urban Environment," *Print* XXIV:III (May/June 1970), pp. 62–63. "The MTA project also includes a consistent signage system for the embattled Long Island Railroad [sic]" with a "standardized" typeface (though photographs show Standard Medium used alongside Helvetica Medium!). There are very few photographs of 1970s and 1980s commuter rail lines signage. For the LIRR see trainsarefun.com/lirr/lirrlogos.htm and trainsarefun.com/lirr/lirrsigns.htm; and for the Hudson and Harlem lines see several photographs by Joe Testagrose at nycsubway.org (1976 Croton-Harmon sign and 1977 Larchmont sign in Unimark style with a black band; 1987 Hudson line with Helvetica Medium Italic and green band). The description of the New Haven line signs is based on my memory of traveling to New Haven between 1978 and 1981. The choice of red for the New Haven line was derived from the colors of its predecessor the New York, New Haven and Hartford Railroad; the blue for the Harlem line was continued from the color of its predecessor the New York Central Railroad, but the green of the Hudson line, another New York Central offshoot, was new, possibly inspired by the scenery along its route. The origin of the colors for the Pascack and Port Jervis lines is unknown.

**MTA Sign
Manual**

**New York City
Transit Authority**

Subway

Graphic Standards

Typography
Alphabet

2.5

Helvetica Medium is the standard typeface for all sign graphics for the New York City Transit Authority. It is to be used on all permanent and temporary signage for stations, rolling stock, garages, yards and other facilities. Helvetica Medium Italic is for limited use on the Platform Edge (Train Information Sign) only (see pages 3.1-2).

The alphabets shown here are for reference only; they should not be reproduced. Reproducable typography for sign production may be obtained from a variety of commercial sources. Alphabets must match exactly the weight of characters illustrated on this page. **Any other form of Helvetica (e.g., condensed, regular, etc.) or other typefaces, are never to be used as a substitute for Helvetica Medium or Helvetica Medium Italic.**

Helvetica Medium

ABCDEFGHIJKLM NOPQRSTUVWXYZ abcdefghijklmnopqrstuv wxyz1234567890$(&.',;:-)

Helvetica Medium Italic

ABCDEFGHIJKLM NOPQRSTUVWXYZ abcdefghijklmnopqrstuv wxyz1234567890$(&.',;:-)

Ⓜ **Metropolitan Transportation Authority**

1989

217

**MTA Sign
Manual**

**New York City
Transit Authority**

Subway

Graphic Standards

Basic Sign Module
Uses

2.2

The standard sign module with the addition of text, route designators, directional arrows, and pictographs are used alone or in combination to make up station signs. Blank panels are used to separate two different messages on the same sign.

Overall length of sign panels must be in increments of one foot (12"). Signs up to 8' long are fabricated as a single panel. For longer signs, place joint on a module division; joints should not break letters or words.

Text may run across two or more modules. Any module containing text must be extended to the next whole foot before other elements are added.

This illustration shows a sign made up of multiple modules containing arrow, text and a route designator. Note that the text modules have been extended to the next whole foot before adding other elements. In the layout and specification of sign sizes, text length must be measured accurately so an adequate number of modules are provided for. Blank modules should be used to separate different messages.

Ⓜ **Metropolitan Transportation Authority**

1989

218

216 Title page, *MTA Sign Manual: New York City Transit Authority, Long Island Rail Road*, **Metro-North Commuter Railroad** (1989).

217 "Typography: Alphabet." *MTA Sign Manual: New York City Transit Authority, Long Island Rail Road*, **Metro-North Commuter Railroad** **(1989), p. 2.5.** "Any other form of Helvetica (e.g., Condensed, Regular, etc.) or other typefaces, are never to be used as a sub-stitute for Helvetica Medium or Helvetica Medium Italic." The manual did not address the issue of Helvetica vs. Neue Helvetica.

218 "Basic Sign Module: Uses." *MTA Sign Manual: New York City Transit Authority, Long Island Rail Road*, **Metro-North Commuter Railroad** **(1989), p. 2.2.**

219

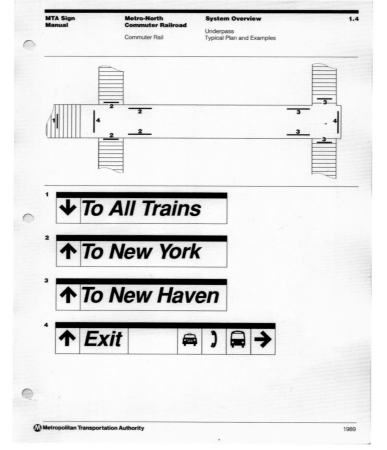

1   ↓ **To All Trains**

2   ↑ **To New York**

3   ↑ **To New Haven**

4   ↑ **Exit**   🚕) 🚌 →

220

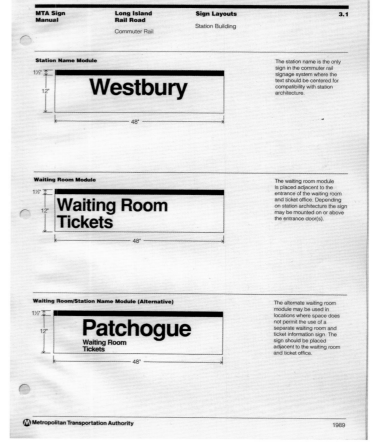

Station Name Module

1½"   3"
12"

Westbury

48"

The station name is the only sign in the commuter rail signage system where the text should be centered for compatibility with station architecture.

Waiting Room Module

1½"   3"
12"

Waiting Room Tickets

48"

The waiting room module is placed adjacent to the entrance of the waiting room and ticket office. Depending on station architecture the sign may be mounted on or above the entrance door(s).

Waiting Room/Station Name Module (Alternative)

1½"   3"
12"

Patchogue
Waiting Room
Tickets

48"

The alternate waiting room module may be used in locations where space does not permit the use of a separate waiting room and ticket information sign. The sign should be placed adjacent to the waiting room and ticket office.

221

A second reason is that by the end of the 1980s most MTA buses were using LED displays which rendered the whole Standard/Helvetica debate moot. (A similar situation is now occurring with the newest subway cars which have LED displays instead of disks and roll-ups for route designations (figs. 273–275).) Since 1972 MaBSTOA, a subsidiary of the NYCTA, had used Standard for the route designations on the front of its buses. The signs were originally white letters on a black background but at some point they changed to white letters on a combined blue and red background—blue for the number/letter code and name and red for the route description. Several of the 1970s-era buses continued to operate into the early 1990s, but from 1980 on they were increasingly supplanted by boxy Grumman Flxible and sleek General Motors RTS buses with LED displays [70]

A third reason is that technological changes in typesetting and graphic design were overtaking the MTA Marketing Communications Division. By the end of the 1980s the full effects of the desktop publishing (DTP) revolution—touched off in 1984 by the conjunction of the Apple Macintosh, Apple LaserWriter, Adobe PostScript page description language and Aldus PageMaker software—had begun to be felt in the graphic design community. The typesetting choices faced by Unimark in 1966 had increased. The 1989 *MTA Sign Manual* listed the following equipment: digital type (Linotronic), phototype (Compugraphic and typositor), tape-based lettering systems (Kroy and Merlin), computer-driven letter- and stencil-cutting systems (Gerber Signmaker, figs. 205, 208) vinyl self-adhesive letters (from various manufacturers), and fabricated or cut-out letters in plastic and other materials. The only typeface that was available for all of these systems and methods was Helvetica. Furthermore, Standard had virtually "disappeared". It was still listed in the VGC Typositor library but not in specimen books from Compugraphic, Linotype or Adobe. They offered either Berthold Akzidenz Grotesk—the true identity of Standard—or a revised version called AG Old Face. The mix-and-match mentality of the mid-1960s was no longer an option. Helvetica (or Neue Helvetica) was the logical choice. [71]

219 Porcelain enamel station sign. **Woodlawn (Metro-North Hudson line).** Note the redundant NYCTA sign at the right. (2009)

220 "System Overview: Underpass, Typical Plan and Examples." *MTA Sign Manual: New York City Transit Authority, Long Island Rail Road, Metro-North Commuter Railroad* (1989), p. 1.4.

221 "Sign Layouts: Station Building." *MTA Sign Manual: New York City Transit Authority, Long Island Rail Road, Metro-North Commuter Railroad* (1989), p. 3.1.

222 Porcelain enamel station sign. **Larchmont (Metro-North Hudson line), 1970s.** Prior to the official standards of 1989 this sign copied the Unimark style of the TA.

70. No one has taken credit for the transference of the NYCTA subway signage standards to the buses, though Michael Hertz worked on bus route maps in 1973. This discussion of type used on the bus route designators is based on photographs found at nycsubway.org: e.g. 1972 Amsterdam, 1973 Eastchester, 1974 Bronx BX26, 1976 M41 Culture Loop). The "New Look" General Motors Coach, Model T6H-5309A, was first made in 1972 and the General Motors RTS in 1977. The first Flxible was introduced in 1973. By 1981, when the RTS004 version made its debut, Grumman had taken over the company. For detailed information on the various buses that MaBSTOA has employed over the years see en.wikipedia.org/wiki/Buses_used_by_NYCTA_before_1980.

71. The term DTP was coined by Paul Brainerd of Aldus in 1985. The methods of setting type for signs is outlined in Metropolitan Transportation Authority. *MTA Sign Manual: New York City Transit Authority, Long Island Rail Road, Metro-North Commuter Railroad.* (New York: Metropolitan Transportation Authority, 1989), p. 2.8. AG Old Face was designed by Günter Gerhard Lange in 1984 for Berthold AG as a regularized version of its Akzidenz Grotesk. Even Helvetica posed a problem at the time. "Compugraphic should not be used for signs because their version of Helvetica Medium does not match the version shown in this manual," according to the 1988 working draft. See *Graphic Standards: Signage.* (1988), n.p. Peter Joseph says that the lack of Standard on CAD-CAM systems that drove signmaking machines was a primary hurdle. Peter

Joseph interview with author, 15 August 2008. These systems (such as Gerber Signmaker) were used to produce "all types of signs, including both cut-out, applied letters for temporary signs and shop-drawings and stencils for porcelain enamel signs". See *Graphic Standards: Signage.* (1988), n.p.

222

223 Porcelain enamel station sign. Beach 36 Street / Edgemere (A). (2010)

224 Porcelain enamel station sign. Jackson Avenue (2/5). (2009)

225–229 Porcelain enamel column signs, post-1989. Despite detailed guidance on proper spelling, hyphenation and abbreviation in the 1989 and 1995 signage manuals, column signs continue to pose problems.

225 Porcelain enamel girder column sign. Kingsbridge Road (4). The second syllable of Kingsbridge has been improperly capitalized. (2009)

226 Porcelain enamel cast-iron column sign. Third Avenue / 149th Street (2/5). Periods have been incorrectly added to the abbreviations for both Avenue and Street. (2010)

227 Porcelain enamel girder column sign. Burnside Avenue (4). (2009)

228 Porcelain enamel girder column sign. Pelham Bay Park (6). The letterspacing is too loose. Compare to (**227**). (2009)

229 Porcelain enamel girder column sign. 42 Street / Port Authority (A/C/E). 2008)

223–224

Kings-
Bridge
Rd

225

Av.
49 St.

226–227

Pelham
Bay
Park

Burn-
side
Av

42 St
Port Authority
Bus Terminal

228–229

230 Congery of signs. Elmhurst Avenue (G/R/V). A porcelain enamel exit sign in Helvetica Medium joins signs in wood, mosaic and tile. (2008)

231 Porcelain enamel station entrance sign. 23rd Street (B/F). (2008)

232 Porcelain enamel station entrance sign. Ft. Hamilton Parkway (F). (2009)

233 Porcelain enamel station entrance sign. 23rd Street (1). (2008)

234 Porcelain enamel platform sign. 15th Street–Prospect Park (F). (2009)

235 Porcelain enamel exit sign with sheet metal addition. Annadale (SIR). SIR is the Staten Island Railway portion of the subway system. (2010)

236 Porcelain enamel platform sign with peeling vinyl coating. 34th Street–Herald Square (B/D/F/V). Since the early 1990s a clear vinyl coating has been added to porcelain enamel signs to make it easier to clean graffiti. Yellowing of the coating causes variations in whiteness among signs. John Montemarano, email to author 22 June 2009. (2009)

Helvetica actually appeared officially on signs in the subway system at least a few months prior to the release of the 1989 *MTA Sign Manual*. In October of that year, when the long-delayed 63rd Street tunnel was finally opened, its three new stations—63rd Street/Lexington Avenue, Roosevelt Island and 21st Street/Queensbridge—all sported 1968-designed interiors and signage in Helvetica Medium. [**72**]

Siegel + Gale rebranded the MTA in 1994, replacing the two-toned M logo with the letters "MTA" rendered in perspective within a circle (fig. 239). "A unifying identity system embracing subways, buses, commuter trains, and bridges was needed to facilitate employment of the MetroCard, an electronic payment card that replaced tokens, transfers, and exact change," according to partner Alan Siegel. The new logo accompanied the development and introduction of the MetroCard.

The electronic farecard—first used on buses in 1994 and then extended to the entire transportation system in 1995—forced the Marketing & Communications Division, led by Alicia Martinez, to revise its signage manual once again and to expand its design guidelines beyond signage to all forms of communication. Michael Hertz Associates was hired to handle the signage manual while the *Service Identity Manual* was done in-house. The latter included not only the MetroCards but stationery, maps, kiosks, booths, and vehicles. Lock-ups for the new logo in combination with the existing logos for each of the MTA's sub-units (e.g. Staten Island Railway, Bridges and Tunnels) were created using Helvetica Medium and Helvetica Medium Italic. But for printed material the typographic options were opened up to include other weights of Helvetica as well as Times Roman. Most likely, the ready availability of Helvetica and Times Roman as core fonts on PCs was the prime factor in this decision. Dull but easy to administer. [**73**]

72. It is possible that the 1988 Archer Avenue line extension signage was also set in Helvetica Medium from the start but there are no reliable photographs to support this idea; and Michael Hertz does not recall the signage for those stations specifically. Some of the signs that exist today are in Standard Medium. As has already been noted, Helvetica (in various incarnations) had already been used in limited and inconsistent ways within the system.

In January 1989 the TA set, as one of its goals for the year: "Bring signage on 136 stations up to current standards." New York City Transit Authority, *1989 Goals: Building for the Future*, January 1989, p. iii. Did this mean switching from Standard to Helvetica?

73. *MTA Service Identity Manual*. (1995). Planning for the MetroCard was begun in 1987. It was introduced on buses in 1994 and at two subway stations (Whitehall Street and Wall Street nos. 4 and 5) before being rolled out system wide in 1995. Lisa W. Foderaro, "Fare Cards Make Debut In Subways," *New York Times*, January 6, 1994. Doris Halle, Design Director at the MTA, was responsible for the hiring of Siegel Gale. To accompany the MetroCard the slogan "Going your way" was introduced. siegelonbranding.com/pictures/90/. Also see abriefmessage.com/2007/11/07/gordon/ "Something Gold, Something Blue" by Emily Gordon 7 November 2007 re: problems with the MetroCard design; and "We Don't Want People to Like Us, We Just Want Them to Hate Us Less" in *Reputation Management* July/August 1995, pp. 55–59.

The 1995 manual elevated core fonts to standards status. This may have, intentionally or not, led to the use of such fonts as the basis for new mosaic nameplates in renovated stations. For example, Arial is the basis for the mosaics at Brooklyn Bridge/City Hall (**264**), Times Roman for mosaics at several BMT stations in Brooklyn (e.g. Cortelyou Road) (**261**), and ITC Bookman for the mosaics at Fulton Street (nos. 2 and 3), Broad Street (J/M/Z) and Botanic Garden (S). The BMT stations were renovated in 1994, Brooklyn Bridge in 1996, Broad Street c.1997, Botanic Garden in 1998 and Fulton Street c.2005.

230

231–233

234–236

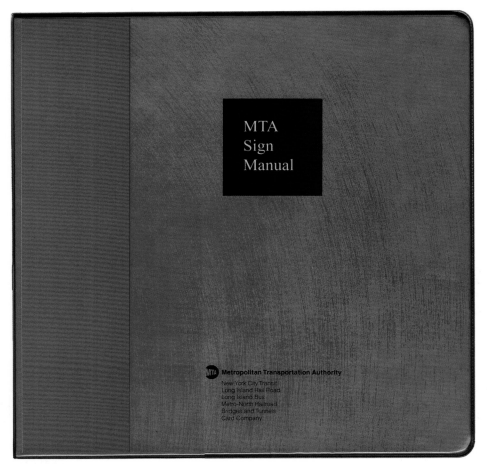

237

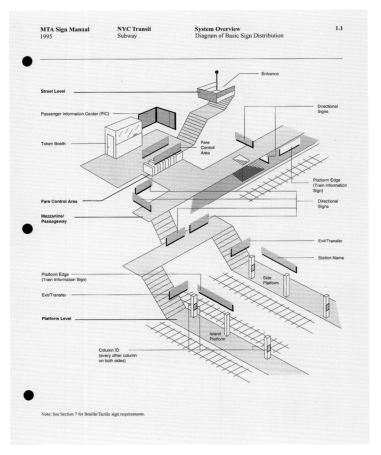

MTA Sign Manual
1995
NYC Transit
Subway
System Overview
Diagram of Basic Sign Distribution
1.1

Entrance

Street Level

Passenger Information Center (PIC)

Token Booth

Fare Control Area

Directional Signs

Platform Edge (Train Information Sign)

Directional Signs

Fare Control Area

Exit/Transfer

Mezzanine/ Passageway

Station Name

Platform Edge (Train Information Sign)

Exit/Transfer

Side Platform

Platform Level

Column ID (every other column on both sides)

Island Platform

Note: See Section 7 for Braille/Tactile sign requirements.

238

239

237–238, 240–241 *MTA Sign Manual: New York City Transit Authority, Long Island Rail Road*, **Metro-North Commuter Railroad (New York: Metropolitan Transportation Authority, 1995).**
Design by the Marketing & Corporate Communications Division, Metropolitan Transportation Authority.

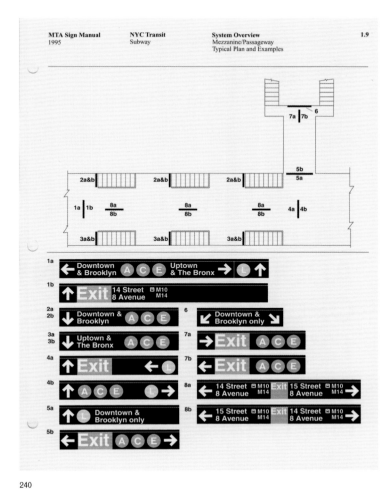

240

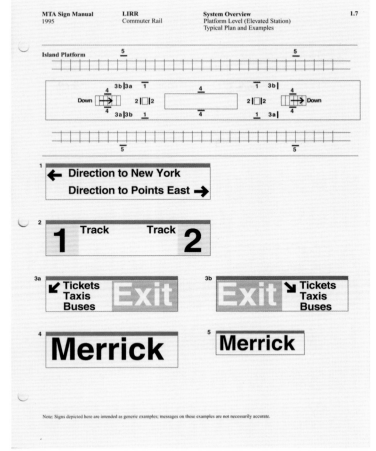

Note: Signs depicted here are intended as generic examples; messages on these examples are not necessarily accurate.

241

237 Binder cover. *MTA Sign Manual: New York City Transit Authority, Long Island Rail Road*, **Metro-North Commuter Railroad** (1995).

238 "NYC Transit: Subway. System Overview: Diagram of Basic Sign Distribution." *MTA Sign Manual: New York City Transit Authority, Long Island Rail Road*, **Metro-North Commuter Railroad** (1995), **p. 1.1.**

239 MTA New York City Subway logo. IRT train. (2009)

240 "NYC Transit: Subway. Mezzanine / Passageway: Typical Plan and Examples." *MTA Sign Manual: New York City Transit Authority, Long Island Rail Road, Metro-North Commuter Railroad* (1995), **p. 1.9.**

241 "LIRR Commuter Rail. Platform Level (Elevated Station): Typical Plan and Examples." *MTA Sign Manual: New York City Transit Authority, Long Island Rail Road*, **Metro-North Commuter Railroad** (1995), **p. 1.7.**

242 Metal Braille sign, 14th Street (A /C/E), post-2003. Braille signs, set in Helvetica, were installed in stations on girder columns in compliance with the Americans with Disabilities Act of 1990. (2010)

242

Helvetica®
bold/halbfett/demi-gras

07130   12 pt Design

Sans Serif / Serifenlose Antiqua / Antiques
Max A. Miedinger 1957, Haas'sche Schriftgiesserei AG/D. Stempel AG
Linotype

abcdefghijklmnopqr
stuvwxyz fiflß&
ABCDEFGHIJKLMN
OPQRSTUVWXYZ
1234567890 .,:;-–— ''
1234567890 „"""•‹›«‹›»*
%‰!?¡¿()[]/†‡§$£¢ƒ

243

Helvetica®
bold No. 2/halbfett Nr. 2/demi-gras No. 2

69130   18 pt Design

Sans Serif / Serifenlose Antiqua / Antiques
1973, D. Stempel AG (Haas'sche Schriftgiesserei AG)
Linotype

abcdefghijklmnopq
rstuvwxyz fiflß&
ABCDEFGHIJKLMN
OPQRSTUVWXYZ
1234567890
.,:;-–— '',""•‹›«‹›»*%‰
!?¡¿()[]/†‡§$£¢ƒ

244

243–247 Examples of various film cuts of Helvetica from *Linotype Collection: Mergenthaler Type Library* (Eschborn bei Frankfurt: Linotype GmbH, 1986).

243 Helvetica Bold (Haas'sche Schriftgiesseri AG / D. Stempel AG, Max Miedinger and Eduard Hoffmann, 1957), 12 pt design, 4220.110. Although labeled Bold this is the typeface that Unimark and other American designers knew as Helvetica Medium.

244 Helvetica Bold 2 (D. Stempel AG, Haas'sche Schriftgiesseri AG, 1973), 12 pt design, 4220.120. Although labeled Bold 2 this is the typeface that Unimark and other American designers knew as Helvetica Bold.

245 Neue Helvetica 65 (Medium) (D. Stempel AG, 1983), 12 pt design, 4200.90. The Medium is now translated as Kräftig in German and Quart-Gras in French (or Quarter-Bold). Note the lightness of the design as well as the tail on the **a**.

246 Neue Helvetica 75 (Bold) (D. Stempel AG, 1983), 12 pt design, 4200.110. The Bold is Halbfett in German and Demi-Gras in French, both of which often translate as Medium in English. This is where the problem in the subway signs began. By 1989 when Helvetica Medium was made the official typeface of the subway system there was Helvetica Bold which was known in this country as Helvetica Medium and Neue Helvetica 65 (Medium). The 1995

MTA Sign Manual specified that the face be Helvetica Medium (p. 2.4) but that for digital sources it should be Neue Helvetica 65 (Medium) (p. 2.5). Yet p. 2.4 explicitly stated that "alphabets must match exactly the weight of characters illustrated on this page" while showing the old Helvetica Medium. It is not surprising that those carrying out new signs initially used Neue Helvetica 65 instead of Neue Helvetica 75 or the old Helvetica Medium (Bold). See **248, 249** for instance.

247 Helvetica Inserat (D. Stempel AG, 1966), 18 pt design, 4220.320, **detail.** Note the **r** which differs from those of Helvetica Compressed and Helvetica Black Condensed.

248 Folio Bold Condensed (Konrad F. Bauer and Walter Baum, Bauersche Gießerei, 1956), 18 pt design, 25101, **detail.** Folio Bold Condensed is nearly identical to Helvetica Inserat—e.g. the cross-stroke of **t** is slightly longer on the right—and may have been used because the latter was unavailable. Helvetica Inserat has a taller x-height. See **247**.

249 Porcelain enamel warning sign. **Borough Hall (4/5).** Set in Neue Helvetica 65 (Medium). (2009)

250 Porcelain enamel warning sign. **Elder Avenue (6).** Set in Helvetica Medium. Note the incorrect shade of red. (2009)

251 Porcelain enamel column sign. **Grant Avenue (A),** c.1986. Set in Helvetica Ultra Compressed. (2008)

252 Porcelain enamel column sign. **Hoyt–Schermerhorn Streets (A/C/G),** c.1986. Set in Helvetica Inserat. (2009)

neue Helvetica® 65
medium/kräftig/quart-gras

06472 12 pt Design

Sans Serif / Serifenlose Antiqua / Antiques
D. Stempel AG, 1983
Linotype

abcdefghijklmnopqr
stuvwxyz fiflß&
ABCDEFGHIJKLMN
OPQRSTUVWXYZ
1234567890
.,:;--— '',"""·‹›«»*%‰
!?¡¿()[]/†‡§$£a¢ƒ

245

neue Helvetica® 75
bold/halbfett/demi-gras

07472 12 pt Design

Sans Serif / Serifenlose Antiqua / Antiques
D. Stempel AG, 1983
Linotype

abcdefghijklmnopqr
stuvwxyz fiflß&
ABCDEFGHIJKLMN
OPQRSTUVWXYZ
1234567890
.,:;--— '',"""·‹›«»*%‰
!?¡¿()[]/†‡§$£¢ƒ

246

abcdefghijklmnop
qrstuvwxyz fiflß&
ABCDEFGHIJKLMN
OPQRSTUVWXYZ
1234567890

247

abcdefghijklmno
pqrstuvwxyz fiflß&
ABCDEFGHIJKLMNO
PQRSTUVWXYZ
1234567890

248

249–252

HELVETICA TRIUMPHANT:
THE SUBWAY SYSTEM TODAY

It took nineteen years for Helvetica to replace Standard as the official typeface of the New York City subway system. But it was only after 1992, when the MTA undertook a major multi-year station renovation program—that the creeping process of 'Helvetica-ization' gained momentum. The program included rooting out older signs, installing new signs in Helvetica Medium and adding artwork, much of it in mosaic tile. In several stations the new artwork—part of the Arts for Transit program begun in the mid-1980s—was accompanied by refurbished or new mosaic tile and terracotta station names (figs. 253, 254, 256, 257, 262–265). The station renovation program, which continues at a slower pace today, also introduced standardized temporary signage to the system that reversed the figure/ground relationship in order to be noticed. (These black-on-white signs are a startling echo of the original Unimark signage (figs. 266, 277).) [74]

The cumulative effect of the changes occasioned by the station renovation program has been to keep the signage of the system in flux even as it becomes more and more uniform. Moreover, the economics and logistics that militated against a complete overhaul of the old signage in the 1970s still pertain today and thus numerous signs in Standard (albeit white on black) remain in place.

The sign system that Noorda and Vignelli first proposed to the NYCTA in 1966 has proved remarkably resilient. It endures today despite a number of severe changes that make one wonder if it can even be attributed to them and Unimark anymore. Their modular system survives but only as graphic units rather than physical components. The black band, mistakenly created by the sign shop but then integrated into the 1970 standards manual, has been replaced by a white stripe to accommodate the reversal of the black-on-white color scheme. The colored disks are still used—some with their original artwork in Standard—but the colors themselves have changed. Finally, Standard Medium has given way to Helvetica Medium—or more accurately to Neue Helvetica 75. Yet, not only is the Unimark DNA still in evidence but it has served as the basis for a much broader transportation system identity. [75]

253 (oposite page) Mosaic artwork. Sutphin Boulevard (E/J/Z), 1988. (2008)

74. Since 1993 John Montemarano has overseen all planning, surveying, fabrication, installation and maintenance of signs as Director of the Station Signage Department within the Division of Stations. The Bergen Street Sign Shop is part of his department. It is responsible for the temporary construction signs, but it does not get involved in the mosaics. The black-on-white signs are intended to call attention to service changes that might go unnoticed by everyday commuters. Signs at construction sites not in Helvetica Medium have been erected by contractors rather than the MTA (266). As long as their information is accurate they are left in place. Louis M. Brill, "Taking the A-Train (or Any Other Train) in New York City Would Be Even Harder Without Directional Signage" at signindustry.com/architectural/articles/2007-11-15-LB-NYC_Subway_WayFinding_Signs_Signage.ph, p.3; and John Montemarano interview with author, 18 June 2009.

75. In 1983 the staff of D. Stempel AG redesigned and reorganized the members of the Helvetica family to make them more internally consistent. The goal was to make the family as harmonious as the Univers family. (The individual faces were even given numbers following Frutiger's system.) The new face was named Neue Helvetica (adjective in front not after) to distinguish it from its famous parent.

A revised version of the 1995 manual is currently underway according to John Montemarano. It will incorporate changes that have occurred in the intervening decade and a half, including signs that are in compliance with the Americans with Disabilities Act of 1990. The white-on-black signs are not at risk since ADA 2002 says, "The greatest readability is usually achieved through the use of light-colored characters or symbols on a dark background." A4.30.4 "Finish and Contrast in ADA Accessibility Guidelines for Buildings and Facilities (ADAAG)" as amended September 2002. To accompany them, Braille signs (242) in Helvetica have been installed on girder columns at most stations over the past five years. John Montemarano interview with author, 18 June 2009.

This broader transportation system identity faces two challenges to its integrity and, by extension, to the dominance of Helvetica. The first is vernacular and the second is technological. "Official" handmade signs—like those that incensed William Lansing Plumb in 1965—continue to appear in subway stations. Token booth clerks, station supervisors, track workers, outside contractors and others hastily erect such signs to solve their immediate needs without regard to the guidelines of a graphics standards manual (fig. 266, 268). Although ostensibly temporary, these signs sometimes remain in place for months. They are unlikely to ever be wholly eradicated.

In the last decade new subway cars equipped with roll-sign line indicators, LCD (liquid crystal display) destination signs and interior strip route guides with LED (light emitting diode) stop indicators have been introduced into the system along with "next-train" annunciators in stations (figs. 269–275). These electronic signs have limited typographic options that bypass Helvetica and reduced color palettes that ignore the familiar PMS colors associated with train routes. However, the vast majority of signs in the subway system will remain resolutely static, set in Helvetica Medium in white on black and fabricated from tin plate or porcelain enamel. They are now as much a part of the New York City subway system's visual identity as its century-old mosaics. [**76**]

76. Subway cars (models R-142A and R-142B) equipped with "New Technology" were first introduced in December 1999. Newer cars (models R-160A and R-160B) with more advanced electronic route maps were added to the fleet in 2005. The first electronic annunciators were installed along the Canarsie Line (L) in February 2007. Computer screens (with text in Helvetica) showing the position of trains along that line—made possible by Computer Based Train Control (CBTC)—were installed in the Myrtle Avenue / Wyckoff Avenue station in October 2008. See nycsubway.org/cars/b-div-new-tech.html;

William Neuman, "How Long Till Next Train? The Answer Is Up in Lights", *New York Times*, February 17, 2007; United States Department of Transportation, Federal Transit Administration, fta.dot.gov/about/news_events_8808.html; and William Neuman, "There Is another Train Right Behind", *New York Times*, October 22, 2008.

254–259

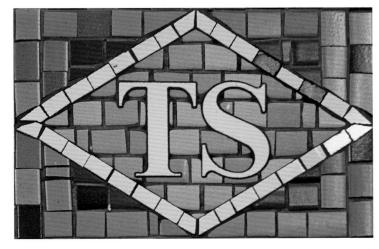

254 Tile directional sign. Queens Plaza (E/G/R/V), 1998. The one-piece tile letters fail to mimic older mosaic ones along the IND Queens Boulevard Line. (2010)

255 Mosaic tile station name. Spring Street (C/E), 1994. (2009)

256 Mosaic tile station name. 161st Street / River Avenue (B/D), 2002. Design by Di Domenico Partners with artist Vito Acconci. Arts for Transit program. This is an imitation of the original IND style mosaics but it is poorly done. The crudeness of the execution is evident in the curves of the **6** and **s**. (2009)

257 Mosaic tile station name. Columbus Circle (1), 2010. This new mosaic is ostensibly a replica of the station's original mosaics. The letters are awkwardly rendered, the spacing is horrific and the green is the wrong shade. Aware of this, the MTA claimed it was only a test design, but months later it was permanently installed. (2010)

258 Mosaic tile station name. 18th Street (1), early 1990s. The letters are a poor attempt to replicate the original mosaic letters at the station. (2005)

259 Mosaic tile station name. Canal Street (N/Q/R/W), 1998. Mosaic by Bing Lee. Except for the **T** the letters are similar to Adobe Garamond. (2007

260 Mosaic tile station name. Broad Street (J/M), c.1997. The mosaic letters, based on ITC Bookman Light, are mechanically cut. (2008)

261 Mosaic tile station name. Cortelyou Road (Q), 1994. The letters are a modified version of Times Roman (note the **y**). (2008)

262 Glazed tile station name. 116th Street (2/3), 1996. The letters are an electronically condensed version of Times Roman. (2007)

263 Glazed tile station name. 125th Street (2/3), 1996. The letters are an electronically condensed version of Bodoni Book. Note the upside down **S**. (2009)

264 Terracotta station wall signs. Brooklyn Bridge / City Hall (4/5/6), 1996. City Hall is set in ITC Cheltenham; Brooklyn Bridge is set in Arial. (2008)

265 Glazed tile station initials. Times Square—42nd Street (N/Q/R/W). **TS** (for Times Square) is an outline version of Times Roman. (2008)

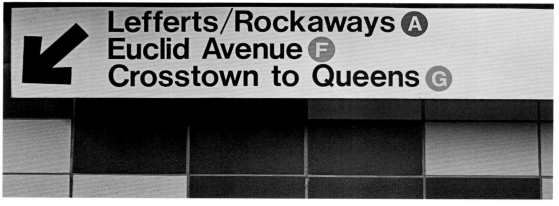

266–267

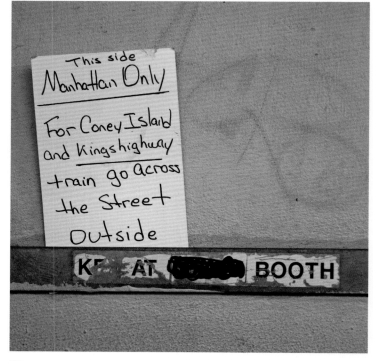

268

266–268 Temporary signs, 2008–2010.

266 Temporary corrugated plastic directional sign. 59th Street–Columbus Circle (1/A/B/C/D), 2008. Created by Judlau Contracting Inc. The typeface is an electronically condensed version of ITC Franklin Gothic Light. (2009)

267 Temporary foamcore directional sign for quick installation and removal during weekend service diversion. Hoyt Street–Schermerhorn Street (A/C/G), 2009. This is close to what the original Unimark signs were designed to look like in 1970. (2009)

268 Handwritten directional sign. Avenue N (F), 2010. (2010)

269–275 Electronic signage, 1999–2008

269 Semi-electronic route map. IRT Lexington Avenue Line (4), 1999. A printed plastic card overlay, derived from a 1970 Unimark design (108), shows the entire route and transfer points. Lights mark each station. The typeface is Helvetica Medium. (2010)

270 FIND (Flexible INformation Display) electronic route map. BMT Broadway / Fourth Avenue Line (N), 2005. Ten stations plus five "further stations" are displayed. The conductor reprograms the route display on the fly. The LED typeface is an approximation of Helvetica. (2009)

271 Train Locator Console. Myrtle Avenue / Wyckoff Avenue (L), 2008. The typeface is Helvetica Medium. (2010)

272 Roll-sign with electronic addition. IRT Flushing Line (7), 1999. A green circle denotes an express train and a green diamond a local train. (2009)

273 LED roll-sign. BMT Broadway / Fourth Avenue Line (N), 2005. (2009)

274 LED roll-sign. IRT Pelham Line (6), 2003. (2010)

275 Electronic annunciator. Atlantic Avenue / Pacific Street, IRT Eastern Parkway Line (4/5), 2010. The typeface mimics Helvetica. (2010)

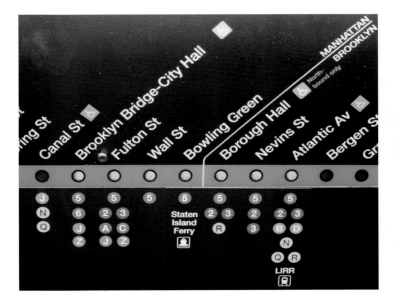

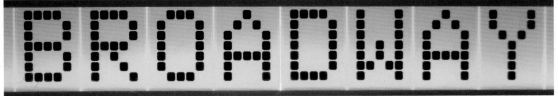

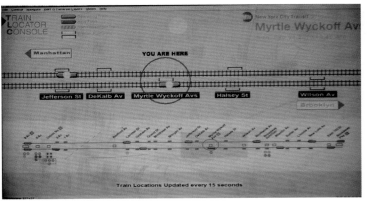

269–271

272–275

119

CHRONOLOGY

1878

Brooklyn, Flatbush and Coney Island
Railway stations that are now part of BMT
Brighton Line
Church Avenue
Newkirk Avenue
Kings Highway
Neck Road
Sheepshead Bay
Brighton Beach

Brooklyn, Flatbush and Coney Island
Railway station that is now part of BMT
Franklin Avenue Shuttle)
Prospect Park

1885

Brooklyn Elevated Railroad stations that are
now part of BMT Jamaica Line
Van Siclen Avenue
Alabama Avenue
Broadway Junction (originally Manhattan
Beach Crossing)
Chauncey Street
Halsey Street
Gates Avenue

before 1888

Brooklyn, Flatbush and Coney Island
Railway stations that are now part of BMT
Brighton Line
Avenue M

1888

Brooklyn Elevated Railraod stations that
became part of BMT Jamaica Line
Kosciuszko Street
Myrtle Avenue
Park Avenue
Flushing Avenue
Lorimer Street
Hewes Street
Marcy Avenue
Driggs Avenue
Broadway Ferry

1888

Union Elevated Railroad stations that
became part of BMT Myrtle Avenue Line
Washington Avenue
Vanderbilt Avenue
Navy Street
Bridge / Jay Streets
Adams Street
Sands Street

1889

Union Elevated Railroad stations that
became part of BMT Myrtle Avenue Line
Wyckoff Avenue
Knickerbocker Avenue
Central Avenue
Broadway / Myrtle Avenue
Sumner Avenue
Tompkins Avenue
Nostrand Avenue
Franklin Avenue
Grand Avenue

1893

Brooklyn Elevated Railraod stations that are
now part of BMT Jamaica Line
Cleveland Street
Norwood Avenue
Crescent Street
Cypress Hills

before 1895

Brooklyn, Flatbush and Coney Island
Railway station that is now part of BMT
Brighton Line
Parkside Avenue

1896

Brooklyn Rapid Transit Company
incorporated

Kings County Elevated Railway stations that
became part of Franklin Avenue Shuttle
Consumer's Park
Dean Street
Franklin Avenue

before 1897

Brooklyn, Flatbush and Coney Island
Railway stations that are now part of
BMT Brighton Line
Avenue H

1898

Union Elevated Railroad that became part of
BMT Myrtle Avenue Line
Park Row

Akzidenz Grotesk halbfett (medium)
(H. Berthold AG, Berlin)

1890s

Brooklyn, Flatbush and Coney Island
Railway station now part of BMT
Brighton Line
Beverley Road

Brooklyn Rapid Transit Company acquired
Sea Beach Railway, Sea View Railroad,
Nassau Electric Railroad, Brooklyn
Elevated Railroad, Brooklyn and Brighton
Beach Railroad, Kings County Elevated
Railroad and Prospect Park and Coney
Island Railroad

1900

Kings County Elevated Railway station that
became part of Franklin Avenue Shuttle
Park Place

277

1904

Interborough Rapid Transit Company (IRT)
begun; 28 stations from City Hall to 42nd
Street and then East Side and West Side
branches north to 145th Street
City Hall
Brooklyn Bridge
Worth Street
Canal Street
Spring Street
Bleecker Street
Astor Place
14th Street [Union Square]
18th Street
23rd Street
28th Street
33rd Street
Grand Central (currently the shuttle)
West Side Branch
42nd Street [Times Square]
50th Street
59th Street [Columbus Circle]
66th Street
72nd Street
79th Street
86th Street
91st Street
96th Street
103rd Street
110th Street
116th Street [Columbia University]
125th Street
137th Street
145th Street
East Side Branch
110th Street [Central Park North]
116th Street
125th Street
135th Street
145th Street

Bronx elevated railway stations now part of
the IRT White Plains Road Line
Jackson Avenue
Prospect Avenue
Intervale Avenue (originally Intervale
Avenue / 163rd Street)
Simpson Street
Freeman Street
174th Street
East Tremont Street / 177th Street
(now West Farms Square / East
Tremont Avenue)
180th Street

1905

IRT East Side Branch extended
Fulton Street
Wall Street
Bowling Green
South Ferry

IRT East Side Branch extended
into the Bronx
Mott Avenue (now 149th Street / Grand
Concourse)
Third Avenue / 149th Street

Franklin Avenue Shuttle
Prospect Park
Parkside Avenue

1906

Brooklyn Rapid Transit Company (BRT)
stations now part of BMT Canarsie Line
Broadway Junction
Atlantic Avenue
Sutter Avenue
Livonia Avenue
New Lots Avenue
East 105th Street
Rockaway Parkway

IRT West Side Branch extended
157th Street
168th Street
181st Street
Dyckman Street
207th Street
215th Street

Lutheran Cemetery Line station now
terminus of BMT Myrtle Avenue Line
Middle Village / Metropolitan Avenue

1907

IRT West Side Branch extended
into the Bronx
225th Street
231st Street

Brooklyn, Flatbush and Coney Island
Railway station now part of BMT
Brighton Line
Avenue J

276 (opposite page) Porcelain enamel
station entrance sign. President
Street (2/5), 1920. Photograph by
Lucia McCreery. This is what IRT
entrance signs looked like prior to
the introduction of the Unimark sign
system. Also see the signs in (**47**,
169.) (2008)

277 Terracotta station name.
103rd Street (1), 1905. (2008)

1908

IRT extended into Brooklyn
Borough Hall
Hoyt Street
Nevins Street
Atlantic Avenue

IRT West Side Branch extended to Van Cortlandt Park
238th Street
Van Cortlandt Park / 242nd Street

Hudson & Manhattan Railroad established (now Port Authority Trans Hudson or PATH)

BMT Nassau Street Line
Essex Street

1911

New York Westchester & Boston Railway stations now part of IRT Dyre Avenue Line
Eastchester–Dyre Avenue
Baychester Avenue
Gun Hill Road
Pelham Parkway
Morris Park

1913

Brooklyn Rapid Transit Company signed Dual Contracts

BMT Nassau Street Line; later joined BMT Jamaica Line
Bowery
Canal Street
Chambers Street
Fulton Street

1915

BMT Myrtle Avenue Line opened
DeKalb Avenue
Canal Street
Metropolitan Avenue
Fresh Pond Road
Forest Avenue
Seneca Avenue

BMT Sea Beach Line; joined BMT West End and BMT Brighton Lines at Coney Island / Stillwell Avenue
Gravesend / 86th Street
Avenue U
Kings Highway
Bay Parkway (originally 22nd Avenue)
20th Avenue
18th Avenue
New Utrecht Avenue
Fort Hamilton Parkway
Eighth Avenue

BMT Fourth Avenue Line opened
Pacific Street
Union Street
9th Street
Prospect Avenue
25th Street
36th Street
45th Street
53rd Street
59th Street
Bay Ridge Avenue

BMT Fulton Street Line opened
80th Street / Hudson Street
88th Street / Boyd Avenue
Rockaway Boulevard
104th Street / Oxford Avenue
111th Street / Greenwood Avenue
Ozone Park / Lefferts Boulevard

IRT Flushing Line opened
Grand Central
Vernon Boulevard / Jackson Boulevard

1916

BMT West End Line opened
25th Avenue
Bay Parkway (22nd Avenue)
20th Avenue
18th Avenue
79th Street
71st Street
62nd Street
55th Street
50th Street
Fort Hamilton Parkway
Ninth Avenue

BMT Fourth Avenue Line
77th Street
86th Street

BMT Culver Line opened
9th Avenue

IRT Flushing Line
Hunters Point Avenue
Court House Square
Queensboro Plaza

BMT Jamaica Line stations closed
Park Avenue
Driggs Avenue
Broadway Ferry

1917

IRT East Side Branch extended (now IRT White Plains Road Line)
East 180 Street
Bronx Park East
Pelham Parkway
Allerton Avenue
Burke Avenue
Gun Hill Road
219th Street
225th Street
233rd Street
238th Street / Nereid Avenue

IRT East Side Branch extended into Bronx (now IRT Jerome Avenue Line)
149th Street / Grand Concourse (originally Mott Avenue)
161st Street / River Avenue [Yankee Stadium]
167th Street
170th Street
Mt. Eden Avenue
176th Street
Burnside Avenue
183rd Street
Fordham Road
Kingsbridge Road

IRT Flushing Line (shared with BMT 1923–1949)
Queensboro Plaza
33rd Street–Rawson Street
40th Street–Lowery Street
46th Street–Bliss Street
52nd Street (originally Lincoln Avenue)
Woodside / 61st Street
69th Street (originally Fisk Avenue)
74th Street / Broadway (originally Broadway)
82nd Street / Jackson Heights (originally 25th Street / Jackson Heights)
90th Street / Elmhurst Avenue (originally Elmhurst Avenue)
Junction Boulevard (originally Junction Avenue)
103rd Street / Corona Plaza (originally Alburtus Avenue)

278

IRT Queensboro Line spur opened (now BMT Astoria Line)
Queensboro Plaza
39th Avenue (originally Beebe Avenue)
36th Avenue (originally Washington Avenue)
Broadway
30th Avenue (originally Grand Avenue)
Astoria Boulevard (originally Hoyt Avenue)
Ditmars Boulevard

BMT Broadway Line opened
Prince Street
8th Street
14th Street / Union Square

BMT West End Line
Bay 50th Street

BMT Brighton Line
Ocean Parkway

BMT Jamaica Line
111th Street
104th Street (originally 102nd Street)
Woodhaven Boulevard
85th Street / Forest Parkway (originally Forest Parkway)
75th Street / Elderts Lane (originally Elderts Lane)

Shuttle service between Times Square and Pennsylvania Station

1918

Times Square / Grand Central shuttle initiated as part of Dual Contracts "H System"

IRT East Side Branch (now IRT Lexington Avenue Line) extended
51st Street
59th Street
68th Street [Hunter College]
77th Street [Lenox Hill Hospital]
86th Street
96th Street
103rd Street
110th Street
116th Street
125th Street

IRT East Side Line extended to Woodlawn (now IRT Jerome Avenue Line)
138th Street (originally Mott Haven)
149th Street / Grand Concourse
Bedford Park Boulevard [Lehman College]
Mosholu Parkway

IRT West Side Branch extended (now IRT Broadway–Seventh Avenue Line)
Times Square
Penn Station
28th Street
23rd Street
18th Street
14th Street
Christopher Street
Houston Street
Canal Street
Franklin Street
Chambers Street
Cortlandt Street
Rector Street

BMT Broadway Line
Whitehall Street [South Ferry] (now Whitehall Street / South Ferry)
Rector Street
Cortlandt Street [World Trade Center]
City Hall
23rd Street
28th Street
34th Street / Herald Square
42nd Street / Times Square

BMT Jamaica Line
168th Street
160th Street
Sutphin Boulevard
Queens Boulevard
Metropolitan Avenue
121st Street

BMT West End Line
Coney Island / Stillwell Avenue

First porcelain enamel column signs made by Nelke Signs (later Nelke Veribrite Signs) and Baltimore Enamel Company

1919

IRT West Side Branch extended to Atlantic Avenue via Clark Street
Clark Street
Borough Hall

IRT Pelham Line opened
Third Avenue 138th Street
Brook Avenue
Cypress Avenue
East 143rd Street
East 149th Street
Longwood Avenue
Hunts Point Avenue

BMT Broadway Line
49th Street
57th Street
Fifth Avenue / 59th Street
Lexington Avenue / 59th Street

BMT Brighton Line
West 8th Street [New York Aquarium]
Coney Island / Stillwell Avenue

BMT Culver Line elevated stations
Avenue X
Avenue U
Kings Highway
Avenue P
Avenue N
Bay Parkway (22nd Avenue)
Avenue I
18th Avenue
Ditmas Avenue
13th Avenue
Fort Hamilton Parkway
Ninth Avenue

1920

IRT East Side Branch extended to city line (now IRT White Plains Road Line)
Wakefield / 241st Street

IRT Eastern Parkway Line opened; joined IRT Broadway–Seventh Avenue Line at Atlantic Avenue
Bergen Avenue
Grand Army Plaza
Eastern Parkway / Brooklyn Museum [Brooklyn Museum of Art]
Franklin Avenue
Nostrand Avenue
Kingston Avenue
Utica Avenue

IRT New Lots Line opened as continuation of IRT Eastern Parkway Line
Sutter Avenue / Rutland Road
Saratoga Avenue
Rockaway Avenue
Junius Street

IRT Nostrand Avenue Line extended to Brooklyn College
President Street
Sterling Street
Winthrop Street
Church Avenue
Beverly [sic] Road
Newkirk Avenue
Flatbush Avenue [Brooklyn College]

IRT Pelham Line extended to Pelham Bay Park
Whitlock Avenue
Elder Avenue
Morrison / Soundview Avenues (originally Sound View Avenue)
St. Lawrence Avenue

East 177th Street / Parkchester (now Parkchester)
Castle Hill Avenue
Zerega Avenue
Westchester Square
Middletown Road
Buhre Avenue
Pelham Bay Park

BMT Fourth Avenue Line
Lawrence Street [Metrotech]
Court Street

BMT Brighton Line
DeKalb Avenue
Atlantic Avenue
Seventh Avenue

New York City Transit Commission formed

1922
IRT New Lots Line completed
Van Siclen Avenue
New Lots Avenue

1923
BRT reorganized as the Brooklyn-Manhattan Transit Corporation (BMT)

1924
Independent Rapid Transit Corporation (IND) established by City of New York

Franklin Avenue Shuttle
Botanic Gardens replaced
Consumer's Park

BMT Canarsie Line opened
6th Avenue
Union Square
3rd Avenue
1st Avenue
Bedford Avenue
Lorimer Street
Graham Avenue
Grand Street
Montrose Avenue

1925
BMT Fourth Avenue Line
Bay Ridge / 95th Street

1926
IRT Flushing Line
Fifth Avenue

1927
IRT Flushing Line
Times Square

1928
BMT Canarsie Line extended
Morgan Avenue
Jefferson Street
DeKalb Avenue
Myrtle Avenue
Halsey Street
Myrtle / Wyckoff Avenues (formerly Myrtle Avenue)
Wilson Avenue
Bushwick-Aberdeen
Broadway Junction (formerly Eastern Parkway)

IRT Flushing Line completed
Main Street Flushing
Willets Point Boulevard
(now Mets / Willets Point)
111th Street

1931
BMT Canarsie Line joined to IND Eighth Avenue Line
8th Avenue

BMT Nassau Street Line
Broad Street

BMT Culver Line extended to Coney Island.
Neptune Avenue (formerly Van Sicklen Street)

279

1932
IND Eighth Avenue Line opened
207th Street
Dyckman Street / 200th Street
190th Street / Overlook Terrace
181st Street
175th Street [George Washington Bridge]
168th Street
163rd Street / Amsterdam Avenue
155th Street
145th Street
135th Street
125th Street
116th Street
110th Street / Cathedral Parkway
103rd Street
96th Street
86th Street
81st Street [Museum of Natural History]
72nd Street
59th Street / Columbus Circle
50th Street
42nd Street [Port Authority]
34th Street / Penn Station
23rd Street
14th Street
Spring Street
Canal Street
Chambers Street [World Trade Center]

London Underground Diagram by Henry Beck published

1933
IND Crosstown Line opened
Nassau Avenue
Greenpoint Avenue
21st Street / Van Alst Avenue
Court Square

IND Church Avenue Line opened
Church Avenue
Fort Hamilton Parkway
15th Street / Prospect Park
7th Avenue / Park Slope
4th Avenue
Smith Street / 9th Street
Carroll Street
Bergen Street

IND Queens Boulevard Line opened
Roosevelt Avenue / Jackson Heights
65th Street
Northern Boulevard
46th Street
Steinway Street
36th Street
Queens Plaza

IND 53rd Street Line opened (continuation of IND Queens Boulevard Line); joined IND Eighth Avenue Line at 50th Street
Lexington Avenue / 53rd Street
5th Avenue / 53rd Street
7th Avenue / 53rd Street

IND Eighth Avenue Line extended to Brooklyn
Broadway / Nassau
High Street / Brooklyn Bridge
Jay Street / Borough Hall

IND Concourse Line opened; joined IND Eighth Avenue Line at 145th Street
155th Street
161st Street / River Avenue [Yankee Stadium]
167th Street
170th Street
174th / 175th Streets
Tremont Avenue
182nd / 183rd Streets
Fordham Road
Kingsbridge Road
Bedford Park Boulevard
205th Street

1936
IND Fulton Street Line; joined IND Eighth Street Line at Jay Street / Borough Hall
Court Street
Lafayette Avenue
Clinton / Washington Avenues
Franklin Avenue
Nostrand Avenue
Kingston / Throop Avenues
Utica Avenue
Ralph Avenue
Rockaway Avenue

IND Queens Boulevard Line extended
Kew Gardens / Union Turnpike
75th Avenue
Forest Hills / 71st Avenue
67th Avenue
63rd Drive / Rego Park
Woodhaven Boulevard / Queens Mall (formerly Slattery Plaza)
Grand Avenue / Newtown
Elmhurst Avenue

IND Sixth Avenue Line extended
Broadway / Lafayette Street
Second Avenue
Delancey Street
East Broadway
York Street

1937
IND Queens Boulevard Line extended
169th Street
Parsons Boulevard
Sutphin Boulevard
Van Wyck Boulevard
(now Briarwood / Van Wyck Boulevard)

IND Crosstown Line extended
Hoyt-Schermerhorn
Fulton Street
Clinton / Washington Avenues
Classon Avenue
Bedford / Nostrand Avenues
Myrtle / Willoughby Avenues
Flushing Avenue
Broadway
Metropolitan Avenue / Grand Street

1939
IRT Flushing Line
Willets Point station rebuilt for World's Fair

IND Queens Boulevard Line
23rd Street / Ely Avenue

1940
Consolidation of IRT, BMT and IND by City of New York

IRT Dyre Avenue Line takeover of New York, Westchester & Boston Railroad interurban line from East 180th Street to the city line
Morris Park
Pelham Parkway
Gun Hill Road
Baychester Avenue
Eastchester / Dyre Avenue

IND Sixth Avenue Line opened
47th-50th Streets (Rockefeller Center)
42nd Street
34th Street / Herald Square
23rd Street
14th Street
West 4th Street / Washington Square

1944
BMT Myrtle Avenue Line stations closed
Adams Street
Sands Street
Park Row

1945
IRT Lexington Avenue Line station closed
City Hall

1946
IND Fulton Street Line
Broadway / East New York (now Broadway Junction)

1948
IND Fulton Street Line extended
Liberty Avenue
Van Siclen Avenue
Shepherd Avenue
Euclid Avenue

IRT Lexington Avenue Line station closed
18th Street

Amsterdam Continental Types & Graphic Equipments, Inc. established—American import office in New York for Amsterdam Type Foundry (Lettergieterij N. Tetterode)

1949
Martin Freund complains about confusing signs in the subway system and suggests using color coding (*New York Times*, October 7, 1949)

1950s and 1960s
IRT and BMT stations lengthened to accommodate longer trains

1950
IND Jamaica Line
179th Street

1952
IRT White Plains Road Line station closed
180th Street / Bronx Park

1953
New York City Transit Authority (NYCTA) created to oversee subways, buses and trollies; often known simply as the TA

1954
Culver Ramp opened; connected IND Church Avenue Line to BMT Culver Line at Ditmas Avenue allowing IND trains to reach Coney Island–Stillwell Avenue

Mildred Constantine curates Signs in the Street exhibition at the Museum of Modern Art

1955
Metropolitana Milanese (4 lines) planned

1956
IND Rockaway Line took over LIRR Far Rockaway Branch (1892)
Aqueduct Racetrack
Aqueduct / North Conduit Avenue
Howard Beach [JFK Airport]
Jamaica Bay Crossing
Broad Channel
Hammels Wye

IND Rockaway Line Far Rockaway Branch
Beach 67 Street / Gaston Avenue
Beach 60th Street / Straiton
Beach 44th Street / Frank Avenue
Beach 36th Street / Edgemere
Beach 25th Street / Wavecrest
IND Rockaway Line Rockaway Park Branch
Beach 90th Street / Holland
Beach 98th Street / Playland
Beach 105th Street / Seaside
Rockaway Park / Beach 116th Street

IND Fulton Street Line
Grant Avenue

IND Fulton Street Line extended to Lefferts Boulevard by incorporating 1915 BMT Fulton Street Line stations
80th Street / Hudson Street
88th Street / Boyd Avenue
Rockaway Boulevard
104th Street / Oxford Avenue
111th Street / Greenwood Avenue
Ozone Park / Lefferts Boulevard

1957

"Out of the Labyrinth: A plea and a plan for improved passenger information in the New York subways" by George Salomon; suggests new terminology for names, new route numbers/letters, new map colors, and standardized design; urges consistency among maps, signs and trains

Neue Haas Grotesk by Max Miedinger and Eduard Hoffmann (Haas'che Schriftgießerei, Münchenstein, Switzerland)

Univers by Adrian Frutiger (Deberny & Peignot, Paris and Lumitype)

Folio by Konrad Bauer and Walter Baum (Bauersche Giesserei, Frankfurt)

Albert Hollenstein (Swiss) set up studio in Paris; later imported Helvetica

1958

IND Far Rockaway Line
Mott Avenue / Far Rockaway

First official NYCTA subway map; designed by George Salomon of Parsons & Nathan; inspired by Henry Beck with color-coded lines: black for IRT, green for BMT and red for IND

Ladislav Sutnar designs exit signs for subway system but not properly implemented by TA sign shop

Massimo Vignelli receives Moholy-Nagy Fellowship, Institute of Design, Illinois Institute of Technology 1958–1959; meets Ralph Eckerstrom

Construction begun on Milano Metro

280

1959

IRT Broadway–Seventh Avenue Line station closed
91st Street

Art Directors Club of Chicago competition jurors: Leonard Rubenstein, Ralph Eckerstrom, Mildred Constantine, Charles Coiner, Massimo Vignelli (for collateral material); Herbert Bayer, Bob Gage, Arnold Varga (magazines and newspaper); Georg Olden, Thomas Gory, Jack Roberts (TV commercials); Carl Reger, Chairman

1960

Neue Haas Grotesk licensed by Stempel from Haas and renamed Helvetica; matrices available from German Linotype in mager and halbfett weights only

Lella and Massimo Vignelli establish Office of Design and Architecture in Milan

Peter Knapp becomes art director of *Elle* magazine in France; uses Helvetica in layouts

1961

Airport, based on Standard, designed by Matthew Carter for Colin Forbes; for sign system at The Oceanic Terminal, Heathrow Airport

Helvetica available from German Linotype; foundry Helvetica shipped by Haas and Stempel to European countries

Sign Language for Buildings and Landscape by Mildred Constantine and Egbert Jacobson

1962

IRT Lexington Avenue Line station closed
Worth Street (Brooklyn Bridge station renamed Brooklyn Bridge / Worth Street) [until 1980 when renamed again as Brooklyn Bridge / City Hall]

Letraset added Neue Haas Grotesk to instant lettering range

Milano Metro contract for station designs by Franco Albini and Franca Helg; signage by Bob Noorda

Peter Chermayeff founded Cambridge Seven Associates, Inc. together with Louis J. Bakanowsky, Paul Dietrich, Terry Rankine, Alden Christie, Ivan Chermayeff, and Thomas Geismar.

1963

Stempel adapted Helvetica for the pica point system

German-made Linotype mats imported to United States

First American advertisement for Helvetica (*Print* XVII:6 November/ December 1963)

New version of Akzidenz Grotesk proposed by Karl Gerstner; drawn from photographic prints of the 36 pt version by Christian Mengelt: bigger x-height, darker weight, no tail on **a**, **R** with Helvetica leg, Univers-style ampersand, serif on **1** as alternate; coordinated family called Gerstner Program intended for Berthold Diatype machine

Type and Typography by Ben Rosen; includes Standard but not Helvetica

1964

TA map competition judged by Harmon H. Goldstone (Commissioner, New York City Planning Commission) and Jerry Donovan (cartographer for *Time* magazine)

Sundberg-Ferar designed TA logo in red and blue lowercase letters as part of contract to design new subway cars

MBTA (Massachusetts Bay Transportation Authority) modernization program begun; Chermayeff & Geismar and Cambridge Seven Associates given assignment

Milano Metro M1 (red) line opened

Mergenthaler Linotype released first Helvetica mats (10 pt) in February

Ralph Eckerstrom left Container Corporation of America (CCA)

Massimo Vignelli created first posters for Teatro Piccolo Milano using Helvetica

Mildred Constantine on United States selection committee for 13th Triennale in Milano

Design Quarterly 60 "Swiss Design"

1965

Metropolitan Commuter Transportation Authority (MCTA) created to oversee commuter railroads including Long Island Rail Road and New York, New Haven & Hartford Railroad

Prof. Stanley Goldstein retained by NYCTA as a consultant for 6 months; submitted "Methods of Improving Subway Information"

"Telling People Where to Go: Subway Graphics" by William Lansing Plumb (*Print* XIX:V September/October 1965)

MBTA signage—including the graphics and the T symbol—publicly introduced in August

Schiphol Airport signage by Benno Wissing of Total Design; used modified Akzidenz Grotesk

Rail Alphabet [based on Helvetica Bold] designed by Jock Kinneir and Margaret Calvert of Kinneir, Calvert Associates for British Railways; first used in signing tests at London's Liverpool Street Station; adopted by Design Research Unit (DRU) as part of rebranding of company as British Rail

New York Central used blue color coding on its Harlem Line

Mergenthaler Linotype completed release of Helvetica mats

First advertisement by Amsterdam Continental Types offering Helvetica (*Print* XIX:I / January/February 1965)

Unimark International founded by Ralph Eckerstrom, James Fogleman, Massimo Vignelli and Bob Noorda; Herbert Bayer a board member but inactive; firm combined American marketing know-how with European design in a strong, modernistic bent; Helvetica was its house face

Unimark opened office in New York with Walter Kacik in charge; office in Milano with Bob Noorda in charge

Massimo Vignelli moved to New York at end of 1965

1966

New York City subway strike January 2–14

Unimark International awarded contract to study NYCTA subway signage; Noorda does study of traffic flow at key stations (Times Square, Grand Central Station, Jay Street, Broadway/Nassau, and Queensborough Plaza)

Washington Metropolitan Area Transit Authority established; architect Harry Weese proposed routes and made a map

Massimo Vignelli replaced Walter Kacik in New York office of Unimark in early 1966; office in Seagram Building

Massimo Vignelli designed Stendig calendar (set in Helvetica but with type composed in Milano); began work for Knoll using Helvetica

Industrial Design November 1966 "Mass Transportation" section

Dot Zero published by Unimark; "Corporate Identity as a System" by Nan Adams (*Dot Zero* no. 2 1966) re: Varian; Helvetica used

1967

Metropolitan Transportation Authority (MTA) took over Long Island Rail Road (LIRR)

IND station opened
Grand Street

Chrystie Street Connector opened November 26; unified BMT and IND lines

Manhattan Bridge connection opened

Sixth Avenue Line express tracks opened from 34th Street–Herald Square to West Fourth Street–Washington Square

New through service to The Rockaways in July

Route designations overhauled: AA, CC, GG, HH, QB, RR and TT already in use; B, EE, JJ, LL, M, Mj, NX, QJ, RJ, SS and no. 8 introduced; BB, Q, QT and T discontinued; new color coding adopted for all routes

Chrystie edition subway strip map

Unimark International received contract to prepare graphics standards manual for NYCTA; survey work done in December

Mayor John V. Lindsay asked commissioners who had programs in which signage was used to coordinate their plans through the Urban Design Group in the City Planning Department

Walter Kacik redesigned New York City Sanitation Department sprinkler trucks; also created "Curb Your Dog" sign; both set in Helvetica Medium

Unimark International hired in October as consultants by New York City Planning Commission to coordinate design of street furniture, graphics and lighting; East 53rd Street prototype used Helvetica Medium

"Transportation Graphics: Where am I Going? How Do I Get There?" symposium at Museum of Modern Art and Donnell Library; hosted by Mildred Constantine, moderator: George Nelson; participants: Lowell K. Bridwell, Jock Kinneir, Pierre Bourgeau, Theodore Karagheuzoff, Henry A. Barnes (talk read by Theodore Karagheuzoff), Will Burtin, Donald Appleyard, Peter Chermayeff, Bob Noorda, Jock Kinneir, Charles Haar, Daniel T. Scannell, Harmon H. Goldstone; sponsored by MoMA Department of Architecture and Design; Dot Zero; Transportation Displays, Inc.

Exhibition on MBTA design program at Institute of Contemporary Art in Boston

Schiphol Airport opened

New Yankee Stadium graphics designed by Lou Dorfsman and Peter Palazzo; used mixture of Helvetica Medium and Standard Medium due to scale of letters (Helvetica too heavy at big sizes)

Massimo Vignelli designed new logo for American Airlines using Helvetica

1968

MTA took over NYCTA (including MaBSTOA) March 1

IRT Lenox Avenue Line
148th Street / Lenox Terminal (now Harlem / 148th Street)

IND station opened
57th Street

Williamsburg Bridge connection (Essex Street Cut) opened in July; KK route introduced

Two-toned **M** logo designed by Peter Muller-Munk Associates (PMMA); replaced TA logo

Harry Weese hired Unimark to design graphics for Washington Metro

Unified signage for Heathrow airport done by Jock Kinneir; Rail Alphabet used

Will Burtin designed signage for University Circle neighborhood in Cleveland using modified version of Helvetica

"Transportation Graphics" [transcript of 1967 MoMA symposium edited by Mildred Constantine] (*Dot Zero* 5)

"Mass Transit: Problem and Promise" by Patricia Conway George (*Design Quarterly* 71)

1969

BMT Myrtle Avenue Line stations closed
Grand Avenue
Washington Avenue
Vanderbilt Avenue
Navy Street
Bridge Street / Jay Street
Broadway / Myrtle Avenue
Sumner Avenue
Tompkins Avenue
Nostrand Avenue
Franklin Avenue

Milano Metro M2 (green) line opened

Chicago Transit Authority introduced KDR (Kennedy-Dan Ryan) style signage on the new Dan Ryan and Kennedy lines; Helvetica Medium used

1970s

IRT Broadway Line
137th Street [City College] renovated

BMT Broadway–Fourth Avenue Line stations renovated; old mosaics covered in white tile and platforms lengthened
28th Street
23rd Street
8th Street
Prince Street
Canal Street [local]
Broadway [express]
Cortlandt Street
Rector Street
Union Street
9th Street
Prospect Avenue
25th Street
45th Street
53rd Street
Bay Ridge Avenue
77th Street

1970

New York City Transit Authority *Graphics Standards Manual* designed by Massimo Vignelli and Bob Noorda of Unimark International; Standard Medium chosen as the typeface for signage

Roll curtains with new single and double-letter route designation in Standard Medium and 9 colors (replacing black and white versions) introduced for R-16 cars; made by Trans-Lite, Inc.

LIRR vehicle livery by Peter Muller-Munk Associates (PMMA); signage overseen by Kenneth Love; set in Helvetica mixed with Standard

Massimo Vignelli and Peter Delft (Unimark) design signage system for Washington DC Metro system; Helvetica used

A Sign Systems Manual by Crosby/ Fletcher/Forbes

"Language of Signs" exhibition curated by Mildred Constantine and Alan Hurlburt, sponsored by AIGA and the Graham Foundation; participants included Walter Kacik Design Associates, Chermayeff & Geismar and Unimark International

1971

MTA took over Staten Island Rapid Transit Operating Company (SIRT) from Baltimore & Ohio Railroad (B&O); now Staten Island Railroad (SIR) line within the subway system

MTA took over New York, New Haven & Hartford Railroad; now Metro-North New Haven Line

Communication Arts (CA) vol. 13, no. 4 "Arrogance" photo essay praising Walter Kacik's design for New York City Department of Sanitation trucks; seen as "arrogant" in its use of white space

Massimo & Lella Vignelli establish Vignelli Partners in New York

1972

MTA took over Penn Central Railroad; now Metro-North Harlem Line and Metro-North Hudson Line

Diagrammatic subway map in Beck style designed by Massimo Vignelli of Vignelli Associates; used 22 colors for the various lines; debuted August 7, 1972

Fencing for MTA construction projects designed by Howard York using Helvetica

Port Authority airport guides and PATH guides designed by Robert Leydenfrost using Helvetica

Bill McCaffery organized Art Directors Club exhibition Making New York Understandable at the Huntington Hartford Museum; the show toured four other cities

1973

BMT Broadway Line
49th Street / Seventh Avenue renovated. Experimental prototype with new sound absorbing ceilings over tunnels, new safety token booths (with bullet resistant glass), welded rails, and fluorescent lighting; white tiles replaced by flame-red glazed brick; redesign by Johnson/Burgee Associates

Inter-agency Marketing Committee established; "MTA gets you there" marketing campaign to stem ridership decline: coordinated transit map, new bus map, Transit Information Center at Grand Central Station, timetables for LIRR and Penn Central Metropolitan Region; Culture Bus loop service inaugurated

281

1974

IRT Lexington Avenue Line
Bowling Green station redesigned by Paul Katz, NYCTA architect; copied look of BMT 49th Street station

BMT Myrtle Avenue Line
Metropolitan Avenue station rebuilt

Signage for São Paolo subway system by Bob Noorda of Unimark International

1975

BMT Culver Line stations closed
9th Avenue
13th Avenue
Fort Hamilton Parkway

1976

IRT Broadway Line
Cortlandt Street station renovation completed as part of World Trade Center construction; renamed Cortlandt Street / World Trade Center

Washington Metropolitan Area Transit Authority (Metrorail) opened March 27

New York Transit exhibit opened July 4; became Transit Museum

"This Typeface Is Changing Your Life" by Leslie Savan (*Village Voice*, 7 June 1976)

Type and Typography (rev. ed.) by Ben Rosen; Helvetica (Mergenthaler VIP version) included as supplement

1977

BMT Jamaica Line stations closed
168th Street
160th Street
Sutphin Boulevard

"Subways" exhibition organized by Lucy Fellowes at Cooper-Hewitt Museum December 8, 1977–February 1978; "New York's Subway" by Stanley Abercrombie displayed at mezzanine level of the 42nd Street / 6th Avenue subway station

Chicago Transit Authority extended KDR (Kennedy-Dan Ryan) style signage to 142 other stations in system; design by CTA's Passenger Controls Graphics section; typeface is Helvetica

Giulio Cittato designed sign system for ACTV vaporetti system in Venice inspired by Milano Metro and New York subway signage systems; typeface is Helvetica

1978

Len Ingalls of MTA instituted program in November to remove obsolete signs and uncover old mosaics hidden by extra signs

Fulton Street Mall transportation information kiosks designed by Samuel Leibowitz

The JFK Express, combined subway/ bus service from Manhattan to John F. Kennedy International Airport (dubbed The Train to The Plane in 1979), inaugurated September 24

Tauranac Committee subway map prototype debuted February 1 at the Cityana Gallery on East 53rd Street; all lines drawn in red

"The New York Subway Map Debate" April 20 at Cooper Union

1979

Diamond Jubilee (75th anniversary of the subway system)

IRT Broadway–Seventh Avenue Line
South Ferry station renovated

Operation Facelift spurred by Phyllis Cerf Wagner, wife of ex-mayor Robert F. Wagner; intended to upgrade old subway stations without major renovations: graffiti removed, stations painted in new colors more attuned to the mosaics, and advertising and other items moved to make mosaics visible

New geographic subway map by the Tauranac Committee and Michael Hertz Associates introduced; accompanied by changes in route designations

"We're Changing..." poster announcing new color coding system designed by Nancy Stahl

1980

IRT Lexington Avenue Line
Brooklyn Bridge / Worth Street renamed Brooklyn Bridge / City Hall

The New York City Transit Authority Graphics Standards Manual Revisions; compiled by Ralph DeMasi

NYCTA subway strike April 1–11

1981

Symbol Signs by American Institute of Graphic Arts; committee consisted of Tom Geismar, Seymour Chwast, Rudolph de Harak, John Lees and Massimo Vignelli

1982

MTA began 5-year capital program to update directional signs at 458 subway stations; 78 stations completed by end of year

1983

Neue Helvetica (D. Stempel AG); Helvetica family redesigned to achieve more unity among members

1984

New York City Transit Authority Graphics Standards Manual Supplement 1984; designed by Michael Hertz Associates

DTP (desktop publishing) coined by Paul Brainerd of Aldus; combination of Apple computer, Apple LaserWriter (by Canon), Adobe Postscript language, and Aldus Pagemaker

"Building Better Transit" station modernization program begun November

AG Old Face by Günter Gerhard Lange (H. Berthold AG); redesign of Akzidenz Grotesk

1985

BMT Jamaica Line stations cloaed
Queens Boulevard
Metropolitan Avenue

Route designations changed from double letters to single letters (e.g. LL to L)

Neighborhood subway maps (set in Helvetica) added to stations; designed by John Tauranac and Michael Hertz Associates; idea originally suggested by Massimo Vignelli in 1972

Akzidenz Grotesk available digitally from Linotype-Hell (but no longer called Standard in Anglo-American markets)

1986

IRT Lexington Avenue Line
Astor Place station renovated; with designs by Milton Glaser

1987

New MTA 5-year station modernization program

BMT Brighton Line
Kings Highway station renovated

1988

IND / BMT Archer Avenue Line opened
Jamaica Center / Parsons Boulevard
Sutphin Boulevard / Archer Avenue
Jamaica / Van Wyck (IND only); first stations with signage officailly in Helvetica Medium

IRT Lexington Line
23rd Street station renovated

MTA–Graphic Standards Manual (NYCTA Signage) Outline [Working Copy]; designed by Michael Hertz Associates; compiled between June and October

1989

IND 63rd Street Line opened
Lexington Avenue / 63rd Street
Roosevelt Island
21st Street / Queensbridge

IRT Broadway–Seventh Avenue Line
86th Street station renovated

MTA Sign Manual: New York City Transit Authority, Long Island Rail Road, Metro-North Commuter Railroad designed by Michael Hertz Associates for MTA Marketing & Corporate Communications Division; Helvetica Medium replaced Standard Medium as the NYCTA typeface; Helvetica Medium and Helvetica Medium Condensed used for LIRR; Helvetica Medium Italic and Helvetica Medium used for Metro-North Railroad

1990s

IND Sixth Avenue Line
34th Street / Herald Square renovated

282

1990

IRT Lexington Avenue Line
103rd Street renovated

IRT Broadway–Seventh Avenue Line
23rd Street renovated

Modular sign system for MTA Bus Stops designed by MTA New York City Transit Graphics Unit; typeface is Neue Helvetica 77 (Bold Condensed)

Milano Metro M3 (yellow) line opened

1991

Signage for Napoli subway system designed by Bob Noorda; lines opened 1993

1992

IRT White Plains Road Line
Intervale Avenue station rebuilt

IRT Broadway–Seventh Avenue Line
Canal Street station renovated

IRT Flushing Line
Queens Boulevard Viaduct renovated

Station Signage Department created within the Division of Stations to oversee all planning, surveying, fabrication, installation and maintenance of signs as part of 5-year capital program to renovate stations

---

1994

IRT Lexington Avenue Line
96th Street renovated

IRT Broadway–Seventh Avenue Line stations renovated
Houston Street
50th Street (Broadway)

BMT Brighton Line stations renovated
Beverley Road
Parkside Avenue
Prospect Park

MTA logo (MTA within circle) designed by Siegel + Gale; replaced two-toned M; intended to unify transportation system beyond the subway

1995

IRT White Plains Road Line
135th Street station renovated

MTA Service Identity Manual designed by Marketing & Corporate Communications Divison; official typefaces are Helvetica and Times Roman; MetroCard and new MTA logo introduced

MetroCards first used on buses

SubTalk marketing campaign designed by Korey Kay & Partners

1996

BMT Franklin Avenue Shuttle
Dean Street station closed

IRT White Plains Road Line stations renovated
Third Avenue / 149th Street
125th Street

IRT Lexington Avenue Line
110th Street station renovated

1997

MetroCards introduced to rest of MTA transportation, including the subway system

BMT Brighton Line
Sheepshead Bay station renovated

BMT Broadway Line
5th Avenue station renovated

IND Fulton Street Line
Lefferts Boulevard station renovated

1998

IRT Lexington Avenue Line stations renovated
116th Street
Union Square
Canal Street

BMT Fourth Avenue Line
36th Street station renovated

IRT Flushing Line
Main Street Flushing station renovated

IRT Broadway–Seventh Avenue Line
18th Street station renovated

1998/1999

BMT Franklin Avenue Shuttle
4 stations rebuilt or restored

BMT Broadway Line
Cortlandt Street / World Trade Center station renovated

1999

IRT Broadway–Seventh Avenue Line
Times Square station renovated

IRT White Plains Road Line
116th Street station renovated

IRT Flushing Line stations renovated
33rd Street / Rawson Street
40th Street / Lowery Street
46th Street / Bliss Street

BMT Canarsie Line
8th Avenue station renovated

IND Eighth Avenue Line stations renovated
110th Street / Cathedral Parkway
81st Street / Museum of Natural History

R-142 subway cars with "New Technology" delivered December 1999: LED exterior line indicator signs, LCD destination signs (in windows), LED interior next stop/variable message signs

2000

BMT Broadway Line
Whitehall Street station renovated

BMT Fourth Avenue Line
DeKalb Avenue station renovated

2001

V Sixth Avenue Local created to link 71st Avenue, Queens with Second Avenue, Manhattan

63rd Street Line extended from 21st Street to 36th Street; merged with the Queens Boulevard Line

BMT Broadway Line
Cortlandt Street / World Trade Center station closed

IRT Broadway–Seventh Avenue Line
Cortlandt Street / World Trade Center station closed

2002

BMT Broadway Line stations renovated; 1970s colored tiles removed
Prince Street
8th Street
23rd Street; hat mosaics designed by Keith Godard
28th Street

IRT Lexington Avenue Line
125th Street station renovated

IND Concourse Line
161st Street / Yankee Stadium station renovated

2003

Pedestrian Subway Transfer from 51st Street (IRT Lexington Avenue Line) to 53rd Street (IND 53rd Street Line); designed by Keith Helmetag of Chermayett & Geismar, Inc.

2004

Subway Centennial

IRT Broadway–Seventh Avenue Line
66th Street station renovated

BMT Sea Beach, West End and Brighton Lines
Coney Island / Stillwell Avenue station renovated

IRT Flushing Line
74th Street / Broadway station renovated

IND 6th Avenue Line
Delancey Street station renovated

2005

IRT White Plains Road Line
116th Street station renovated

R-160 subway cars delivered; include new electronic interior route/stop display sign called "FIND" (Flexible INformation Display)

2007

Massimo Vignelli asked by *Men's Vogue* to revisit and redesign his 1972 subway map

Electronic annunciators installed in Canarsie Line stations

2008

BMT Canarsie Line
Train Locator Control computer screens installed at Myrtle Avenue / Wyckoff Avenue station

2009

IRT Broadway–Seventh Avenue Line
South Ferry station closed; new South Ferry station opened; joined to Whitehall Street (BMT Broadway Line)
New Rail Alphabet by Henrik Kubel with Margaret Calvert (A2/HK/SW)

2010

June 27 V and W discontinued; M re-colored orange and re-routed to replace Vin Manhattan and Queens; G terminates at Long Island City / Court Square; Q terminates at Astoria Boulevard

SOURCES

BOOKS

Aaron Burns & Company. *Typositor Typography*. New York: Aaron Burns & Company (Rapid Typographers, Inc.), 1965.

Ambasz, Emilio et al. *design: Vignelli*. New York: Rizzoli International Publications, Inc., 1981.

American Institute of Graphic Arts. *Fifty Advertisements of 1967*. New York: American Institute of Graphic Arts, 1967.

American Institute of Graphic Arts. *The Federal Design Response*. New York: American Institute of Graphic Arts, 1977.

American Institute of Graphic Arts. *Symbol Signs*. New York: Hastings House and American Institute of Graphic Arts, 1981.

Atkinson, Frank H. *Atkinson Sign Painting: A Complete Manual Self-Education*. Chicago: Frederick J. Drake & Company, 1909).

Aynsley, Jeremy. *A Century of Graphic Design*. Hauppauge, NY: Barron's Educational Series, Inc., 2001.

Baglee, Christopher and Andrew Morley. *Street Jewelry: A History of Enamel Advertising Signs*. rev. ed. London: New Cavendish Books, 1988.

Biggs, John R. *Basic Typography*. London: Faber and Faber, Ltd., 1968.

Broos, Kees. *design: Total Design*. Utrecht: uitgeverij Reflex, 1983.

Celant, Germano, Mildred Constantine, David Revere McFadden and Joseph Rykwert. *design: Vignelli*. New York: Rizzoli International Publications, Inc., 1990.

Chalfant, Henry and James Prigoff. *Spraycan Art*. London: Thames and Hudson, Ltd., 1987.

Chermayeff, Ivan, Tom Geismar and Steff Geissbuhler. *designing*. New York: Graphis Inc., 2003.

Composing Room, Inc., *The CRT Typebook*. New York: The Composing Room, Inc., 1965.

Conradi, Jan. *Unimark International: The Design of Business and the Business of Design*. Baden, Switzerland: Lars Müller Publishers, 2010.

Constantine, Mildred and Egbert Jacobson. *Sign Language for Buildings and Landscape*. New York: Reinhold Publishing Company, 1961.

Cooper, Martha and Henry Chalfant. *Subway Art*. New York: Holt, Rinehart and Winston: An Owl Book, 1984.

Coppola, Philip Ashforth. *Silver Connections*. vol. II. Maplewood, New Jersey: n.p., 1990.

Coppola, Philip Ashforth. *Silver Connections*. vol. IV. Maplewood, New Jersey: n.p., 1999.

Crosby, Fletcher, Forbes. *A Sign Systems Manual*. New York and Washington: Praeger Publishers Inc., 1970.

Diethelm, Walter. *Signet, Signal, Symbol*. Zurich: ABC Verlag, 1984.

Finke, Gail Deibler. *City Signs: Innovative Urban Graphics*. New York: Madison Square Press, 1994.

Finke, Gail Deibler. *Urban Identities*. New York: Madison Square Press, 1998.

Fiorvanti, Giorgio, Leonardo Passarelli and Silvia Sfligiotti. *La Grafica in Italia*. Milano: Leonardo Arte, 1997.

French, Thomas E. and Robert Meiklejohn. *The Essentials of Lettering: A Manual for Students and Designers*. New York: McGraw-Hill Book Company, Inc., 1909.

Friedman, Mildred, ed. *Graphic Design in America: A Visual Language History*. Minneapolis: Walker Art Center and New York: Harry N. Abrams, Inc., 1989.

Garland, Ken. *Mr. Beck's Underground Map: A History*. Middlesex: Capital Transport Publishing, 1994.

Gray, Nicolete. *Lettering on Buildings*. London: Architectural Press, 1960.

Hefting, Paul, Koosje Serman and Dingenus van de Vrie. *Benno Wissing: Grafische & ruimtelijke ontwerpen*. Rotterdam: Museum Boijmans Van Beuningen and NAi Uitgevers, 1999.

Herdeg, Walter, ed. *Who's Who in Graphic Art: An Illustrated Book of Reference*. Zurich: Amstutz & Herdeg Graphis Press, 1962.

Herdeg, Walter, ed. *Archigraphia: Architectural and Environmental Graphics*. Zurich: Graphis, 1981.

Herdeg, Walter, ed. *Graphis Diagrams*. Zurich: Graphis Press, 1984 (4th expanded edition).

Hillebrand, Henri, ed. *Graphic Designers in the USA 2*. New York: Universe Books, 1971.

Hood, Clifton. *722 Miles: The Building of the Subways and How They Transformed New York*. New York: Simon & Schuster, 1993

Howes, Justin. *Johnston's Underground Type*. London: Capital Transport, 2000.

Lauwen, Toon. *Bob Noorda*. Eindhoven: [Z]OO Producties, n.d. [1994?].

Leach, Mortimer. *Lettering in the Graphic Arts*. New York: Reinhold Publishing Corporation, 1960.

Malsy, Victor and Lars Müller, eds. *Helvetica Forever: Geschichte einer Schrift*. Baden: Lars Müller Publishers, 2008.

McGrew, Mac. *American Metal Typefaces of the Twentieth Century*. 2nd, rev. ed. New Castle, Delaware: Oak Knoll Books, 1993.

Mergenthaler Linotype. *Akzidenz Grotesk. 54 unit General Typefaces from Mergenthaler Linotype, Stempel and Haas*. Melville, NY: Mergenthaler Linotype, n.d. [c.1974].

Middendorp, Jan. *Dutch Type*. Rotterdam: 010 Publishers, 2004.

Morgan, Ann Lee, ed. *Contemporary Designers*. London: MacMillan Publishers, 1984: 455.

New York Transit Museum [Carissa Amash]. *Subway Style: 100 Years of Architecture & Design in the New York City Subway*. New York: Stewart, Tabori & Chang, 2004.

Noorda, Bob and Francesco Dondina. *Bob Noorda: Una vita nel segno della grafica*. Milano: Editrice San Raffaele, 2009.

Osterer, Heidrun and Philipp Stamm, eds. *Adrian Frutiger Typefaces: The Complete Works*. Basel, Boston & Berlin: Birkhäuser Verlag AG, 2008.

Ovenden, Mark. *Transit Maps of the World*. 2nd rev. ed. Edited by Mike Ashworth. London: Penguin Books, Ltd., 2007.

Remington, R. Roger and Robert S.P. Fripp. *Design and Science: The Life and Work of Will Burtin*. London and Burlington, Vermont: Lund Humphries, 2007.

Rose, Douglas. *Tiles of the Unexpected Underground: A Study of Six Miles of Geometric Tile Patterns on the London Underground*. London: Douglas Rose, 2007.

Rosen, Ben. *Type and Typography: The Designer's Type Book*. New York: Reinhold Publishing Corp., 1963.

Rosen, Ben. *Type and Typography: The Designer's Type Book*. rev. ed. New York: Van Nostrand Reinhold, 1976.

Stewart, Jack. *Graffiti Kings: New York City Mass Transit Art of the 1970s*. New York: Melcher Media–Harry N. Abrams, Inc., 2009.

Stookey, Lee. *Subway Ceramics: A History and Iconography of Mosaic and Bas Relief Signs and Plaques in the New York City Subway System*. New York: Lee Stookey, 1994.

Tauranac, John. *Seeing New York: The Official MTA Travel Guide*. New York: Metropolitan Transportation Authority, 1976.

Type Directors Club. *TDC XIII*. New York: Type Directors Club, 1967.

Ventura, Nico, ed. *Bob Noorda Design*. Ferrara: MusArc, 2005.

Visual Graphics Corporation. *The World Famous Photo Typositor Alphabet Library*. Tamarac, Florida: Visual Graphics Corporation, 1973.

von Moos, Stanislaus, Mara Campana and Giampiero Bosoni. *Max Huber*. London and New York: Phaidon Press, 2006.

Wallis, L.W. *A Concise Chronology of Typesetting Developments 1886–1896*. London: The Wynken de Worde Society and Lund Humphries, 1988.

PERIODICALS

"3 Win Transit Authority Prizes for Designs of Subway Maps." *New York Times*, October 17, 1964.

"Advertising News and Notes." *New York Times*, April 12, 1950.

"Advertising News and Notes." *New York Times*, April 14, 1966.

"Arrogance." *Communication Arts* vol. 13, no. 4 (1971): 24–31.

"Business Notes." *New York Times*, February 17, 1947.

Classified advertisement. *New York Times*, August 22, 1966.

Classified advertisements. *New York Times*, August 6–13, 1967.

"Daniel T. Scannell Dies at 87." *New York Times*, February 25, 2000.

"Designers and Politicians Gather on the Mall to Explore City Ills." *New York Times*, May 12, 1967.

"Making New York Understandable." *Print* XVI:IV (July/August 1972).

"Mass Transportation." *Industrial Design* (November 1966): entire issue.

"Molto Bene Italiano." *Transit* no. 11 (December 1970)

"The New York Subway Map Debate." *Skyline* no. 1 (April 1, 1978): 6

"Poster USA/73." *Print* XXII:V (September/October1973).

"Rapid Transit: A Tri-State 20-Year Plan." *New York Post*, May 18, 1966.

"Rerouted Subways a Little Late, Lost." *Newsday*, November 27, 1967.

"Sanitation Department Changes Aspect of Its Sprinkler Trucks but They're Still Cool." *New York Times*, August 8, 1967.

"Second Federal Design Assembly." *Design Quarterly* 94/95 (1975).

"Subway Changes Set for Jan. 2 Praised." *New York Times*, November 25, 1972

"Subway Studying Color-Centric Guide." *New York Times*, May 20, 1966.

"Subway Suits Are Rejected." *New York Daily News*, November 25, 1967.

"Subways Can Be Beautiful." *Time*, October 20, 1967.

"The Subway: One Tough Brake after Another." *New York Post*, November 29, 1967.

"Unified New York Transit." *New York Times*, January 20, 1966.

"We Don't Want People to Like Us, We Just Want Them to Hate Us Less." *Reputation Management*, July/August 1995

Abelman, Lester. "Subways: Straps and Maps." *New York Daily News*, November 26, 1967.

Abelman, Lester. "Confusion Day on Subways." *New York Daily News*, November 27, 1967.

Abercrombie, Stanley. "New York's Subway." In *Subways*. Edited by Peter Blake. New York: Cooper-Hewitt Museum, 1977.

Adams, Nan. "Corporate Identity as a System." *Dot Zero* 2 (1966): 14–21.

Barnett, Jonathan. In "Transportation Graphics." *Dot Zero* 5 (Fall 1968): 23–25.

Biemann, Emil O. "Univers." *Print* XV:1 (January/February 1961): 32–36.

Blake, Peter. "Get Off at N, 1, 2, 3, 7, SS, QB, RR, NX, EE—The Crossroads of the World." *New York Magazine*, April 8, 1968, 108–109.

Blake, Peter. "Boston's MBTA." In *Subways*. Edited by Peter Blake. New York: Cooper-Hewitt Museum, 1977.

Bronzaft, Arline L., Stephen B. Dobrow and Timothy J. O'Hanlon. "Spatial *Orientation in a Subway System*." *Environment and Behavior* vol. 8, no. 4 (December 1976): 575–594.

Bronzaft, Arline L. and Stephen B. Dobrow. "Improving Transit Information Systems." *Journal of Environmental Systems* vol. 13, no. 4 (1983–1984): 365–376.

Burks, Edward C. "Subways' Colored Tile Gets Cover Up Job." *New York Times*, February 21, 1970.

Burtin, Will. In "Transportation Graphics." *Dot Zero* 5 (Fall 1968): 18–22.

Cahn, Joel G. "Yankee Stadium Gets a Facelifting." *Print* XXI:V (September/October 1967): 23–26.

Carmody, Deirdre. "To Gunn, City's Transit Is Better, But Not Best." *New York Times*, November 25, 1985.

Carpenter, Edward K. "Travelers' Aid, Courtesy DOT and AIGA." *Print* XXIX:II (March/April 1975): 25–31.

Chermayeff, Peter. In "Transportation Graphics." *Dot Zero* 5 (Fall 1968): 32–37.

Cittato, Giulio. "La via d'acqua." *Rassegna* (1981): 84–87.

Clarke, Geoffrey. "The plate that outlasts all others." *Penrose Annual* 64 (1971): 38–46.

Constantine, Mildred, ed. "Transportation Graphics." *Dot Zero* 5 (Fall 1968).

Conway, Patricia. "Subway Graffiti: The Message from Underground." *Print* XXVI:III (May/June 1973): 25–32.

Day, Kenneth. "Types of the Sixties." *Penrose Annual* 61 (1968): 241–256.

DeNeve, Rose M. "MTA Gets You There." In *The Best in Posters. The Print Casebooks: First Annual Edition* edited by Martin Fox. (Washington, DC: RC Publications, Inc., 1975): 46–48.

DeNeve, Rose M. "Peter Muller-Munk: Design for the Urban Environment." *Print* XXIV:III (May/June 1970): 60–65, 76.

Druckrey, Inge. "Signs." *Design Quarterly* 92 (1974).

Epstein, Jason. "The Last Days of New York." *The New York Review of Books* vol. 23, no. 2 (February 19, 1976). Online version.

Fenton, John H. "Imported Ideas Improve Boston Subways." *New York Times*, November 27, 1967.

Foderaro, Lisa W. "Fare Cards Make Debut In Subways." *New York Times*, January 6, 1994.

Fowler, Glenn. "Subway Signs Often Sidetrack Riders." *New York Times*, March 14, 1982.

Fox, Sylvan. "Lindsay Names 2 to M.T.A. Board." *New York Times*, March 8, 1968.

Freund, Martin. "Letters to the Editor." *New York Times*, July 16, 1949.

Freund, Martin. "Letters to the Editor." *New York Times*, October 7, 1949.

George, Patricia Conway. "Mass Transit: Problem and Promise." *Design Quarterly* 71 (1968).

Goldberger, Paul. "Design Notebook." *New York Times*, February 9, 1978.

Goldberger, Paul. "Design Notebook." *New York Times*, May 3, 1979.

Goldberger, Paul. "Design Notebook: At Last, A Usable Subway Map." *New York Times*, August 2, 1979.

Goldman, Ari. "JFK Train: Wasteful or Wonderful." *New York Times*, June 5, 1980.

Goldstone, Harmon. "Transportation Graphics." In *Dot Zero* 5 (Fall 1968).

Greisner, Walter. "The History of the Most Successful Sans Serif." *Linotype Matrix* vol. 4, no. 3 (Winter 2008): 64–79.

Huxtable, Ada Louise. "Doing the Hard Things First." *New York Times*, September 24, 1972.

Kelly, Scott. "Boston transit: team design and fractious fans." *Industrial Design* 14/5 (June 1967): 64–70.

King, Seth. "City Hall Parley on Subways." *New York Times*, November 22, 1967.

Kinneir, Jock. In "Transportation Graphics." *Dot Zero* 5 (Fall 1968): 5–11.

Kneebone, Peter, ed. "International Signs and Symbols: Special ICOGRADA Issue", *Print* XXIII:VI (November/December 1969)

Lahr, John. "The Cities: New York Is New York—Alas." *Print* XXII:II (March/April 1968): 50–57, 122 and 130.

Lichtenstein, Grace. "New Funds Unlikely to Alter New York's View on Subway," *New York Times*, May 8, 1978.

Lichtenstein, Grace. "Carey Announces Express Service to Kennedy by Bus and Subway." *New York Times*, June 28, 1978.

Lindsey, Robert. "The Subway Prospect: Better Service, Fewer Riders and Clamor for Subsidy." *New York Times*, October 12, 1973.

Lukach, Joan M. "Transportation: Design in Transit: Boston's Revitalized Subway System." *Print* XXII:II (March/April 1968): 62–67.

MacLeod, Hope. "The View from the Subway." *New York Post*, October 16, 1967.

Mancini, Anthony and Jean Crafton. "Oh, Those Subways" and "Riders Burn as TA Pulls the Switch." *New York Post*, November 26, 1967.

Mancini, Anthony and Jean Crafton. "Note to Straphangers—No, It's Not a Noose." *New York Post*, November 28, 1967.

McKinley, Jr., James C. "What's in a Symbol? A Lot, the M.T.A. Is Betting." *New York Times*, August 28, 1994.

McCoy, Katherine. "How I Lost My Faith in Rational Functionalism." *AIGA Journal of Graphic Design* vol. 9, no. (1990); reprinted as "Rethinking Modernism, Revising Functionalism" in *Looking Closer: Critical Writings on Graphic Design*. Edited by Michael Bierut, William Drenttel, Steven Heller and D.K. Holland. New York: Allworth Press and the American Institute of Graphic Arts, 1994: 49–50.

Micha, Emil and Karen Micha. "Staten Island Rapid Transit." *Print* XXVII:I (January/February 1973): 34–37.

Nemy, Enid. "Phyllis Wagner's New Job Is Hard, Which Suits Her Fine." *New York Times*, July 21, 1978.

Neuman, William. "How Long Till Next Train? The Answer Is Up in Lights." *New York Times*, February 17, 2007.

Neuman, William. "There Is another Train Right Behind." *New York Times*, October 22, 2008.

Noorda, Bob. "Studies for Signs and Indicator Board in the Milan Underground–Studi per la segnaletica della Metropolitana Milanese–Etudes pour la signalisation du Metropolitain Milanais." *Pagina* no. 4 (Gennaio 1964): 4–13. Introduction by P.C.S. [Pier Carlo Santini].

Noorda, Bob. In "Transportation Graphics." *Dot Zero* 5 (Fall 1968): 38–41.

Oreskes, Michael. "Analysts Expect M.T.A.'s Projects to Aid Economy." *New York Times*, November 28, 1982.

Ovink, G.W. "German-speaking countries." *Print* XV:2 (March/April 1961).

Pelleck, Carl J. "Subway Switch Set to Go—Here's How to Keep Track" *New York Post*, November 25, 1967.

Penrose Annual, The 58 (1965): typeface advertisements.

Penrose Annual, The 59 (1966): typeface advertisements.

Perlmutter, Eugene. "BMT–IND Changes Bewilder Many." *New York Times*, November 27, 1967.

Plumb, William Lansing. "Telling People Where to Go: Subway Graphics." *Print* XIX:V (September/October 1965): 13–23.

Plumb, William Lansing. "Graphic Design in the Human Environment." *Print* XXII:II (March/April 1968): 24–25.

Poston, Ted. "Mayor Blasts TA Foulup." *New York Post*, November 30, 1967.

Poynor, Rick. "Introduction." *Typography Now: The Next Wave*. Edited by Poynor and Edward Booth-Clibborn London: Booth-Clibborn Editions, 1991; reprinted as "Type and Deconstruction in the Digital Era" in *Looking Closer: Critical Writings on Graphic Design*. Edited by Michael Bierut, William Drenttel, Steven Heller and D.K. Holland. New York: Allworth Press and the American Institute of Graphic Arts, 1994: 83–87.

Print XIV:3 (May/June 1960) to XXVIII:1 (January/February 1974): typeface advertisements.

Rawsthorne, Alice. "Helvetica: The little typeface that leaves a big mark." *International Herald Tribune*, April 1, 2007.

Roberts, Steven V. "Subway Stations to Be Redesigned." *New York Times*, September 30, 1967.

Roberts, Steven V. "Mayor Hires Consultants to Study Street Design." *New York Times*, November 14, 1967.

Robertson, Keith. "Starting from Zero." *Emigre* no. 19 (1991); reprinted in *Looking Closer: Critical Writings on Graphic Design*. Edited by Michael Bierut, William Drenttel, Steven Heller and D.K. Holland. New York: Allworth Press and the American Institute of Graphic Arts, 1994: 77–80.

Ross, Edwin, Frank Mazzi and Richard Henry. "Subways Are for Weeping & Tears Are Bitter" and "TA Acts to Clear the Flubway Tracks." *New York Daily News*, November 28, 1967.

Salomon, George. "Letters to Editor." *New York Times*, 1946.

Savan, Leslie. "This Typeface Is Changing Your Life." *Village Voice*, June 7, 1976. Reprinted in *Looking Closer 3: Classic Writings on Graphic Design*. Edited by Michael Bierut, Jessica Helfand, Steven Heller and Rick Poynor, 256–259. New York: Allworth Press, 1999.

Scannell, Daniel T. In "Transportation Graphics." *Dot Zero* 5 (Fall 1968): 45–47.

Sewell, Chan. "On Its Last Wheels, No. 9 Line Is Vanishing on Signs." *New York Times*, May 25, 2005.

Sheehan, Neil. "Subways a Maze to Uninitiated." *New York Times*, September 18, 1964.

Sims, Calvin. "Plans and Costs Expand to Fix Subway Stations." *New York Times*, June 9, 1990.

Spark, Robert. "Face-lift for BR." *Design 1965 Journal*: 46–51.

Smit, Gees-Ineke. "Schiphol: The development of an airport." In *Holland in Vorm: Dutch Design 1945-1987*. Edited by Gert Staal and Hester Wolters, 35–37. 's-Gravenhage: Stichting Holland in Vorm, 1987.

D. Stempel AG. "Helvetica." *Print* XVII:6 (November/December 1963), insert.

Unimark International. "Segnaletica–Signs projects." *Casabella: rivista di architettura e urbanistica* 339/340 (August/September 1969): 56–59.

Witkin, Richard. "MTA Takes Over Transit Network." *New York Times*, March 2, 1968.

Wolf, Henry. "Foreword." *#1 Handbook by Haber: Helvetica*. New York: Haber Typographers, [November] 1971.

Wyman, Lance. "Subway Signage." In *Subways*. Edited by Peter Blake. New York: Cooper-Hewitt Museum, 1977.

REFERENCE WORKS

New York Telephone Company. Manhattan Telephone Directory: White Pages, 1956/1957. Westchester Telephone Directory: White Pages, 1956/1957. Manhattan Telephone Directory: White Pages, 1964/1965. Manhattan Telephone Directory: White Pages, 1966/1967. Manhattan Telephone Directory: White Pages, 1967/1968. Manhattan Telephone Directory: White Pages, 1969/1970. Manhattan Telephone Directory: Yellow Pages, 1965. Manhattan Telephone Directory: Yellow Pages, 1966.

PUBLIC DOCUMENTS

City of New York, Office of Midtown Planning and Development, and New York City Planning Commission. *New York Streets for People: New Designs for City Spaces*. May 1975.

DeMasi, Ralph, comp. *New York City Transit Authority Graphics Standards Manual Revision*. New York: New York City Transit Authority, 1980.

Metropolitan Transportation Authority. *Transportation Progress: An Interim Report* Number One, December 1968.

Metropolitan Transportation Authority. *1968 Annual Report. 1969 Annual Report. 1970 Annual Report. 1971 Annual Report. 1973 Annual Report. 1974 Annual Report. 1976 Annual Report. 1977 Annual Report.*

1978 Annual Report.
1984 Annual Report.
1987 Annual Report.

Metropolitan Transportation Authority. *Graphic Standards: Signage.* New York: Michael Hertz Associates, 1988.

Metropolitan Transportation Authority. *MTA Sign Manual: New York City Transit Authority, Long Island Rail Road, Metro-North Commuter Railroad.* New York: Metropolitan Transportation Authority, 1989.

Metropolitan Transportation Authority, Marketing & Corporate Communications Division. *MTA Service Identity Manual.* New York: Metropolitan Transportation Authority, 1995.

New York City Transit Authority. *Annual Report 1966–1967.*

New York City Transit Authority. *Annual Report 1967–1968.*

New York City Transit Authority. *New York City Transit Authority Graphics Standards Manual.* New York: Unimark International, 1970.

New York City Transit Authority. *New York City Transit Authority Graphics Standards Manual Supplement 1984.* New York: Michael Hertz Associates, 1984.

New York City Transit Authority. *New York City Transit Authority 1989 Goals: Building for the Future* (January 1989).

UNPUBLISHED MATERIAL

Barrington and Company. "A Survey of Prospective User Reaction to the New Subway Map." May 31, 1966. Typescript, courtesy of Peter B. Lloyd.

Clough, James. "Relazione sulle proposte Inarea per la segnaletica della Metropolitana di Milano." May 2009.

Constantine, Mildred, organizer and **George Nelson,** moderator. "Transportation Graphics: Where Am I Going? How Do I Get There?" a symposium at the Museum of Modern Art, October 23, 1967. Museum of Modern Art audio archives 67.9–11. (The talks by Harmon Goldstone and Daniel T. Scannell are missing from the digital copy of the original tapes which are no longer playable.)

Goldstein, Stanley A. "Methods of Improving Subway Informaton." New York City Transit Authority, 1965. Typescript, courtesy of Prof. Goldstein.

Helms, J.C. [Jan Conradi]. "A Historical Survey of Unimark International and Its Effect on Graphic Design in the United States." M.F.A. thesis, Iowa State University, 1988.

Hodder, Kenneth C. (New York City Transit Authority). "Invitation to submit original designs for a subway route map and bus map", July 30, 1964. Typescript.

Salomon, George. "Out of the Labyrinth: A plea and a plan for improved passenger information in the New York subways." [1957]. Typescript. Archives, New York Transit Museum, Brooklyn, NY.

INTERVIEWS

Bronzaft, Arline. Telephone interview by author. 19 August 2008.

Calvert, Margaret. Email to author, 24 June 2009.

Conradi, Jan. Telephone interview by author. 26 July 2008.

Constantine, Mildred. Interview by Sharon Zane. The Museum of Modern Art Oral History Project. New York, April–June 1991. Telephone interview by author. 15 May 2008.

Crouwel, Wim and Massimo Vignelli. Interview by Alice Twemlow. "Modernism on Two Planes: A Conversation with Wim Crouwel and Massimo Vignelli." AIGA–NY. New York, 25 October 2007.

Fox, Martin. Telephone interview by author. New York City, 8 August 2008.

Goldstein, Stanley A. Telephone interview by author. 6 August 2008.

Halle, Doris. Telephone interview by author. 14 August 2008.

Hertz, Michael. Telephone interview by author. 25 August 2008. Telephone interview by author. 26 August 2008.

Joseph, Peter. Interview by author. New York City, 15 August 2008.

Lloyd, Peter B. Conversation with author. New York City, 28 August 2008.

McDonald, Rod. Interview by author. Buffalo, NY, 19 July 2008.

Montemarano, John. Interview by author. New York City, 18 June 2009.

Noorda, Bob. Interview by author and Alessandro Colizzi. Milano, 30 May 2008.

Parker, Mike. Telephone interview by author. 30 April 2008.

Tauranac, John. Interview by author. New York City, 9 August 2008. Interview by author. New York City, 14 August 2008.

Vignelli, Massimo. Telephone interview by author. New York City, 29 April 2008.

CORRESPONDENCE

Alb, Erich. Email to author, 12 March 2005. Email to author, 1 May 2008. Email to author, 2 May 2008. Email to author, 15 May 2008. Email to author, 6 June 2008. Email to author, 30 June 2008.

Bosniak, Michael. Email to author, 18 August 2008.

Brignall, Colin. Email to author, 1 May 2008.

Bronzaft, Arlene. Email to author, 5 February 2010.

Carter, Matthew. Email to author, 5 May 2008. Email to author, 7 May 2008. Email to author, 5 July 2008.

Charysyn, Joan Email to author, 21 October 2009. Email to author, 22 October 2009.

Clough, James. Email to author, 15 December 2009.

Conradi, Jan. Email to author, 25 July 2008. Email to author, 27 July 2008. Email to author, 29 July 2008. Email to author, 30 July 2008. Email to author, 31 July 2008. Email to author, 1 August 2008. Email to author, 5 August 2008.

D'Adamo, R. Raleigh. Email to author, 22 August 2008. Email to author, 23 August 2008.

D'Onofrio, Greg. Email to author, 9 July 2008.

Fripp, Robert S.P. Email to author, 11 November 2008.

Geismar, Tom. Email to author, 30 April 2008.

Guzowski, Barbara. Email to author, 30 July 2008.

Joseph, Peter. Email to author, 12 August 2008. Email to author, 13 August 2008. Email to author, 14 August 2008. Email to author, 19 August 2008.

Lahr, John. Email to author, 2 August 2008.

Lloyd, Peter B. Email to author, 28 August 2008. Email to author, 29 August 2008.

McCaffery, Bill. Email to author, 6 July 2008.

Spiekermann, Erik. Email to author, 18 July 2008.

Tauranac, John. Email to author, 6 August 2008. Email to author, 15 August 2008. Email to author, 27 August 2008.

Vignelli, Massimo. Email to Erich Alb, 30 April 2007. Email to Erich Alb, 25 August 2007. Email to author, 2 May 2008. Email to author, 6 May 2008. Email to author, 15 May 2008. Email to author, 16 May 2008. Email to author, 6 August 2008. Email to author, 10 August 2008. Email to author, 15 August 2008. Email to author, 18 August 2008.

York, Howard. Email to author, 3 August 2008. Email to author, 11 August 2008.

FILMS

Hustwit, Gary. *Helvetica: A Documentary Film.* Swiss Dots Production in association with Veer, 2007.

WEBSITES

Brill, Louis M. "Taking the A-Train (or Any Other Train) in New York City Would Be Even Harder Without Directional Signage" at signindustry.com/architectural/ articles/2007-11-15-LB-NYC_Subway_WayFinding_Signs_Signage.php3 Conradi, Jan. "Unimark International: A History of the World's Largest Design and Marketing Firm 1964–1977." at unimark-international.com. 2004.

Feinman, Mark S. "The New York Transit Authority in the 1970s." at nyc.subway.org/articles/history–nycta.1970s.html. 2002.

Hogarty, Dave. "Michael Hertz, Designer of the NYC Subway Map." at gothamist.com/2007/08/03/michael_hertz_d.php

allposters.com

designarchives.aiga.org

forgotten-ny.com

fta.dot.gov/about/news_events_8808.html

metronexco.com/research.htm

mic-ro.com/metro/metrofonts.html

milesfaster.co.uk/information/heathrow-airport/heathrow-history.htm

new.idsa.org

nycsubway.org

patentstorm.us

railroad.net

siegelonbranding.com/pictures/90/

songdo.com

subway.com.ru

sundbergferar.com

trainsarefun.com/lirr/lirrlogos.htm

trainsarefun.com/lirr/lirrsigns.htm

ursasoft.com

vads.ahds.ac.uk

xrite.com

278 Painted station sign. 103rd Street–Corona Plaza (7), c.1917. (2010)

279 Mosaic tile station name. Smith Street–9th Street (F/G), 1933. This is a unique mosaic tile design. (2009)

280 New York City Transit System Substation. Avenue O, c.1941. (2009)

281 Porcelain enamel girder column sign. Middletown Road (6), 1970s. Set in Standard Medium. (2008)

282 Porcelain enamel girder column sign. Wall Street (4/5), early 1990s. Set in Helvetica Medium. (2009)

283 Porcelain enamel warning sign. Rockaway Park–Beach 116th Street.(A/S), 1950s? (2009)

284 Porcelain enamel route sign. 34th Street–Penn Station (B/D/F/V), c.1967. Set in Standard Medium. Note the struts and the non-structural "black bar" (1970)

283

ACKNOWLEDGEMENTS AND CREDITS

284

Massimo Vignelli graciously answered my questions and encouraged me to dig further into the story of Unimark and the NYCTA. Bob Noorda took time out from his busy schedule to talk to me on short notice. He also kindly supplied me with images of his signage work for both the Milano and New York subway systems. Alessandro Colizzi not only made the interview with Noorda possible, but also helped with translation as the conversation shifted from English to Italian to Dutch. I owe much to Jan Conradi, who has studied Unimark for over twenty years, for her willingness to help me figure out exactly what happened between Unimark and the NYCTA. Mildred Constantine graciously consented to discuss her role in helping Unimark receive the initial NYCTA contract. Tom Geismar clarified details of the renovation work he and Cambridge Seven Associates did for the Boston "T". Matthew Carter, Mike Parker, Erich Alb and Colin Brignall all provided me with useful information on the technological history of Helvetica in the 1960s. Rod McDonald tipped me off to the existence of Brightype and explained the process to me. The story

of the transformation of the Unimark signs from the early 1970s through the mid-1990s was made possible by much help from Michael Hertz and Peter Joseph, both of whom provided me with copies of the various revised graphics standards manuals. Michael Bosniak and R. Raleigh D'Adamo gave me invaluable information on the shift from white to black signs. John Tauranac, Arline Bronzaft and Michael Hertz all provided insights into the close connection between the 1979 map and the signage. Prof. Stanley Goldstein kindly sent me a copy of his 1965 report. I want to thank Doris Halle, Howard York, Ron Kane, Peter B. Lloyd and Stephanie Aaron for their help. Dave Pirmann's nycsubway.org website has been invaluable in understanding the convoluted history of the New York City subway system and in providing a wealth of images that have played an instrumental role in shaping my account of its evolving signage. The great majority of those photographs were taken by Joe Testagrose who has kindly allowed me to reproduce them. I am grateful to Charles Sachs, Senior Curator at the New York Transit Museum who found a revelatory

photograph of a transformed Unimark sign and later allowed me to visit the museum's store room. Thanks are also in order to Carey Stumm, Archivist at the New York Transit Museum; MacKenzie Bennett, Assistant Archivist in the Museum Archives of The Museum of Modern Art; and the staffs of the Rare Book and Manuscript Collection, Butler Library and Avery Architectural & Fine Arts Library at Columbia University. Throughout the research and writing of this story Steve Heller was consistently supportive. Greg D'Onofrio and Patricia Belen of Kind Company were the first to suggest that the essay become a book. They also provided scans of several critical items. Jamie Lemoine did a wonderful job retouching my snapshots of the subway system; and James Puckett provided indispensable production assistance. Abby Goldstein not only helped design and produce this book, but her steady enthusiasm for it was a much-needed boost. She also served as an invaluable sounding board regarding its content.

The text of this MIT Press edition is improved thanks to the sharp-eyed proof-reading of Jackson Cavanaugh and Lucia McCreery. The accuracy of the chronology has benefited from Herb Schonhaut's detailed comments. Ornella Noorda, Catherin Noorda and Duška Karanov kindly provided additional material from the Bob Noorda Archives. Without Carey Stumm's continued support and gracious assistance, I would not have discovered new photographs of early Unimark signs. As my literary agent, Scott-Martin Kosofsky was instrumental in seeing that this book had a second life; and, as its producer, he used his prepress expertise, to insure that the high quality of the first edition has been maintained. I am grateful to Roger Conover, executive editor at the MIT Press, for recognizing the potential of a book that might otherwise have reached only a select few.

As before, Abby Goldstein has continued to share with me an unswerving dedication to make this book as good as possible in every detail. Finally, to my wife Bronwen who, as ever, exhibited the "patience of Job" and provided steady encouragement.

Photographs and scans courtesy of the following individuals and institutions. All other photographs or scans are by Paul Shaw

Margaret Calvert: 67, 68
Matthew Carter: 60, 61
Chris Calori, Calori & Vanden-Eynden: 205, 208
Brian Cudahy: 48, 49, 50
Greg D'Onofrio and Patricia Belen, Kind Company: 62, 63, 64, 65, 80, 196
Tom Geismar, Chermayeff & Geismar: 72
Dr. Stuart Gitlow: 146
Emily Gordon, Print: 59, 73, 77, 78, 90, 91, 113, 121, 122, 127, 129, 188–190
Michael Hertz, Michael Hertz Associates: 204, 206, 207, 209, 210–214
Otmar Hoefer, Linotype Library: 243–248
Alfred Hoffmann and Lars Müller Publishers: 117–119

Peter Joseph: 97–109, 112, 159, 160, 161, 162–164, 173, 174, 175, 182, 216–218, 220, 221, 237, 238, 240, 241
Lucia McCreery: 276
Roger Conover, The MIT Press: 124, 125
Lars Müller: 120
Jon Naar: 140
NAGO, the Dutch Archive of Graphic Design: 71
New York Times: 92
New York Transit Museum: 3, 5, 39, 52–57, 76, 79, 93, 94, 96, 110, 111, 137, 142, 147, 148, 150, 167, 169, 186, 187, 191, 195, 284
Bob Noorda: 83–89
Dave Pirmann, nycsubway.org: 58 and 193 (photographs by Eric Oszustowicz); 222 (photograph by Ed McKernan)
Charles Sachs, New York Transit Museum: 25, 42, 45, 52 (photographs by Paul Shaw)
Regina Stewart: 138, 139 (photographs by Jack Stewart)

John Tauranac: 143, 165, 170–172, 201
Teatro Piccolo da Milano: 81, 82
Joe Testagrose: 136 (photograph by Doug Grotjahn), 141, 186, 187
Massimo Vignelli: 95
Howard York: 185

285

285 **Porcelain enamel and sheet metal
warning signs. Middletown Road
(6), after 1990.** Both signs are
set in Helvetica Medium. Note
the changes in line breaks, word
spacing and scale as well as the
addition of the pictogram (2009)

286 **LED roll-sign. IRT Pelham Line (6),
2003.** Photographed at the last stop
(Brooklyn Bridge–City Hall) on the
line. (2010)

274 **Metal entrance sign. Grant Avenue
(A), 1956.** (2009)

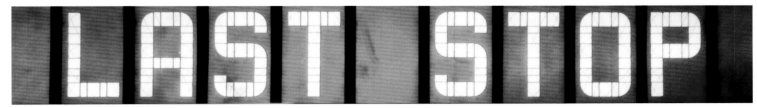

286